WOMEN IN CHAINS:
ABANDONMENT IN LOVE RELATIONSHIPS
IN THE FICTION OF SELECTED WEST AFRICAN WRITERS

BY

DR. ROSE URE MEZU

WOMEN IN CHAINS:
ABANDONMENT IN LOVE RELATIONSHIPS
IN THE FICTION OF SELECTED WEST AFRICAN WRITERS

BY

DR. ROSE URE MEZU

WOMEN IN CHAINS:
ABANDONMENT IN LOVE RELATIONSHIPS
IN THE FICTION OF SELECTED WEST AFRICAN WRITERS

BY

DR. ROSE URE MEZU

Women in Literature, Women in Chains, Abandonment, African novels, African Literature, West Afrrican Literature, Chinua Achebe, Sembene Ousmane, Elechi Amadi, Henri Lopes, Alkali Zaynab, INC Aniebo, Mariama Bâ, Mongo Beti, Buchi Emecheta, Aminata Sow Fall, Flora Nwapa, Ifeoma Okoye, Isidore Okpewho, Feminism, Womanism

All Rights Reserved Including the
right of reproduction in whole or
in part in any form

Copyright © 2013 by Black Academy Press, Inc.
ISBN 0-87831-179-3   978-0-87831-179-8 Paper

4015 OLD COURT ROAD
PIKESVILLE, MARYLAND 21208 USA

DEDICATION

TO

an unusual husband/chum and a loving brood of ten
whose
team support and encouragement saw this work to its
successful completion.

TO

the memory of my father,
John Oguguo Okeke,
whose unparalleled love of sound education
led him to invest in the education of all his children -
male and female -
and be a community other father to others not his but
who showed promise.

TO

my mother, Bessie Chiege Okeke,
whose resourcefulness and strength have made her a
rallying point for all.

TO

Mary, the Blessed Mother,
under whose patronage this work
for the enhancement of family love was undertaken
.

ACKNOWLEDGMENTS

I acknowledge an inexpressible debt of gratitude to my family: my husband, Dr. S. Okechukwu Mezu, whose friendship, inspiration, support - material and otherwise - ensured the completion of this task and whose commitment to excellence, industry and the right to individuation remains unparalleled; to my beloved children, Chinyere and Nnenna in the U.S.A. and my daughters, Kelechi and Olachi of Abia State University, Nigeria.

I acknowledge, with immeasurable gratitude, the contribution of Professor Charles Nnolim, whose critiqes gave me much needed insight. A debt of love to Dr. Augustine Okere for his unremitting interest in the work. Similar gratitude goes to my brother-in-law, Charles Mezu whose wealth of experience guided me in building up an effective bibliography.

Further thanks go to my sisters, Mrs. Margaret. Nwaobia, Mrs Anne Okoli,and her husband Fabian. My immense gratitude goes to Rev. Frs. J.C Okoye and Philip Obinna Aguh, CSSP, who while in Rome and France, provided some of the out of print French texts sorely needed for this comparative study.

I am also grateful to Dr. Chioma Opara of the Rivers State University of Science and Technology, Port Harcourt, and to Mrs. Theresa Njoku of Alvan Ikoku College, Owerri for very stimulating discussions. They provided real life sisterly bonding necessary among women.

I acknowledge the inestimable help of Dr. Shirley Donwa-Ifode of the Dept. of Linguistics, University of Port Harcourt, as well as the support given to me by Profs. Sunday Anozie, Wilfried Feuser and T. Maduka of the English and Comparative Literature Department,

University of Port Harcourt.

Never to be forgotten is the very concrete presence of my eleventh and last born, Master Ikechukwu Mezu, whose advent during the first year of this research made it clear that his birth and nurturance must take precedence over those of this work.

My warm appreciation to numerous friends and relatives whose encouragement spurred me on, and who considered me a role model worthy of emulation since quite a few went iback to college for their doctoral education.

And finally, to the Greatest. I exalt the bountiful Triune Lord God, Gracious Majesty, who despite almost insuperable difficulties, has led me on to see the completion of this study.

FOREWORD

Women in Chains; Abandonment in Love Relationships in the Fiction of Selected West African Writers examines selected works of Anglophone and Francophone feminist and gynandrist authors who have demonstrated immeasurable concern for the dehumanizing conditions under which the African woman in a familial construct is forced to function in a subcategory role. This study, therefore, considers abandonment as an aberration from the most enduring form of love relationship - marriage. The following hypotheses are consequently set forward:

a That by nature, man and woman are created to live in mutual support, comfort and companionship in a stable, fruitful, love relationship - marriage being its most enduring form - and this is a universal phenomenon.

b. That this stable, heterosexual union which constitutes the bedrock of any progressive society can be threatened by certain socio-cultural norms and practices. These can be abused, thereby promoting female exploitation and abandonment.

c. That a crop of West African writers with a lively social conscience have used the popular, protean genre of the novel to dramatize the cause of wronged womanhood by delineating in fiction the tensions and strictures immanent in a gender-structured society. Thus, through their writings, they create empathy amongst the literati who are so well-placed to redress these injustices that destabilize homes and promote the process of abandonment.

d. That these writings, constituting the core of the

literature of abandonment, are inextricably linked to the "woman question" and being a protest literature, it fittingly serves a consciousness-raising purpose by drawing attention to the position of women placed as passive receptacles of patriarchal injustices.

e. That the aim of this study is positivistic since it seeks to encourage women to transcend the immanence of abandonment by recognizing opportunities for self-improvement and reclamation, exercising the will to change negative circumstances and ultimately achieving self-healing and wholeness, a life of self-worth and happiness within a familial construct freed from the limiting traditional expectations and usages such as portrayed in the novels.

f. That qualities such as mutual understanding, tolerance and forgiveness are *sine qua non* for sustaining a companionate union so that all concerned - man or woman, young or old, rural or urban, educated or illiterate, will live and operate in an ambience of mutual trust and unhindered personal growth. The work therefore emphasizes the need for sufficient public enlightenment which can promote a revalorisation of the factors that create disharmony in the home.

g. That, finally, as distilled from the authors studied, this study underscores the liberating ideals of education, hard work, resourcefulness as well as economic independence as avenues for survival and transcendence for all oppressed people, and for women in particular.

TABLE OF CONTENTS

TITLE PAGE 3
DEDICATION 15
ACKNOWLEDGEMENT 16
FOREWORD.. 18
TABLE OF CONTENTS 20

CHAPTER 1
    Women in Chains: The Universal Canvas................ 21

CHAPTER 11
    Infertility: Catalyst for Self-Discovery 74

CHAPTER 111
    Polygamy and Abandonment 120

CHAPTER 1V
    Infidelity, Incest and Abandonment....................... 167

CHAPTER V
    Feminist Awareness and the Abandoned Female .. 218

CHAPTER VI
    Conclusion: The Will to Change 267

BIBLIOGRAPHY 289

POSTFACE
Women in Chians: A Review by Prof. Peter I. Okeh 294

CHAPTER ONE

WOMEN IN CHAINS: THE UNIVERSAL CANVAS

Patriarchy is the power of the fathers: a familial, social, ideological, political system in which men, by force, direct pressure, or through tradition, law and language, customs, etiquette, education and division of labor, determine what part women shall or shall not play, and in which the female is everywhere subsumed under the male (Adrienne Rich, *Of Woman Born* 57-58).

WHAT IS ABANDONMENT?

The word **to abandon** comes from an old French word, "mettre à bandon" which means "to reduce under control, to subdue" (*Oxford Dictionary* 2). To abandon is to renounce, to leave without support and consideration and it is therefore the antithesis of to love or to respect. Lipking traces the word even further back to a Latin base - "*ad*" meaning "to," "*bandon*" meaning "power or control," and signifying a submission to power as in bowing to the will of a monarch. The person who owns you can also toss you away. This definition accords, of course, with the patriarchal concepts of Roman law where the husband, the only person who was "*sui juris*" regards the - wife or daughter or sister - as his property and can dispose of her in any way he sees fit, reserving the right to punish, beat, imprison or abandon her.

Abandonment is a universal literary theme and the abandoned woman, a universal figure, is represented in the pantheons of many national literatures including Africa. It is an aberration from any love relationship and is usually fraught with psychological and emotional traumas. Abandonment, like love, can occur in any human milieu and is not the exclusive prerogative of any one sex; therefore, man as well as woman can initiate it. It is tantamount to an extreme form of alienation presupposing, by implication, a pre-existing intimate and reciprocal relationship.

Abandonment thus represents the reverse side of the love coin and love connotes an intense desire for an interpersonal union or fusion with some other person. Love denotes a desire to transcend an emotional prison of separateness. C. S. Lewis' theory of love comprises four constituent parts, viz - Affection, Friendship, Eros ["being in love" - romantic or sexual] and Charity [*agape* or Divine love] (Lewis 148). Erich Fromm, evidently merged these "four loves" to produce that one love whose integral qualities he gives as - active concern (for the life and growth of that which we cherish), care, responsibility, respect and knowledge. He insists that to speak of "love" is not preaching for the simple reason that it means to speak of the ultimate and real need of every human being. He continues,

> *That this need has been obscured does not mean it does not exist. To analyze the nature of* love *is to discover its general absence today and to* criticize *the social conditions which* are *responsible for this absence* (Fromm 95).

Those social conditions responsible for the absence of love, which must be criticized because they culminate in the abandonment of a love partner, constitute the core of this study. In the context of this work, therefore, the inability to transcend the emotional prison of separateness equates the utter absence of love, an absence which sets in motion the reality of abandonment. A serious love relationship such as marriage must, of course, be based on more than romantic love, a necessary though transitory phase in sustaining a marriage. Abandonment will, therefore, presuppose an existing serious love commitment between a man and a woman of equal human worth, sincerely committed to promoting each other's happiness. It can, then, be seen how inextricably linked are the themes of love and abandonment which have earlier been said to represent the two sides of a coin. Any meaningful discussion on the theme of abandonment must, therefore, go hand in hand with an examination of the love phenomenon from its earliest record in Western literature.

ABANDONMENT IN WESTERN LITERATURE

Abandonment has formed the theme of significant national literatures. In fact, in some cultures, the role of women in literature has been virtually identified with abandonment, a theme that has preoccupied much of ancient as well as modern literature. The anguished voice of the "unhappy woman" abandoned in love - Medea, Dido, Phaedra, Ariadne, Sappho, *et cetera*, seems invariably to dominate and drown that of the abandoned man hence Lipking asks rhetorically: "Is Criseyde or Troilus the more abandoned" (Lipking 1). The literature of ancient Greece represents one such culture redolent of stories of abandoned women since the type of male/female love celebrated by that civilization can be said to be more akin to *eros* which Macquarrie describes as *"ecstasy, a madness"* (Macquarrie 197) and because *eros* is somewhat irrational, it leaves in its wake that disillusionment and disenchantment normally associated with abandonment. In Greek mythology, as a result of this *genre* of love, Helen abandons Menelaus for the

Trojan prince Paris, and the consequences of her betrayal are recorded in Homer's *Iliad* and Virgil's *Aeneid*. Medea, daughter of King Aeetes of Colchis is abandoned by Jason for the daughter of King Kreon of Corinth. Euripides records in *Medea* that to cause Jason pain Medea vengefully murders Kreon, his daughter and her two sons by Jason. Medea's passion (*eros*) carries her too far "[and] because she finds no redress for her wrongs in society, [she] is driven by her passion to violate that society's most sacred laws in a rebellion against its most typical representative, Jason, her husband... [thus, shaking the Greeks] out of their complacent pride in the superiority of Greek masculinity" (*Norton Anthology* 359). Medea is considered essentially a feminist melodrama as illustrated by her lament: "I am deserted ... thought nothing of, by my husband" (367).

Abandonment featured so heavily in classical Greco-Roman literature because their societies did not place much value on their women. Athenian rights and institutions, for instance, were established for men while women had few privileges and practically no legal rights, hence one can understand Medea's bitter words:

> *of all things which are living and can form a judgment, we women are the most unfortunate creatures (Medea* in *Norton Anthology* 366).

In fact, these societies tended to eulogize homosexual rather than heterosexual love. Plato's *Symposium*, for instance, considered love between males as the only kind "capable of satisfying a man's highest and noblest aspirations" (Plato 12). Buttressing this point further, Ian Watt confirms that "classical Greece and Rome knew little of romantic love in our sense" and women, because of their inferior social status, were considered merely from the utility perspective - for procreation. Even

Euripides himself considered "sexual passion . . . as a violation of the human norm, and has Jason wishing to do away with women even as a means of procreation as he curses Medea:

> *It would have been better far for men*
> *To have got their children some other way,*
> *And women not to have existed* (*Medea* 374).

Therefore, a woman like Medea (to whom love is life itself) and who when Jason tauntingly indicts her for murdering her children "for the sake of pleasure in bed" asks plaintively, "is love so small a pain, do you think, for a woman?" (392), regards love as life itself. Even Jean Racine, French neoclassical dramatist, in his recreation of Greek tragedies, portrays two female characters, Hermione *(Andromaque)* and the eponymous Phèdre as women ruled, like Medea, by an overmastering passion such that, when abandoned by their lovers, they are willing to stoop to anything to get what they want; and when that eludes them, they resort to revenge. For Medea therefore, Jason's betrayal of their conjugal love goads her into the unspeakable violence of the oppressed. Being considered merely as part of a man's possession and procreator of children is inadequate for a woman of great intellectual power such as she is (359). Being a man's chattel may, however, be enough for Penelope for according to C. S. Lewis,

> *Odysseus loves Penelope as he loves the rest of his home and possessions, and Aristotle rather grudgingly admits that conjugal relation may now and then rise to the same level as a virtuous friendship between good men* (*The Allegory of Love* 4).

Generally, therefore, ancient literature was

misogynous. Undue emphasis by a man on sexual / female love denotes weakness rather than strength and Paris is perceived as a figure of derision for bringing down the destiny of a whole country for love of a mere woman, who, as we have already seen, on account of her inferior status is considered an item of property rather than a partner. Germaine Greer, in *The Female Eunuch*, summarily describes the situation thus:

> *indeed, many Platonists believed that women were not capable of love at all, because they were men's inferiors physically, socially, intellectually and even in terms of physical beauty. Love is not possible between inferior and superior, because . . . being lesser, they [women] themselves cannot comprehend the faculties in the superior which are worthy of love. The superior being on the other hand cannot demean himself by love from an inferior. The proper subject for love is one's equal, seeing as the essence of love is to be mutual and the lesser cannot produce anything greater than itself. Seeing the image of himself [another man], recognizes it and loves it out of fitting and justifiable amour propre (The Female Eunuch* 136).

Thus did ancient Greece rationalize abandonment of women in love, gender discrimination and unabashed bias towards homosexual love. It would take the eleventh-century Provençal troubadours celebrating *amour courtois* to inject adequate seriousness to the idea that love between the sexes should be the supreme value of life on earth. This idea will be developed later in this chapter.

As has been said, in Greco-Roman times, sexual love - *eros* - was regarded as madness. Therefore, since sexual passion between man and woman was regarded as an aberration, the victims of this passion (usually women) were considered victims of tragic madness or what C. S. Lewis describes as *an arn* which can plunge otherwise sane people into crime and disgrace. It is a false kind of love and Catullus, Propertius and Ovid, most among classical authors to be indicted for this false treatment of romantic love, portray their women characters as being in the grip of this "*arn.*" This amorous obsession is consequently not regarded as a noble sorrow but as a degrading emotion. Think of the despair of abandonment as painted by Catullus: at the marriage of Thetis and Pelleus, the deserted Ariadne, a portrait of agony and fury, stood naked on the beach, hurling curses after her fleeing love. Underscoring the depth of this emotional bathos, Lipking observes about the woman betrayed and abandoned in love:

> her abandonment begins with a lover and takes on the world eventually. She is barred from happiness, the pillar that sustains her falls away and all conventions of behavior lie in ruins. Even the laws of nature no longer apply, it seems, when love is denied. Medea kills her children, Dido herself. She becomes the outcast of society and God. Laodamia tries to copulate with the shade of her husband and with the castrate she mistakes for her lord. (*The Abandoned Women and Poetic Tradition* 2)

Laodamia begs to be allowed to speak with her dead husband; the request is granted by the gods and she chooses to accompany him to the land of the dead.

However, the figures of abandoned women do insist on a hearing and lot of attention is given to them. The most famous literature on abandonment is probably Ovid's *Heroïdes,* a love letter in verse form involving historical persons which dramatize the hurt feelings of a woman who has been forsaken by husband or lover. In the *Heroïdes,* or (*Heroic Epistles),* the heroine is always an abandoned woman, be it Penelope, Phaedra, Dido, Ariadne, Medea, Laodamia or Sappho. Betrayed, and empassioned, each abandoned woman pours out her sorrow in a letter, castigating or cajoling the lover but hoping against hope to coax him back but never quite succeeding. The *Heroïdes* begins with Odysseus and concludes with the spectacle of Sappho leaping from the Leucadian rock to the waves below in a suicidal bid to purge herself of passion for Phaon, the handsome, young ferryman.

Dido, the legendary queen of Carthage and another victim of desertion, "so broken in mind by suffering ... caught her fatal madness" (*The Aeneid, Norton Anthology* 520) and kills herself when Aeneas, son of Anchises and Aphrodite, leaves her. Aeneas leaves the burning city, carrying his father on his shoulder and leading his son by the hand, emphasizing the continuity of generations - the task for which he abandons Dido. His sacrifice is unlike that of Achilles whose career, however brilliant is one of lonely, meteor-like shortness and of no purpose; it is also unlike that of Odysseus, which however heroic is an individual affair. Aeneas suffers and fights for a greater objective: the glory of a future empire. It is, of course, to be assumed that if Aeneas had stayed with Dido, Rome and *The Aeneid* would never have been accomplished for Latin literature also considered love as a frivolity. The Roman ideal of devotion to duty and seriousness of purpose, naturally, supercedes this great passion of Aeneas' life; his own life is as unhappy as his death is miserable. In chapter VI of *The Aeneid,* unhappy Aeneas, meeting the abandoned Dido in the underworld, confesses, "I left your land against my will, my Queen; the gods' commands drove me to do their will" (*NA* 535). But the implacable Dido "flung away from him and fled," going to join her first love and husband, Sychaeus who returns her love. Thus, her death-wish that Aeneas "shall call and call on Dido's name . . . and I shall be . . . a shade to haunt you" (517) comes true, giving her victory. Evidently, love was not considered a lofty goal in life. Ian Watt records a commentary of Servius on the *Aeneid* to the effect that Dido's love was not considered as serious enough subject for epic dignity, but Virgil had redeemed himself by treating it in an almost comic style (153). The heroic worship accorded the goddess of love - Aphrodite or Venus - was, therefore, done in mockery although in the course of time, it was taken seriously enough by the courtly love troubadours. In the light of this, it can be understood why Euripides (who reverses traditional order by making the tragic hero - "one who is highly renowned and prosperous such as Oedipus" - no longer a king but a woman, Medea), was held in such contempt by his contemporaries and often became the butt of scurrilous humor by comic poets. Later generations of Greeks, however, revered him. Ultimately, the myth of the abandoned woman enters historical times with Sappho.

Turning to the *Bible*, itself, an acknowledged source of rich and varied literature - myth, biography, poetry, short stories, letters, prophecy - there is abundant literature of "unhappy passion" and abandonment: Leah, Jacob's first wife and Michal, King David's first wife and Saul's daughter, are just two famous examples of unloved victims of polygamy and each lived out her days in abandonment. As women chained to the immanence of the socio-cultural mores of their time, each lived out her days as neither wife, mistress nor widow. Just like pre-biblical Greek and Roman literatures, the Christian concept of romantic love is heavily redolent of guilt and is divorced from conjugal felicity. The myth of the great fall of the first man, Adam, had and perhaps will forever blight the character of Eve, the alleged seductress responsible for man's fall from grace. The Teachings of St. Paul and those of the Desert Fathers, the earliest Christian theologians, were all aimed at suppressing lust, incarnated in the figure of woman. Novelist Julien Green summarizes it:

> "The body is the devil,' said the Catharist preachers ... And long before their time, in that mysterious orient where shadow and light commingled, the flesh had been likened to evil and consigned to darkness (150).

Woman was regarded as the agent of the devil in her sensuousness and seductiveness. St. Francis of Assisi, for instance, avoided St. Claire, in charge of the women's monastery, and counseled his *poverelli* (poor friars) to avoid contact with women:

> *Deep down, he [Francis] was as apprehensive as ever about women. Perhaps he noticed a little too much enthusiasm in the charity his brothers showed towards their saintly neighbors. One day, he dropped an ironic and revealing remark: "It is the Lord who has preserved us from taking wives; but who knows, it may have been the devil who has sent us these sisters* (Greene 150).

Funny as it seems, the sexual abstemiousness recommended for the clergy is also considered worthy of practice by the married person who would be saint, hence St. Paul's preference for the celibate state, both for himself and for widows. Even married people like Thomas More, in his quest for sanctity "secretly wore a hairshirt ... until the day before he died" (More 14), while mystics like Edward, the Confessor, King of England, took celibate vows even within marriage. Thus, very strenuous efforts were made to disentangle carnal love from conjugal love. But despite its stated misogyny, the merit of the Christian conception of womanhood is that women were equally considered capable of attaining the highest states of man: salvation and sanctity. Thus, the courtly love tradition which, at first, celebrated in romantic terms the love between the sexes and was generally pro woman in sense of the chivalric had to be purged of all sexual connotations making it, in essence, the result of the transfer of an attitude of religious adoration from a divine to a secular object, from the Virgin Mary to the lady worshiped by the troubadour. Paradoxically, the forms of clerical and bourgeois medieval literature which dealt with everyday life was definitely misogynist, presenting womankind as a "species characterized by an insatiate. Fleshly cupidity" (Watt 153) which characters abound in *The Canterbury Tales.*

The prevailing opinion was that true love was impossible in marriage since theoretically, a husband commands and a wife obeys and as we have already seen from the Platonists, love is, only possible between equals. However, the medieval cult of "woman worship" was platonic and pure only in theory while in actual practice, it was adulterous and antisocial. Germaine Greer insists in *The Female Eunuch:*

> *The body-soul dichotomy which characterizes medieval thought operated to protect the 'status quo.' Servant girls and country bumpkins were debauched without mercy, while the passion for the lady of the manor became exalted into a quasi religious fervor. The literature of adulterous passion was like modern stories of obsession, fetishism and perversion, a series of vicarious peeps into a region so fraught with dangers that only a lunatic would venture there* (Greer 198).

In actual fact, the courtly love tradition lacked realism and this fact, in Jim Hunters's opinion, makes it "a pose, a fashion, an attitude towards love which belonged to literature rather than to life" (Hunter 23). This aristocratic literature was therefore a literary expression of escapism and unrealism which the ruling class espoused so as to continue keeping their vassals in perpetual subjection because the stories functioned to transport their hero and readers to an ideal world of fantasy, illusions and dreams rather than "help [them] cope in a positive way with the business of living" (Kettle 29). Generally therefore, the courtly love convention, whose essential qualities include "humility, courtesy, *adultery* and the religion of love" (Lewis 12) consigns the adulterous woman to a destiny of heartache, degradation and abandonment.

Woman poet and precursor of modern feminism Christine de Pisan (1365-1430) reacted against this treatment of women, reproaching Jean de Meung, author of the second part of *Le Roman de la Rose* (1275-1280) for his crude and vigorous criticism of women, love and marriage. Her *Epître au Dieu d'amours - Letter to the God of Love* (1399) deplored the prevailing vogue of literary invectives against women and the attitude promoted among the populace to reduce love and romance to sexual conquest and *abandonment*. She, earliest advocate of women's rights, further extends the literary theme of abandonment in love, explores the feelings of a woman unhappy in love in her *Cent ballades d'amant et de dame* (One Hundred Ballads of a Lover and his Lady <ca 1410>), a collection of poems in which a man and a woman alternate in describing their love, its consummation, interruption and final decay. Even so, asserts Lawrence Lipking, "abandonment is the destiny written in her (woman's) script. . . . The sexes are not equal in power or justice; the woman will always be the one who pays" (Lipking 3). But Christine de Pisan, said to be France's, and possibly Europe's first woman known to have earned her living by the pen, had by 1399, undertaken to be spokesperson for the dignity of women by attacking ribaldry and misogyny in male-authored works. Consequently, with the publication of *Le Livre de la cité des dames – Book of the City of Ladies* (1405), the three-century long debate on the status of women - *querelle des femmes* was on.

On the other hand, the courtly love traditions greatly aided the flowering of Romanticism with its spirit of humanism, and the free rein given to subjective emotions enabling writers and literary characters - male and female alike - to sing of their love, chagrin, disappointment or abandonment. The achieved objective was the enthronement of the primacy of personal emotions (enthusiasm or the melancholy of *l'âme romantique"*), and the sexual aspect of love was treated without prudery. By this time, of course, the novel had assumed form and marriage had become a matter of free choice instead of an arrangement of social convention. The values of courtly love could now conveniently be combined with those of marriage; and thus, love could validly "dwell in marriage." Richardson's *Pamela* (1740) accomplished this feat by celebrating the love and courtship leading to marriage, thus guaranteeing to women greater freedom of choice in matters of marriage. In this regard, Chaucer can be safely labeled a revolutionary because judging from both the *Knight's Tale* and the *Franklin's Tale*, he obviously thought "that love and marriage were perhaps compatible after all" (Coghill 11).

With Romanticism guaranteeing the unrestrained outpouring of personal feelings and the novel, being structured to enable its characters speak out on love, betrayal or abandonment within or outside marriage, more writings now dealt with the travails of women in love. *Clarissa* (1748) is described by Arnold Kettle as "an assertion of a woman's dignity within the moral jungle of the world of arranged marriages and hypocritical prostitution" (Kettle 29). In, *Madame Bovary*, Emma's distorted perception of reality involves her in amorous situations that render her a pitiable victim of frustrated and betrayed love; Miss Havisham *(Great Expectations)*, abandoned on her wedding day, puts her life just like the clock, on freeze; Hardy's Michael Henchard *(The Mayor of Casterbridge)* in "seeking to shake himself loose of a wife, to discard the drooping rag of a woman... to escape not by a slinking abandonment but through a public sale of her body to a stranger as horses are sold at a fair" (Howe 84) equally becomes victim of his own abandonment scheme as desperate and unmanned by the collapse of the virile façade of his world of authority, he seeks but cannot repossess the supportive love bonds of his wife Susan, and daughter Elizabeth-Jane. We therefore agree with Elaine Showalter's pertinent critique that Henchard had symbolically sold "his entire share of the world of women [and had] severed his bond with his female community of love and loyalty" (*Modern Literary Theory* 94).

Equally, in *Seduction and Betrayal*, Elizabeth Hardwick undertakes a study of women that men have betrayed and abandoned such as Hetty *(Adam Bede)* or Hester Prynne in Hawthorne's *The Scarlet Letter*. A feminist re-reading of Brontë's *Jane Eyre* injects some thought-provoking racial connotations in the polygynously-inclined Edward Rochester's abandonment of the indomitable Creole Bertha Mason who is exploited for her beauty and wealth only to be oppressed as a mad woman and betrayed when eventually considered an encumbrance. In *Wide Sargasso Sea,* Jean Rhys depicts Bertha's situation in a new light. Betrayed and harassed by both white men and women, this female, culturally-defined **Other** spiritedly resists all attempts to render her invisible. Jane's efforts to supplant her meet with a telling reprisal and Thornfield, the white patriarchal edifice, is burnt down and Rochester is reductively rendered helpless and dependent. Thus far, Brontë's treatment of Rochester falls within the female writer's technique of male reductionism, but when Bertha, the cultural Other dies along with the collapse of white patriarchy, saving even the misogynist Rochester, albeit reduced in stature, Nigerian critic Ogunyemi in protest wonders with some justification if feminist utopia is after all only meant for the white women, in which case, black women would do well to redefine universal feminism and maintain their womanist stance. For the "plain and virtuous" Jane, Showalter opines, all that befalls her seems just desserts for she "should know better than to supplant another female to secure a husband" ("Towards a Feminist Poetics," 124).

But despite the almost excessive idealization of romantic love in European literature, when love or marriage fails, it is always the woman who is traumatized. It is perhaps for this reason that many feminists from Simone de Beauvoir to Betty Friedan to Kate Millet to Germaine Greer to Shulamith Firestone consider love a "mania . . . mystic madness" (Ogunyemi 66). Falling in love with men, rather than being a metaphor for happiness, becomes an action which repeatedly reinforces women's subordination, turning them into "female eunuchs." For a radical feminist writer like Firestone, love therefore is "the pivot of women's oppression today" (Firestone 126). Kate Millet in *Sexual Politics* gives a unique re-reading of D. H. Lawrence's *Sons and Lovers.*

Millet makes the point that all the women in Paul Morel's life from his mother to Miriam and Clara Dawes become exploited and ultimately abandoned by him when he no longer needs them. Like a leech, he clings to each for emotional sustenance only to withdraw, when any of them needs him the most. Supporting this viewpoint, it is pertinent that Paul wonders aloud to his mother:

> *I think there must be something the matter with me, that I can't love . . . They seem to want me, and I can't ever give it to them* (Lawrence, *Sons and Lovers* 350-1).

And when the mother's dying becomes too protracted and painful, Millet accuses Paul of rank ingratitude when he asks the doctor: "can't you give her something to put an end to it?" (Lawrence 393).

In the opinion of these radical feminist writers, it would appear that if, like Kate in the *Taming of the Shrew,* women had their wits about them and were of high mettle, shrewd and energetic, they would not always fall victims of abandonment in love relationships especially in marriage, an institution that Shakespeare did not romanticize about, but rather recognized "as a difficult state of life requiring discipline, sexual energy, mutual respect and great forbearance. He knew there were no easy answers to marital problems and that infatuation was no basis for continued cohabitation" (Greer 206). Women, Greer maintains, must recognize "being in love" as a cheap ideology that essentially leads to irrational self-destruction. On this point, we disagree. Arguably, infatuation alone cannot sustain a meaningful marriage yet, some romantic love is a necessary primary basis for nurturing a lasting, meaningful and permanent heterosexual relationship.

On her part, Simone de Beauvoir, in her short story,

La femme rompue [Woman Destroyed] takes a firm, dispassionate look at the issue of abandonment. Monique, the tragic female hero of the story, gradually loses her mind because her husband, Maurice had for eight years lied about his affairs with other women. Beauvoir squarely indicts Monique as the architect of her own downfall. Beauvoir's reasoning is simple: modern woman has been sufficiently sensitized about the ideals of feminism and the need for both emotional freedom and financial independence. Yet, Monique exhibits unpardonable *"mauvaise fois"* by choosing to define herself as a "relative" being, denying herself opportunities for growth through work - (Monique gives up her medical career and rejects opportunities to work, believing that for Maurice and herself, love has welded them into one entity, always and forever. One is persuaded to agree with critic Toril Moi who posits that:

> *her [Monique's] definition of love is also cruelly flawed. Maurice and Monique's interpretation of their marriage are radically opposed... because, he has changed through his struggles to realize his projects in 'the world, whereas she has remained faithful to a static image of herself... in this sense, he represents dynamism, activity and transcendence whereas she represents immanence, passivity and inaction [so], when he longer loves her, she is nobody* (Moi, 69-70).

It is rather obvious that *La femme rompue* is used to illustrate de Beauvoir's thesis enunciated in *Le Deuxième Sexe* that economic liberation is a *sine qua non* for all other forms of freedom. In *All Said and Done,* Beauvoir acknowledges that "she had never written anything more somber than *The Woman Destroyed:* the whole of the second part is one long cry of agony, and the final crumbling of the heroine is sadder than death itself" (142/147). Evidently, the story is meant to serve as a lesson to other women to not willingly create opportunities for their own victimization, and betrayal since love is not a static essence but an active project or, as Germaine Greer puts it, "love is not swoon, possession or mania but a cognitive act, indeed the only way to grasp the innermost core of personality" (Schwarz 20). Thus, I argue that this innermost core of personality must be nourished by and rooted in what Betty Friedan calls "human work" which constitutes life or else one has forfeited oneself. In other words, the woman becomes a parasite, needing the husband to buttress her emptiness of self and demanding too much attention from a husband who ultimately comes to resent so much oppressive need. The end result is betrayal/abandonment. This is what sets off the tragedy of violence, incest and abandonment in Toni Morrison's *The Bluest Eye.* As Pauline Breedlove, new in town, fails to make her own friends and increasingly turns to her husband, Cholly, for company to fill the vacuum. Cholly begins to resent her total dependence on him. Thus, most of the feminist writers' discussion on love/ abandonment rests on the necessity for a woman to develop the *will to change* her negative circumstance, acquire self-respect, self-dependence and strength in order to escape suffering humiliations and contempt: for "women who accepted conditions which degraded them felt contempt for themselves and all women" (Friedan 92).

Thus, exploring Western literary history, it can be seen that abandonment and love have always gone hand in hand, and women have not always received a fair deal from patriarchy. Love, which in the beginning was regarded as a frivolous pass-time game divorced from conjugal living, was in turn romanticized and idealized out of all realism until the rise of the novel restored romance and love within the basic structure of marriage as worthy of serious notice. Henceforth, woman can now be a serious object of love and of abandonment. But when abandonment takes place within marriage, the structure of the family as a primary unit of society is always affected.

ABANDONMENT IN AFRICAN FICTION: A CRITICAL REVIEW

Abandonment, being, as already seen, a universal phenomenon, exists in African literature and in fact, has developed into a significant corpus which *may safely* be termed a literature of *abandonment*. Even though African philosophy of love may not be invested with all the paraphernalia of idealized and romanticized love characteristic of the Western concept, it is nonetheless a heartfelt, personal experience, though rooted in a communal societal structure. Phanuel Egejuru sums it up very succinctly:

> *The point is that Africans conceive of love differently, and they have a very different way of approaching the subject. Indeed, love is very much a part of living, but the expressions of it are more complex than a non-African would care to analyze.*

It is more complex because the African woman is operating from a milieu deeply steeped in sexist norms and mores and she is contending with a plethora of problems which complicate her life and endanger her chances of a felicitous conjugal living. Yet, when she suffers abandonment, she is aware of it and her lament is no less heartfelt and traumatic than that of her Western counterpart. Therefore, the non-overt expression of love by the African woman can be mistaken for the non-existence of love in African marriages. Issues such as barrenness, polygyny, dowry system, lack of free choice in marriage, and gender discrimination are also directly linked to the societal conception and perception of the status and value of the woman, to her own self-perception and consciousness of her individual rights. This consciousness has produced a wave of a literature of abandonment as seen in, Flora Nwapa's *Efuru*, Sembène's *Xala, Véhi-Ciosane,* Emecheta's *The Joys of Motherhood, Second Class Citizen*, Mongo Beti's Perpétue, Henri Lopes' *La Nouvelle Romance,* Ifeoma Okoye's *Behind the Clouds,* Elechi Amadi's *Estrangement,* Ngugi wa Thiongo's *Petals of Blood, Devil on the Cross*, Mariama Bâ's *Une Si Longue Lettre, Un Chant Ecarlate,* Aminata Sow Fall's *La Grève des Battus,* among many other novels.

Consequently, the abundance of this body of literature, the relevance and urgency of issues treated therein make a research on the theme of abandonment in love relationships imperative. But unlike in European and American literatures in which, as we have seen, abound critical materials on the theme of abandonment in love, there is a dearth of research writings in African literature on the traumatic consequences of abandonment (especially to the woman) in a love relationship. Yet, concerned critics are trying to sensitize African *literati* on this new wave of the literature of abandonment which is generating such concern to African novelists. Consequently, existing critical materials will be reviewed. Katherine Frank broaches the topic in her 1987 article entitled "Women Without Men: The feminist Novel in Africa" (*Women in African Literature 15*; 14-34). She discusses among other works, Mariama Bâ's *So Long a Letter*, Nwapa's *One is Enough* and Emecheta's *Double Yoke*. Frank sets out to identify female characters with a destiny of their own by examining the bitterness and cynicism, born of the unflinching vision and hard struggle that inform the works of a growing number of women novelists in Africa; she delineates the restrictive cultural mores that oppress and marginalize the female protagonists of the novels under discussion. An obvious limitation is her ideological thrust which is directed towards lauding female separatism and its implied militancy. Women, she says

> *must spurn patriarchy in all its guises and create a sane, safe, supportive world of women; a world of mothers and daughters, sisters and friends. This, of course, amounts to female separatism* (Frank 15).

Her overt admiration for these urban women living in a world without men, spurning patriarchy "in all its guises" and whose "heroinism appears to be courageous, indeed a daring act," impinges seriously on the stated objective of this study which primarily aims at restoring a healthy balance in the relationship between men and women. "Heroinism" is used in this sense to underpin the courage involved in "the conscious, deliberate rejection of marriage by women" (Frank 17). Ellen Moers first uses the term "heroinism" to describe what she calls "literary feminism" - a massive, revolutionary change in literary pattern where women now occupy center stage as principal characters, enjoying "all the adventures and alarms that masculine heroes had long experienced... in fiction" (Moers, *Literary Women* 123-126). This praxis is reminiscent of Virginia Woolf's radical mandate (endorsed by Elaine Showalter) for the creation of a feminine sub-culture in *A Room Of One's Own*. In the same vein, Mary Daly in *Gyn /Ecology* advocates total liberation of women from the chains of a repressive, sexist society in order to seek female autonomy in a female world separated from the male sphere. Though written in persuasive language, we disagree with Frank's conclusions.

Since the realism of the novel as a genre resides principally in verisimilitude - the novelist being able to convincingly depict a world as close to the real world as possible, such "a world of (only) mothers, daughters, sisters and friends" is far from being "safe and sane," is neither realistic nor indeed a realizable ideal; such exotic flights from the male world to a culture defined in opposition to male tradition are reminiscent of the Amazon's female utopia. But I argue that the real world contains men, and "men" form an inextricable part of living reality and must be accommodated in the emancipated African woman's vision of self-actualization and quest for wholeness. In this respect, in spite of his usual cynicism towards feminist issues, one agrees rather with critic Femi Ojo-Ade that freedom, not rooted in the couple and family is sham and only results in solitude (Ojo-Ade 84). Consequently, happiness within a conjugal unit and not separatism, is the goal of this study.

Another exploration into the factors that blight the happiness of the woman within a marital set-up is contained in Charles Nnolim's article, "The Unhappy Woman in Nigerian Fiction: A mythic Interpretation of the Archetypes" published in the journal *Calabar Studies*.

In it, women are examined as archetypes and ascribed the reductive anima image of

> *femme fatale or the dangerous woman, who either denies a man his manhood or acts as a "castrating" figure who castrates a man by making him a slave to her beauty* (Nnolim 2).

The above exemplifies the archetypal image of womanhood decried by feminists everywhere. These *femmes fatales* must have a flaw, the superstitious patriarchal milieu insists. Among such flaws, Nnolim identifies barrenness as a biological and social malady that constitutes one of woman's chains and turns familial happiness into ashes in her mouth. For African women, he maintains, barrenness is "the ultimate affliction." On the other hand, the reverse is no better for

> *...if these women are fecund and prolific in childbearing, that blessing becomes the source of their unhappiness. If they are very beautiful and perfect models among their kind, their very perfection brings them unhappiness, for they are denied what every woman longs for -- children (*Nnolim 20*).*

So, either way, these jinxed women are in for trouble, being placed as it were, between two Greek misogynist symbols - the *Scylla* of infertility and the *Charybdis* of fecundity. Nnolim's article further highlights some of the cultural practices that forge chains of unhappiness for the woman: the use of superstitious divination in explaining various myths -- such as Elechi amadi's symbolism of the sea-king (*The Concubine*), the myth of *ogbanje* or *iyiocha* (Onuora Nzekwu's *Wand of Noble Wood),* et cetera. But the present study regards such *marked* women as being removed from the pale of normalcy because they are literally hamstrung both in the life here and in the beyond by inscrutable, capricious and insuperable mystic forces.

In addition, the causes of woman's chains of suffering and unhappiness are subjected to mythic interpretations that ally the stories more with romances than with novelistic realism. The merit of Nnolim's article and its relevance to this study lie in the fact that it identifies and isolates some of those socio-cultural constraints which vitiate the attainment of both personal and familial happiness for the woman, which destabilize the conjugal construct and lead to abandonment. But we insist that these problems be confronted by normal women whose fates are not in the least determined by mystic and supernatural forces that confine them more firmly in their sexual identity, a fact that Naana Banyiwa-Horne, with our concordance, sees as "a further projection of the male perspective of African womanhood" (Banyiwa-Horne 128). Women must transcend not mythic but realistic proscriptions and fall or survive only on their own strengths. And here again, only the Nigerian literary field comes in for consideration in Nnolim's essay.

A study that appreciates the weaknesses and strengths of abandoned female heroes as portrayed by a gynandrist is Jennifer Evans "Women and Resistance in Ngugi's *Devil on the Cross*." Ngugi's female characters stand as embodiments of the highest feminist ideals. Evans persuasively argues the fact that Ngugi uses the position of women as a parameter to measure the ills plaguing modern Kenyan society, placing them in historico-cultural settings as actual resistance heroines and agents of change, a position that opposes Soyinka's treatment of women. For Soyinka, the agents of change are male like his dentist while women serve as symbolic essences.

Ngugi's Wanja (*Petals of Blood*), and Wariinga (*Devil on the Cross*) are more than revolutionary symbols. They are revolutionaries themselves. And these females defined the terms of their own emancipation. They are both early victims of love relationships. They get pregnant by older men who abandon them. Wanja kills her baby, but Warringa with the solidarity shown by her family keeps hers. Warringa can be seen as an update on Wanja for she exercises positively the *will to change* and thus avoids the downward slide into bars and prostitution. Jennifer Evans appreciates Ngugi's principal intention in creating "his strong, determined woman [women] with a *will to resist and to struggle* against the conditions of her [their] present being" (Evans 131) (emphases, mine). We consequently agree with her opinion that Warringa serves primarily "as a radical example of how a woman can resist being pushed or tempted into accepting subservient, degrading or decorative roles" (Evans 134). This is in keeping with one of the tenets of feminism as defined by Ogundipe Leslie who maintains that the most significant challenge facing the African woman is her own self-perception "since it is she who will have to define her own freedom" (Boyce-Davis 7). For the woman suffering abandonment, values like survival, freedom and transcendence are not to be handed to her on a platter of gold but must be earned. To that end, we agree with Evans that "Warringa is a positive model for a new generation of Kenyan [African] women" (Evans 134). This study, recognizing the limited geographical and linguistic purview of Jennifer Evan's meritorious article, seeks to extend this analysis of women coping with abandonment to encompass much wider comparative, linguistic and geographical *spectra*.

Love in Nigerian Fiction by Rose Acholonu is equally promising in its analyses of the obstacles to happiness in love which beset women. Her study constitutes the positive side of the love coin because the nuisible conditions which chain women to the immanence of abandonment in a love relationship such as infertility, infidelity, polygamy, high bride price, lack of free choice in marriage, issue of virginity, *et cetera*, are the same factors of which the successful resolution unfetters those chains and promotes love in a marital union. Acholonu examines in depth these features that mar the enthronement of a more "egalitarian and balanced love relationship." These cultural mores that militate against the harmony of a couple receive comprehensive coverage. In fact, *Love in Nigerian Fiction* bubbles with happiness like fresh palm wine frothy with energy and life; but also her literary tentacles do not go beyond the Nigerian national literature and so fail to make the work truly comparative.

The article which most pertinently prefigures, albeit in a limited scope, the themes treated in this study is Edris Makward's article, "Marriage, Tradition and Women's Pursuit of Happiness in the novels of Mariama Bâ" (Makward 272). Reading *0 pays!, mon beau Peuple* (1957), Makward salutes Sembène for being one of the first creative writers to treat the couple as a central and exalting entity and to indict polygamy as a principal cause of disharmony in marriage. But, it is in Makward's critique of Mariama Bâ's two novels that his ideology finally approaches that envisaged in the present study. In *Une Si Longue Lettre*, he explores the search for "personal happiness by Bâ's abandoned female protagonists. He brings out Ramatoulaye's and Aissatou's "strong belief in social and political change and progress" (Makward 272). *"In Un Chant Écarlate,* Makward summarizes the storyline and concludes that the pursuit of happiness as conceptualized by Bâ means

> happiness -- and not just women's but men's as well, a whole society's happiness [which] must be

based on a monogamous marriage . . .a close *association between two equals, and the sharing of pains, joys, hopes, disappointment and successes. The foundation of this happiness is without doubt in* the *couple, a concept that is clearly new in Africa (*Makward 272).

Makward participates further in the idealism of *Abandonment in Love Relationships* by supporting Bâ's disapproval of certain glaring abuses of tradition which impede familial stability. In denouncing Ousmane's base and poltroonish treatment of his Frenchwife Mireille and his sexual excesses, he reiterates Lamine's castigation of Ousmane who wishes to be happy

> *sans rien sacrifier. Tu ne veut rien céder et tu exiges des concessions. La vie conjugale est plutôt humaine approche et tolérance.* (Bâ, *Un chant E carlate* 28)

> [*without sacrifice. You do not want to give up anything and [yet] you demand concessions. Married life applies above all humane approach and tolerance*]

These desirable ideals are, of course, vitiated by the marital incubus that is polygamy which negates the female protagonists' free choices in marriages not prearranged by their parents. In upholding Bâ's concept of the couple, Makward reiterates that "family success depends on the continued harmony of the founding couple and it was the grouping of all these successful and happy families that would constitute the nation" (Makward 274). Thus, Makward lends support to Bâ's visionary panegyric of the happy family, that is the microcosm of the nation "where men and women would share equally in the duties as well as in the joys and rewards of a harmonious partnership between **one** husband and **one** wife." In employing the word **one** (my emphasis), Makward underpins the fact that "polygamy" blights the harmony of the couple. But there are other factors not treated by him.

By way of conclusion Makward quotes Fatna Ait Sabbah, a Muslim woman writer who believes firmly that progress in society implies changes which should involve both men and women and that it is possible

> *de vivre mieux, d'aimer mieux. Les femmes, ne sont pas condamnées à vivre mutilées* Sabbah 15).
>
> [*to live better, to love better. Women are not condemned to live as mutilated beings.*]

Pursuit of happiness and self-fulfillment, free choice in marriage, concept of the couple, tolerance in marriage, a happy family, a stable nation, transcending the fettered state of immanence produced by socio-cultural norms -- these are the ideals which inspired this study, *Women in Chains: Abandonment in Love Relationships.* The flaws in Makward's sparkling work reside only in its lack of sufficient depth, its linguistic and geographical limitations and its failure to consider other factors besides polygamy and infidelity as contributory causes of abandonment.

Mbye Cham's article, "Contemporary Society and the Female Imagination: A study of the Novels of Mariama Bâ" deals squarely with the problem of abandonment in her two novels. However, the thrust of the critique is on the form, significance and influence of culture vis-a-vis the stability/success of, or betrayal/abandonment in, a marriage. The female heroes of *Une Si Longue Lettre*, faced with the specter of abandonment, undergo transformative influence and emerge stronger, more aware and better equipped to deal with "the problems, challenges and aspirations not only of women but of society in general" (Cham 67). But confronted with a similar problem, Mireille *(Un Chant Écarlate)*, coming from a different culture, reacts differently, thus becoming the sad and distressed personification of the tragedy and destruction attendant on the problem of abandonment. So far so good. But Mbye Cham had in the second paragraph already established that abandonment in the works of Bâ is primarily a female condition that is both physical and psychological, "transcending race, class, ethnicity and caste" - an assertion which again, we accept. But the contrasting reactions of the female protagonists of the works - reactions to abandonment defined by culture - do, however, cast doubts on the universalism of the problem of abandonment as conceived by Bâ since responses to it depend on cultural formation. This fact does seem to bear out the rightness of the insistence by African-American and other Third World countries like Caroline Ramazanoglu who in *Feminism and the Contradictions of Oppression* insist that women can not develop universal political practices if their oppression takes culturally specific forms, struggles and solutions, that the feminist ideology must be bent to reflect the specificities of race, culture and class.

We, nonetheless, are in accord with Mbye Cham's statement that the primary reality of the women depicted in this literature of oppression and repudiation is that of abandonment and the necessity and determination to transcend and overcome it. The critic aptly calls "the dialectic of oppression and struggle/regeneration" - a dialectic highlighting the political and socio-cultural framework from where one sees the exploitative relationship between man and woman (as conceived by Bâ) in patriarchal African societies. The two critiques of Bâ's work examined above are both scintillating studies, only limited by the need to extend the exercise to encompass other works from other cultural and linguistic entities, a lacuna the present study intends to fill.

In the "Divorce Dilemma," Beatrice Stageman, analyzing two novels - Aluko's *One Man, One Wife* and R.S. Easmon's *The Burnt-out Marriage* -- argues that divorce or destruction of the familial construct is what results when unprogressive traditional values come into conflict with rapid social change. The changing face of society produces a new African woman who "wishes to assume responsibility for her life, to reason about the basic values of life... she sets her own goals rather than assuming a stereotyped role" (Stageman 92). That every woman should assume individual responsibility for the direction of her life is acceptable and, as Stageman also points out, the locus of ethical responsibility which has shifted from the group is tantamount to a theory of personhood and is therefore highly individualistic. She however fails to demonstrate how this new African woman can bend her newly-acquired freedom and self-determining existence to accommodate the family as a corporate structure or, are we to assume that this personalized happiness is preferable to the happiness of a couple (as an entity and, as a unit cell of a larger social structure) in a stable, mutually appreciative union? To counter this view of divorce as the only laudatory means of the new African woman achieving a sense of personhood and self-actualization is the additional objective of this study.

Evidently, no noteworthy, in-depth, comprehensive and comparative research has thus far been carried out in the topical area of abandonment -- its many causes taken up as separate but related themes and dealt with exhaustively within a cohesive study, and possible remedial measures suggested as well. It is thus imperative to fill up the lacuna in this area of African feminist scholarship. This study as a comprehensive, book-length, comparative study that gives close, critical attention to the plethora of problems keeping women in chains and robbing them of much-desired peace of mind and love can hopefully become a launching pad for further critical investigation into this area.

For this study, the critical method used is sociological. The approach will also involve close textual reading and an underlying feminist interpretation of texts. Sociological criticism analyzes the relationship between the text and society. René Wellek and Austin Warren do acknowledge that much light has been thrown on literature by a proper knowledge of the conditions under which it has been produced. And so, this dynamic and complex relationship between literature and society forms the bedrock of the sociological approach. Philip Rice and Patricia Waugh observe that while:

> *the task of literature is to render life, experience and emotion in a potent way, the job of criticism is to reveal the true value and meaning of that rendition - a rendition at once contained within the literary work and yet paradoxically needing the critical act to reveal it* (*Modern Literary Theory* 2-3).

Our investigation will thus appreciate and employ textual evidences to reveal and deliver up the true value of the literary "life, experience and emotion" contained in the works to be studied. Additionally, the feminist perspective will contribute to the illumination and apprehension of these female experiences by showing how literature, in the words of Cheri Register, "comprehends, transmits and shapes female experience and is in turn, shaped by it" ("Literary Criticism," in *Signs* 29). The organizing principle of this study of men and women in love relationships will be that of woman-consciousness which is a first step in feminist scholarship.

FEMINISM: A LITERARY BACKDROP

The core of this study deals with the happiness or misery, survival or abandonment of the woman involved in a love relationship as well as the fate of the family as a primary unit of the social structure. All that concerns the woman is tied up in the *woman* question, hence the entire study has feminism as a literary backdrop. The beginnings, development and establishment of Western feminism as both a socio-political ideology and a literary perspective are too well-known to require further recapitulation. Suffice it to say that after a long struggle, feminism was able to draw on all three dimensional areas of freedom: political, sexual and economic which had been at issue. If it was a struggle, it was not fought with guns but with pens. Eventually, however, this theme of conflict between man and woman found its way into African literature with differing degrees of stridency. The result is a protest literature which invariably dealt with the woman and her oppression because unsong but deeply etched on the canvas of the African novel is the plight of the other half of humanity - womankind.

Earlier African male writers, unashamedly chauvinistic, had no time to treat issues concerning women with any seriousness. This should not be so surprising, for since literature is a reflection of culture, at this time, culture was still predominantly male. The awakening of female writers to a sense of their own identity was yet to come. Early novelist Cyprian Ekwensi's preoccupation, for instance, was with creating sensational melodrama and the result is a portraiture of women that is considered bigoted. Wole Soyinka's presentation of women, usually courtesans, is that of "symbol and essence" (Bryan 119). Carole Boyce Davies insists that portraiture even on a symbolic plane "does not shield a writer from negative or limiting portrayals" (75-88). Achebe himself, with a new-found humility, acknowledges in *The Anthills of the Savannah* that women form the oldest if not "the biggest single group of oppressed people in the world" (*Anthills* 98). From being cast in a scapegoat anima image (Eve causing Adam's fall), archetype of the temptress -- mysterious, alluring, tantalizing and destructive - woman becomes idealized and enshrined on a pedestal (from the Christian Virgin Mary to the Igbo "*Nneka*" - "Mother is supreme"), resorted to only in an extremity and ultimately denied participation in the actual running of human affairs in the public domain. In her remarkable essay, "The Talented Woman in African Literature," Juliet Okonkwo protests that women are brought in to provide a literary background picture, drawing legitimacy only as wives, daughters, mothers or mistresses, coming and going

> with mounds of foo-foo, pots of water, market baskets, fetching kola, being scolded and beaten before they disappear behind the huts of their compound (African Quarterly 36).

In short, women were to be seen, not heard and the Lévi-Straussian theory of two worlds, where, as Okonkwo further observes, "the physiological differences between men and women dictate complete, distinct, social roles for the sexes" (36) was reflected in these novels. It was obvious that women themselves and sympathetic male writers, gynandrists [christened "literary mid-wives" by Charles Nnolim in "A House Divided" 4) had to do something about the situation. Slowly therefore, emerged, a nascent body of writing committed to giving women a voice in the scheme of things and a chance to assume charge of their individual destiny. Thus, the literature of abandonment is a significant part of feminist literature.

The first spur was given in the middle sixties when Flora Nwapa and Ama Ata Aidoo burst into the literary scene to register female presence. Nwapa's *Efuru* (1966) introduced, for the first time, an eponymous female protagonist grappling squarely with the tensions and conflicts that shape her life, instead of living the hitherto peripheral, tangential role of a passive victim of a masculine-based cultural universe, already described by Adrienne Rich (Rich 57-8).

It was a long-awaited departure from the stereotypic female portraiture in male-authored literature; a long wait brought about by the kind of male-favored educational policy implemented by erstwhile colonial administrators. Other novels by Flora Nwapa followed: *Idu, One is Enough, Women are Different*. Nwapa's thought shows evidence of a diachronic progression. From accepting the limiting societal view of woman's sole culpability for infertility in *Efuru*, Nwapa in *Idu* lays the blame squarely on the man and Amarajeme accepts responsibility: "they are men, I am not a man" (23), and promptly hangs himself; while in *One is Enough,* Amaka represents the acme of Nwapa's feminism as following one disastrous marital experience, Amaka radically does away with even the formality of marriage in order to achieve motherhood.

The expatriate Nigerian writer Buchi Emecheta also registered her presence with *In the Ditch*. She has since been prolific: *Second Class Citizen, The Joys of Motherhood, The Bride Price, The Slave Girl, Double Yoke, et cetera*. All of these novels invariably harp on the theme of female oppression, the "slave girl" becoming her leitmotif - the archetypal African woman buried alive under the heavy yoke of traditional mores and customs. Later feminist novelists like Zaynab Alkali, Ifeoma Okoye, and others, though they temper their language and moderate their styles to achieve a reconciliation of the sexes, nevertheless, graphically depict the customary practices and injustices that overburden woman's existence and lead to misery and abandonment.

Conversely, women writers in the Francophone areas of West Africa arrived belatedly on the literary scene. Their progress was somewhat hampered by the nature of French educational policy in her colonies which encouraged assimilation and identification with French culture; their progress was also retarded by the non-functional, psycho-analytical, language-based brand of French feminism (influenced by Derrida's deconstruction and the psychoanalysis of Jacques Lacan) which showed obsession with the nurturant image of woman. Notable French feminist writers coming after de Beauvoir include Luce Irigaray *(Speculum de l'Autre Femme* <1974>); Hélène Cixous *(With ou L'Art de l'Innocence* <1981>); Monique Wittig *(Les Guérillères, Le corps Lesbien* <1973>, *l'Opoponax);* French professor of Linguistics and Psychoanalysis, Julia Kristeva ("Le Temps de femmes" <1981>), *et cetera*. French feminism did not make much impact at first (the Anglo-American, functional feminism influenced Anglophone African countries early enough). Aminata Sow Fall brought out *La Grève des Battu* in 1979, pleading for women suffering abandonment under polygamy as well as pleading for the beggars - "the wretched of the earth". Mariama Bâ's *Une Si Longue Lettre* (1980), *Un Chant Écarlate* (1981) focused her feminist lenses on abandonment, on the destruction of the couple as a unit cell of the larger human family by factors and customs (under patriarchy) which pander to man's egotism. Her analysis of what society should do and the kind of courage needed by woman to achieve a life of self-worth and happiness remains unparalleled. In *Le Fort Maudit,*

Nafissatou Niang Diallo like Buchi Emecheta in *The Rape of Shavi*, imaginatively and successfully deconstructs male-authored literary history and in the reconstruction (according to the principles of *gynocritique*[2] demanded by Elaine Showalter), portrays women endowed with beauty, courage, strength and undaunted will. *Le Fort Maudit* is a kind of female epic in which the power of patriarchy crushes women. Thiane, the female protagonist, possesses as Jacques Chevrier remarks "un sens aigu de sa dignité qui caracterise d'ordinaire, les protagonistes mâles des récits héroiques" - [a sharp sense of her dignity which usually characterizes male protagonists of heroic tales] (*Littérature Nègre* 97-153). This heightened sense of her humanity enables Thiane to achieve glory and vindication.

These and other writings by women are obvious responses to Elaine Showalter's[1] injunction to put right "what men have thought women should be" (Showalter 25-33) - responses in answer to African feminist critic, Ogundipe-Leslie's call to tell us about being a woman: "... [her] personality and the way she feels and knows her world" (Ogundipe-Leslie 9), demand that responds to Hélène Cixous' call to "l'écriture féminine" - feminine writing (Cixous 250) in order to give, says Katherine Frank, "female characters .... a destiny of their own." (Frank 14-34).

Early African feminism, it can be seen, faced similar historical realities as, say Négritude or early African literature. Achebe confesses to espousing a revolution "to help my society regain belief in itself and put away the complexes of years of denigration and self-denigration" (*Morning Yet On Creation Day* 44). Similarly, early African feminism faced the same colonial problem of correcting misconceptions, misrepresentations, outright neglect, sub-category roles and reversing women's own self-created negative self-image engendered by what Carole Boyce Davies calls "centuries of interiorization of the ideologies of patriarchy and gender hierarchy" (Davies, 8). It would be an uphill task stripping off the layers of generations of oppressive burdens that have chained woman - the six mountains on her back, so succinctly outlined by Ogundipe-Leslie[2] and described in detail by Carole Boyce Davies in her "Introduction: Feminist Consciousness and African Literary Criticism" (*Ngambika* 7).

In any case, the terms of woman's freedom and what her new role would be depend solely on the woman herself. This last point is, in itself, a fact of irony because as is pointed out in Ogunyemi's "womanism[3]," the illiterate woman most often used as protagonist is, in reality, so beset by problems of survival that she is hardly aware of her sexist predicament. Therefore, raising her consciousness so as to effect any kind of re-socialization would be hard indeed. In any case, radical feminism (especially, the kind that promotes lesbian / gay rights) as advocated by Western feminists must, of essence, be modified before being acceptable to the generality of black and African women, who are aware of the social primacy of wifehood and motherhood. For this reason, "feminism" is being spoken of in more pliable terms such as "femalism" which is the hybrid of feminism and "femininism" with consciousness-raising forming the bedrock of the femalist theory. Femalism because of its non-opposition to man is diametrical to radical feminism, which makes "man" its principal enemy. Femalism merely seeks to claim for women recognition, opportunities for self-actualisation and self-reclamation. Ogunyemi arrives at another term, "womanism" which parallels Alice Walker's ideology. Ogunyemi's ideology

celebrates black roots, the ideals of black life

while giving a balanced presentation of black womanhood..... Its ideal is for black unity where every black person (man or woman) has a modicum of power ... its aim is the dynamism of wholeness and self-healing... (Ogunyemi in Signs 72).

However, a rose by any other name will still smell as sweet. In the context of this study, feminism is used as an enveloping term since feminism, femalism or womanism -- all center on the "woman question." Thus, as an ideology, modern new wave feminism takes cognizance of the specificities of race, milieu and culture. Therefore, the apprehension of feminism by this writer is the multiple dimensional brand which, to quote Julia Inyang Essin Oku, does not seek

to castrate the men or which is reminiscent of the vocal and sometimes histrionic suffragettes. While ... these responses are vital to any coherent understanding of feminism, they are significant in so far as they provide stepping-stones to the kind of feminism which explores, without bias, self-pity or recrimination, the weaknesses, traumas, defeats and glories, all of which make up a woman ("Courtesans and Earthmothers: A Feminist Reading...." *Calabar Studies in African Literature 3;* 225).

WOMEN IN CHAINS:
AIMS AND METHODOLOGY

This research effort, therefore, is anchored on the need to investigate and gauge the extent of abandonment as a literary phenomenon, its causes and its consequences. This study is organized on a set of themes that conduce to the incidence of abandonment. The following will form the working hypotheses:

This literature of suffering, oppression and abandonment is dialectical in nature and possesses discernible organic phases. Its reach is pervasive and is irrespective of social *milieu* and ranks, stretching from rural to urban, illiterate to the educated. Abandonment is an aberration from any love relationship and its prevalence can be reduced only when its causes and dire consequences are sufficiently highlighted to prompt a rethinking in the society.

There are thematic and stylistic affinities as well as differences in the treatment of the subject matter obvious in both the Anglophone and Francophone texts. What are these similarities and differences?

Consequently, the identifiable causes of abandonment have been delineated into broad categories, namely: (1) childlessness, or, infertility; (2) polygamy (3) infidelity and, (4) those other *"nuisible"* factors such as -- high bride price, greed and competition by younger women, opposition from and manipulation by older women, cruelty arising from inferiority complex on the part of the man -- which are considered together as *exploitation*. Sometimes as in *Une Si Longue Lettre, Un Chant Écarlate, La Grève des Battus, Behind the Clouds* and *One is Enough*, the distinction between two causes like infidelity and polygamy may not be very sharp as they tend to overlap and merge. For instance, to Aissatou, Mireille, Ije and Lolli, infidelity and polygamy are one and the same -- *a grave act of betrayal*. Some protagonists like Ramatoulaye, Amaka, Lolli, or Ije may swallow their pride, put on a brave face and be willing to accommodate to polygamy whereas others like Aissatou and Mireille will outrightly reject any compromise. To Aissatou, polygamy equates "procréer sans aimer" [to procreate without loving]. The subtle distinction between heartfelt, idealistic love and plain physical lust remains unappreciated by her because, "la communion charnelle ne peut être sans l'acceptation du coeur, si minime soit-elle" (50), [there can be no union of two bodies without the hearts acceptance, however little that may be]. To Mireille of *Un Chant Écarlate,* Ousmane, by his infidelity and polygamous marriage to Ouleymatou has become "sale Traître! Adultère! Infidèle!" Killing their only son and attempting to slay Ousmane constitute acts of revolt and a symbolic intent to extirpate, in her madness, both present and future generations of patriarchy with all its entrenched and institutionalized injustices that keep a woman in the kind of chains that precipitate her into an abyss of insane despair.

Certain salient facts crystallized in the course of researching this topic -- there are different levels of abandonment and it wears many faces:

(a) Abandonment can result in both an emotional and physical act of separation as in the case of Li *(The Stillborn),* Ramatoulaye *(USLL),* Nnu Ego *(The Joys of Motherhood),* Ije *(Behind the Clouds), et cetera,* where the husbands or wives move or are forced into moving away.

(b) Abandonment or alienation can remain on an emotional and psychological level as in *The Victims, The Journey Within, Xala, La Grève des Battus, Vèhi-Ciosane and Sous l'Orage* where the protagonists remain within the familial construct but in total alienation from their spouses. Again, even where women like Efuru, Amaka *(One is Enough),* Wali *(La Nouvelle Romance),* Aissatou *(USLL), et cetera,* initiate the physical act of separation, it can still be argued that the men concerned by their infidelities have already removed themselves emotionally from their spouses long before their wives became aware of that fact.

There are even cases of abandoned husbands (outside the purview of this study) as in *Idu,* or, *The Burnt-Out Marriage* where Ojiugo and Makallay Touray abandon their respective husbands, Amarajeme and Chief Francis Briwa, conceive for their lovers and actually turn their backs on their marriages. Both are cases of infidelity by women brought about by infertility arising from each husband's impotence.

Abandonment wears many faces:

(1) There are rural, illiterate and helpless females with no economic base like Nwabunor *(The Victims),* Ngonè War Thiandum (*Vèhi-Ciosane*) who really get trampled upon. Nwabunor's utter helplessness and dire poverty evoke the pathetic situation of Aku (*In The Last Duty,*) whom extreme need leads into a degrading kind of infidelity; Ngonè War Thiandum, because of caste pride and the ancestral Ceddo[4] spirit, believes, she can only wipe out the stain on the paternal honor by suicide. In any case, with the theme of incest as a revolting form of infidelity (though a popular theme in Black American fiction as exemplified in Ralph Ellison's *Invisible Man* and Toni Morrison's *The Bluest Eye* or Alice Walker's *(The Color Purple),* Ousmane Sembène broke new ground in West African fiction.

(2). There are rural, illiterate but economically strong females like Efuru, who survive and turn to other pursuits, deciding that life is worth living after all, despite barrenness and failed marriages.

(3). There are the urban, helpless and economically dependent females like Lolli (*La Grève des Battus*), Adja

Awa Astou (*Xala*) and Perpétue, who, trodden upon, have no choice but to accommodate themselves to the situation.

(4). There are also the urban, economically strong but emotionally dependent females like Ije, Ramatoulaye, Mireille, Jacqueline and Wali, who, their happiness obliterated, either perish or are forced to survive somehow.

(5). There is yet the group of the urban, employed, tough-minded, resilient and economically resourceful abandoned females, who refuse to allow life's vicissitudes and vagaries to overwhelm and defeat them. These are Amaka, Aissatou, Li, Adaku and Adah.

The different categories of abandonment correspond also to the level of awareness that the individual female protagonist has with regard to her condition.

1. Some are conservative, passive traditionalists like Adja Astou in *Xala* and Lolli in *La Grève des Battus*.

2. The second group is quite aware of their rights to happiness and self-actualization. This group includes outright rebels like Aissatou (*Une Si Longue Lettre*), Amaka in *One is Enough,* Efuru, and on a symbolic plane even Mireille in *Un Chant Ecarlate* and Ngoné War Thiandum in *Vèhi-Ciosane.* The latter, an illiterate, conformist Muslim is forced by incredible events into being conscious of institutionalized, systemic female exploitation and to ultimately think for herself. She chooses to die; her suicide is an extension of her awakening, the ultimate act of free will open to her through which she can elude those who would torment her and drag her down.

3. Finally, there is a third group - the accommodationists - the self-actualized and emancipated females, aware of their rights to bliss and personhood but more than that, aware of the fact that compromise and tolerance are indispensable conditionalities to a successful conjugal living. In the words of Nnolim in "A House Divided: Feminism in African Literature," they aim at "a pooling together of resources not a scattering, a building together not destruction...." These therefore, consciously choose to place the happiness of the hearth above that of self and save themselves an intolerable abyss of solitude. Thus, Ramatoulaye, proved, tried and refined like gold in the furnace of suffering, yet declares herself still committed to this search for "*bonheur* - happiness" while yet manifesting a subtle radicalism truly subversive in a Muslim milieu. Thus, also, Li, having found her identity, is willing to hazard another try with a now chastised and crippled Habu Adams "and side by side, we will learn to walk" (105).

Which then is the archetype of the new African woman: the passive traditionalist who, fettered by patriarchal strictures and cultural mores, allows herself to get done in? or the radical, self-achieving, no-nonsense female, ready to go it alone if things do not work out right? or is it the compassionate and enlightened accommodationist, still willing to try again and again for the sake of the family?

This study thus assumes immense significance in underscoring the need for the human family which primarily is a microcosm of any nation, to achieve stability. Any condition creating rancor and disunity becomes a kind of cankerworm eating deep into the fabric of an entire society.

The novel will be the genre examined in this study.

Being new and a kind of catch-all genre, its utilitarian possibilities are limitless. This study of abandonment in love relationships aims at pointing out to society where some of the inequities lie, aims at correcting what may be termed a literature of *suffering* by helping to highlight its lamentable causes. This will be effected through synthesizing from the literary texts of the revisionist authors, messages and recommendations as to how the abandoned females, chained to constricting social factors and cultural mores, can acquire "**the will to change**" (Chapter Six of this work), and thus transcend their oppressed state. Thus may be brought about the kind of "social transformation ... that will change all human relationships for the better" (Eisenstein 14) - a social transformation that will operate in a new society such as described by A. R. Wadia in *The Ethics of Feminism:*

> *the society of the future will have to give a new vigor and a new color to family life by reconstructing its very foundations on the basis of mutuality and not on the relation of male superiority and female inferiority; justice not might; love not fear; confidence not suspicion; frankness not hypocrisy*... (Wadia 34).

This may be utopian, perhaps. Thomas More's *Utopia*, was derived from the Greek words "outopia" (no place) and "eutopia (the good place) – [the good place that exists no where], as a result of which the word has come to stand for an idealistically perfect society which is not practical. But out of dreams, concrete realities can be shaped.

In determining how abandonment undermines happiness in a familial construct, the traumas the abandoned women go through as well as its causes, this study limits itself to the West African literary region. The works of six Anglophone writers -- Flora Nwapa, Buchi

Emecheta, Isidore Okpewho, I. N. C. Aniebo, Ifeoma Okoye and Zaynab Alkali have been chosen for study. On the Francophone side, works to be examined include those of three Senegalese writers - Ousmane Sembène, Mariama Bâ and Aminata Sow Fall; the works of the Cameroonian author, Mongo Beti and the Congolese author and former Prime Minister, Henri Lopes are also featured. *La Nouvelle Romance* is included because it belongs to the "Yaounde Group"- products of the Camerounian publishing house, Editions CLE (Centre de Littérature Evangelique) established in 1965. Nigerian authors have been chosen as representatives of the Anglophone sector because they, more than any other cultural or linguistic group, have contributed the most towards the emergence and propagation of both the fictional genre and African literature in general. On the other hand, that the Francophone authors come mainly from Senegal and Cameroun proves that Senegal as well as Cameroun have both been at the vanguard of French West African letters.

My choice of authors includes gynandrists. The gynandrist is a male writer who creates his characters from the feminine view-point, thus, joining forces with the femalist in her effort to slough off restrictive patriarchal norms that impede growth and happiness of woman. As even Emecheta herself has confessed, "we need our men" (Solberg 247-262). The choice of texts is subjective, prompted both by propinquity and ready availability of materials. The critical discussion becomes textually interpretative because I share Hester Eisenstein's dictum that understanding of texts springs from immersion, from empathy and commitment and because "it is impossible to eliminate the human being, the mind and the heart from life's essential realities" (Eisenstein, xx) Empathy and commitment become desiderata for the

African female writer who should strive to live up to the charge by Molara Ogundipe-Leslie to be committed in three ways: "as a writer, as a woman, and as third World person and her biological womanhood is implicated in all three" (Ogundipe-Leslie 10).

Consequently, this study is organized, on the basis of a set of themes that have been identified as the main causes of abandonment of the woman in a marital construct; these themes fall into four broad categories which are translated into chapters.

Chapter one serves as the introductory chapter. It defines the subject-matter, conducts a literature search, tracing the literary history of abandoned women through the ages; furthermore, it provides a literary overview of feminism as an ideology and the degree to which it influenced the development of the African literature of abandonment, which is delineated in its many faces; its principal causes are highlighted.

Chapter two pinpoints barrenness or childlessness - *the ultimate affliction* - as a precipitant of abandonment in love relationships. In a heavily child-centered society with high sex-role traditionalism, marital stability is sometimes anchored on a woman's procreative ability while infertility becomes a scourge and a curse.

Chapter three examines polygamy, a tradition-based, sometimes religiously-sanctioned feature of African and Muslim societies, as the most common theme unifying the works of many of the Anglophone and Francophone writers, as they explore the plight of the abandoned woman in polygamy. Hitherto depicted by earlier male writers, Achebe, Elechi Amadi, *et cetera*, as receiving unquestioning acquiescence and complaisance, a crop of feminist and gynandrist writers now ask questions, raise objections and proffer alternate arrangements.

Chapter four examines the act of infidelity as the

harbinger of ill-tidings and which culminates ultimately in abandonment. Sometimes the line of demarcation between infidelity and polygamy gets blurred as the female protagonists concerned fail to grasp the subtle nuances between the two themes, regarding both polygamy and infidelity as one -- *a grave act of betrayal.*

Chapter five critically questions whether feminist awareness exacerbates the process of abandonment. It examines the levels of the awareness of their condition by the female protagonists concerned. The eponymous Perpétue, bartered into an incompatible marriage with the mediocre, ambitious and exploitative Edouard, makes a fruitless effort at self-determinism. Ada (*Second Class Citizen*) and Wali (*La Nouvelle Romance*) as emancipated new African women, living in Europe and impelled by their new environment to become aware of their basic human rights to dignity and individuation, resolve to end marriages whose traditionalism is incompatible with the realities of their new milieu; while Nko, spurned with patriarchal scorn for her generous gift of love, self-emancipates to redeem the onslaught on her "individuality and dignity." A few myths are demolished before the "double yoke" of tradition and modernism find a common ground.

Chapter six, serving as the conclusion, recapitulates the salient points made in the course of the study and hazards suggestions towards stemming the tide of abandonment in love relationships. There are suggestions for further research.

And finally, this literature of abandonment, therefore, anchors its roots on this quest for wholeness and self-healing, for recognition and opportunities for self-actualization and self-worth, for happiness within a familial construct, freed from constricting traditional expectations and usages. To be able to achieve these ideals, it is committed to exploring without bias or recriminations, the *constraints and traumas that impede the woman's goal of living up to her supreme destiny.*

Notes

1. The term, *gynocritique* is used by Elaine Showalter to cover the entire *gamut* of female creativity and representation as in: (a) feminist critique, or woman as reader of male-produced literature, decoding the significance of sexual codes so as to change our apprehension of a given text; (b) *gynocritique*, or woman as writer and producer of textual meaning using history, themes, genres and structures of literature by women and gynandrists to recreate from the female subjectivity as delineated in "Towards a Feminist Poetics" (*Women Writing About Women.*"

2. For a detailed description of Ogundipe-Leslie's six mountains on the African woman's back, see Carole Boyce Davies,s "Introduction: Feminist Consciousness and African Literary Criticism" in *Ngambika: Studies In African Literature.* (1986), eds. Carole Boyce Davies and Anne Adams Graves.

3. A term coined by Alice Walker and which Okonjo Ogunyemi claims to have arrived at independently of lice Walker's Womanism. See "Womanism: the Dynamics of the Contemporary Female Novel in English." *Signs*, 11, 1 (Autumn 1985).

4. The Ceddo or Tiėdos represent medieval Senegalese warriors who fought valiantly and determinedly against slavery in order to maintain their honor. In 1977, Sembène released the film "Ceddo" as a social commentary against Black slavery and Islam. See Chioma Opara, *Towards Utopia: Womanhood in the Fiction of Selected* West *African Writers.* An unpublished Ph.D dissertation at the

University of Ibadan, Nigeria (1987).

WORKS CITED

Achebe, Chinua. *Anthills of the Savannah.* Nigeria: Heinemann, 1988.

_____. *Morning Yet On Creation Day: Essays.* London: Heinemann, 1975.

Acholonu, Rose. *Love in Nigerian Fiction.* Owerri: Achisons Publications, 2000.

Banyiwa-Home, Naana. "African womanhood: the Contrasting Perspectives of Flora Nwapa's *Efuru* and Elechi Amadi's *The Concubine*" in *Ngambika: Studies of Women in African Literature.* Eds. Carole Boyce Davies & Anne Adams Graves. Trenton, New Jersey: Africa World Press, Inc., 1986.

Bryan, Sylvia. "Images of Women in Wole Soyinka's Work," *African Literature Today,* 15.

Chevrier, Jacques. *Littérature Nègre.* Paris: Armand Colin Collection, 1974.

Cham, Mbye. "Contemporary Societv and the Female Imagination: A study of the Novels of Mariama Bâ" in *African Literature Today,* 15.

Cixous, Hélène. "Le Rire de la Méduse, *L'Arc,* 61. (Trans. as "The Laugh of the Medusa") in Marks and de Courtivron, Davies, Carole Boyce & Graves, Anne Adams. Eds. *Ngambika: Studies In African Literature.* Trenton, New Jersey: Africa World Press, Inc; 1986.

_____. "Introduction: Feminist consciousness and African Literary criticism" in *Ngambika.*

_____. "Maidens, Mistresses and Matrons: Feminine Images in Selected Soyinka's Works" in *Ngambika: Studies of Women in African Literature.* Eds. Carole Boyce Davies & Anne Adams Graves. New Jersey: Africa World Press, 1986.

Diallo, Nafissatou. *Le Fort Maudit.* Paris: Hatier, 1980.

de Beauvoir, Simone. *Tout Compte Fait.* Coll. Folio. Paris: Gallimard, 1972. Trans. as *All Said and Done,* Patrick

O'Brien. Middlesex:: Penguin, 1987.

_____. *La femme rompue*. Paris: Editions Gallimard, 1967. Trans. by Patrick Brian as *The Woman Destroyed* London: Fontana, 1957.

de Pisan, Christine. *Book of the City of Ladies by Christine de Pizan*. Trans. Earl Jeffrey Richards. Persea Press, 1994

Egejuru, Phanuel. "The Absence of the Passionate Love Theme in African Literature." In *Design and Intent*. Eds. David Dorsey, Phanuel Egejuru and Stephen Arnold. Washington D. C: Three Continent Press, 1979.

Eisenstein, Hester. Contemporary *Feminist Thought*. London: Unwin Paperbacks, 1984.

Evans, Jennifer. "Women and Resistance in Ngugi's *Devil on the Cross*" in *Women in African Literature Today* 15. Trenton, New Jersey: Africa World Press, 1987.

Frank, Katherine. "Women Without Men: The Feminist Novel in Africa." In *Women in African Literature*. Trenton, New Jersey: 1987.

Friedan, Betty. *The Feminine Mystique*. New York: W. W. Norton, 1973.

From, Erich. *The Art of Loving*. London: Unwin Books, 1972.

Firestone, Shulamith. *The Dialectics of Sex: The Case for Feminist Revolution*. N.Y.: Bantam Books, 1970.

Greer, Germaine. *The Female Eunuch*. New York: McGraw-Hill Book Co., 1971.

Greene, Julien. *God's Fool: The Life and Times of St. Francis of Assisi*. Trans. by Peter Heinegg. San Francisco: Harper & Row, 1983.

Howe, Irving. *Thomas Hardy*. London, 1968.

Hunter, Jim. *The Metaphysical Poets*. London: Evans Brothers Ltd., 1965.

Irigary, Luce. *Sepeculum de l'Autre Femme*. Paris: Éditions de Minuit, 1974. Trans. Gillian C. Gill.

Kettle, Arnold. *An Introduction* to the *English Novel*, Vol. 1. London: Hutchinson & Co. Ltd., 1951.

Lawrence, D. H. *Sons and Lovers*. London: Heinemann Educational Books, 1982.

Lerner, Gerda. *The Creation of Feminist Consciousness: From the Middle Ages to Eighteen-seventy.* Oxford: Oxford University Press, 1993.

Lewis, C. S. *Allegory of* Love. Coghill, Nevill. "Introduction" to *The Canterbury Tales.* London: Penguin Books, 1958

_____. *The Four Loves.* London, New York: Harcourt Brace Jovanovich, 1960.

_____. *The Allegory of Love.* Oxford, New York:: Oxford University Press, 1936.

Lipking, Lawrence. ed. *The Abandoned Woman and Poetic Tradition.* London: The University of Chicago Press, 1988.

Lopes, Henri. *Nouvelle Romance.* Yaounde: Editions CLE, 1976.

Moi, Tori. *Feminist Theory & Simone de Beauvoir.* Massachusetts: Basil Blackwell, 1990.

Morrison, Toni. *The Bluest Eye.* New York: Washington Square Press, Pocket Books, 1973.

Macward, Idris. "Marriage, Tradition and Woman's Pursuit of Happiness in the Novels of Mariama Bâ" in *Ngambika:Studies of Women in African Literature.* eds. Davies and Graves. Trenton, N.J.: Africa World Press, Inc.

Macquarrie, John. *A Dictionary of Christian Ethics.* London: SCM Press Ltd., 1967.

Mack, Maynard. General Ed. *The Norton Anthology of World Masterpieces.* New York. London: W. W Norton & Co., Inc., 1987. Subsequent references will be to this edition and the pages will be inserted into the text.

More, Thomas. *Utopia.* Trans. Paul Turner. London: Penguin Books, 1965.

Nnolim, Charles. "Mythology and The Unhappy Woman in Nigerian Fiction," in *Calabar Studies.* Calabar, Nigeria, 1989.

_____. "A House Divided: Feminism in African Literature." *Feminism in African Literature* Ed. Helen Chukwuma. University of Port Harcourt, Nigeria.

Ogundipe-Leslie, Molara. "The Female Writer & Her Commitment" *African Literature Today*, 15.

_____. "The Female Writer and her Commitment," *African Literature Today*. 15.

Ogunyemi, "Womanism: The Dynamics of the Contemporary Black Female Novel in English." In *Signs* Chicago: The University of Chicago Press, 1985.

Ojo-Ade, Femi. "Still A Victim? Mariama Bâ's *Une Si Longue Lettre*." *African Litterature Today* 12, 1982.

Okonkwo, Juliet. "The Talented Woman in African Literature." *African Quarterly,* 15, 1&2. 1975.

Oku, Julia Inyang Essin. "Courtesans and Earthmothers: A Feminist Reading of Cyprian Ekwensi's *Jagua Nana's Daughter* & Buchi Emecheta's *Joys of Motherhood.*" *Calabar Studies in African Literature,*3.

Opara, Chioma. *Towards Utopia: Womanhood in the Fiction of Selected* West *African Writers.*An unpublished Ph.D dissertation at the University of Ibadan, Nigeria (1987).

Plato. *The Symposium.* Trans. Walter Hamilton. Hammondsworth, England: Penguin Books Ltd. 1951.

Register, Cheri. "Literary Criticism," *Signs*, vol.6, no.2. University of Chicago.

Rhys, Jean. *Wide Sargossa Sea.* New York: W. W. Norton & Co., 1967.

Rice, Philip & Waugh, Patricia. eds. *Modern Literary Theory: A Reader.* London: Hodder & Stoughton, 1989.

Rich, Adrienne. *Of Woman Born: Motherhood as Experience and Institution.* New York: W. W, Norton, 1976

Sabbah, Fatna Ait. *La Femme dans l'Inconscient* musulman. Paris: Edition Le Sycomore, 1982.

Schwarz, 0. *The Psychology of Sex.* London, 1957.

Showalter, Elaine. *A Literature of Their Own: British Women Novelists from Brontë to Lessing* London: Virago Ltd., 1977.

_____. "Towards a Feminist Poetics" in *Women Writing about Women,* ed. Mary Jacobus. Cited in *Modern Literary Theory,* eds. Philip Rice & Patricia Waugh. London: Hodder & Stoughton, 1989.

Solberg, Rolf. "The Woman of Black Africa, Buchi Emecheta: The Woman's Voice in the New Nigerian Novel." *English Studies,* 64, 3 (June 1983): 247-262.

Stageman, Beatrice. "The Divorce Dilemma: The New Woman in Contemporary African Novels" in *Critique*, vol. 15, 81-93.
The Oxford University Dictionary. London: Oxford University Press, 1985.
Virgil, *The Aeneid.* N.Y.: Bantam Classics. 1981.
Wa Thiong'o, Ngugi. *Detained:A Writer's Diary.* Nairobi: Heinemann, 1981.
Wadia, A. R. The Ethics of *Feminism: A Study of the* Revolt of *Woman.* George Allen & UnWin Ltd. London: 1923.
Watt, Ian. *The Rise of the Novel.* Hammondsworth, England: Penguin Books, 1957.
Willard, Charity Cannon. *Christine de Pizan:Her Life and Works, A Biography by Charity Cannon Willard.* New York: Persea Press, 1984.
Wilson, Katharina M. *Medieval Women Writers.* Athens, G., USA: U. of Georgia Press, 1984.
Woolf, Virginia. *A Room of One's Own.* Hammondsworth: Penguin, 1929.

CHAPTER TWO

BARRENNESS: CATALYST FOR SELF-DISCOVERY

> *Yes, Indeed! A woman with a fruitful womb is most precious to a man; contrariwise, a woman without a fruitful womb is of scant value to a procreative man and holds little power over him* (Chinweizu 10).

Childlessness, known variously as barrenness, infecundity or infertility, possesses in African traditional and modern *milieux* a peculiarly central importance. Its peals of signification resound with telling effects on the institution of marriage as it is integrally linked to the stability of most marriages. Infertility is one of the socio-cultural factors that forge chains of iron for African women, robbing them of self-fulfilled conjugal existence and more often than not, leading to polygamy and abandonment. That a woman bears a child (preferably sons) fortifies her *locus standi* in her husband's home, enhances her value before her kinsmen and wards off for her, excessive interference from an overbearing mother-in-law and *umu ada* or *umu mgboto* (female relations of the husband) as poignantly depicted in Munonye's *Obi*.

The centrality of procreation is also underpinned by the fact that man is driven to survive through his progeny: *des héritiers en qui se prolongera sa vie terrestre [heirs through whom his earthly life is prolonged]* (de Beuvoir 112-132). Filomena Steady obviously concurs when she observes that women's "reproductive capacity is crucial to the main-tenance of the husband's lineage..." (*The Black Woman Cross-Culturally* 7-36). Motherhood, in fact, defines womanhood / selfhood since without pregnancy, a woman's humanity is doubted and she is referred to as a "man" due to her inability to conceive (Bello, *Sunday*

Vanguard 8). Christie Achebe further expatiates

> In other words, fulfilment as a human being is measured by the number of children (especially males) she bears... (*Présence Africane* 7).

In addition, the African woman is socialized by a male-supremacist society into believing herself culpable hence in novel after novel -- *Efuru, Idu, One is Enough, The Victims, La Nouvelle Romance, Les Soleils des Indé pendances, O pays, mon beau Peuple!* -- it is invariably the woman who makes the round of herbalists, prayer-homes and medical facilities for treatments amidst immense danger to her life and its attendant loss of indignity. It hardly occurs to anyone to attribute the infertility to the man as actually is the case in *Idu* and *Behind the Clouds*. Onuora Nzekwu's female character Agom laments her early barrenness:

> If only she'd had a child! What shall I tell my ancestors when I go to them? That while the dance lasted, all I did was make preparations to join in it? (*Highlife for Lizards* 54).

Thus, the lot of the barren African woman in African society, irrespective of cultural, linguistic or geographical distinctions, is often fraught with tensions, insecurity, heartache and grief. Tormented by the heartless, gossipy taunts of neighbors, co-wives or an insensitive husband, the pains suffered by the barren woman are long and lingering as without doubt (except for the few fortunate ones), she has the destruction of her marital bliss and abandonment as her lot.

Ironically, infertility often seen as the lamentable state of the barren by outsiders, has quite often in the novels to be studied turned out to be a catalyst for self-discovery.

Most of the barren women in these novels decide to do something about their barrenness and consequent abandonment. Some pack up and leave the homestead (Aissatou in *USLL*; others run to more virile men (Ije in *Behind the Clouds*) and Amaka (*One is Enough*); some (Ojiugo in *Idu*) re-marry or prove their fecundity in unconventional ways (Amaka *One is Enough*). Education and the changing society encourage these trapped women to take some form of action that reflects their changed circumstances. Some even start a rebellion while others end up becoming radical feminists.

In the works discussed in this chapter, barrenness turns out to be a major cause of abandonment. A general trend also appears to emerge. It is seen that most barren and abandoned women, especially the uneducated or unenterprising, accept their fate and end their days in grief. For a second group, especially, the educated or enterprising ones, abandonment becomes a catalyst for self-discovery, for self-awakening, for self-reclamation, for self-assertion as new doors in life become open and a seeming curse is turned into a blessing, even if in the process some moral codes are broken. Consequent upon this, a certain kind of African feminism emerges, being built on the foundation of what initially seems a disaster, or the end of the road. In the process also, what seems like a curse, an albatross, turns into a personal moral victory over a destructive patriarchal system, and for some women like Wali (*La Nouvelle Romance),* childlessness becomes a fulcrum for an ideologically self-rewarding crusade for themselves and for women of like mind. It becomes apparent also that childlessness and monogamy are more often, mutually exclusive. Oladele Taiwo acknowledges that "a childless marriage has no place in African traditional (and often modern) life *(Female Novelists of Modern Africa* 2). Thus, childlessness directly leads to infidelity and polygamy which are examined in subsequent chapters. Often, the woman (whether Efuru, Idu or Agom) actively conforms to tradition by marrying wives for the husband to simply perpetuate his lineage. Any wonder that infertility stamps its indelible seal of doom on many an African marriage as it chains the woman to the immanence of unfulfilment, misery and abandonment.

In pursuit of the stated objective of this study, this chapter therefore pinpoints barrenness - the ultimate affliction - as a precipitant of abandonment in marriage. The African societies under study are heavily child-centered with a high sex-role traditionalism that is aggravated by ignorance, prejudices, and fetishistic practices. Marital stability is therefore predicated on the woman's procreative ability while infertility becomes a scourge and a curse. The major works to be examined are: Emecheta's *The Joys of Motherhood,* Nwapa's *One Is Enough,* Henri Lopes' *La Nouvelle Romance,* and Ifeoma Okoye's *Behind the Clouds.* There is a pattern of spatial and temporal progression discernible in these four Works. Nnu Ego's early base is entirely rural; Nwapa's Amaka goes from rural-urban Onitsha to fully urbanized Lagos; Ije's base is entirely urban while Lopes' Wali migrates from a rural-urban to a sophisticated, international milieu - Brussels. Their levels of feminist consciousness can therefore be said to be modulated by the degree of their individual contact with urban, progressive ideas. This chapter follows this progression in time and space, from the rural and traditional to the urban and the radicalized. There is also an ideological transformation as the protagonists in the various novels move from an attitude of quiescence to moderate and eventually to modern feminist radicalism as abandonment proves to be not a chain on the woman but a catalyst for self-discovery and self-realization such that even when she decides to stay on in the marriage, her decision is based on the ideological principle of accommodationism (her own terms) rather than on the fetters of marriage or on the traditional concept of the inferior role and place of the woman in the home.

11

Nnu Ego, the heroine of Emecheta's *The Joys of Motherhood,* is so thoroughly subsumed under such a plethora of sociocultural ills ind practices that this novel is considered by non-Africans to be the lexicon for all the traditional mores keeping *women in chains* in a sexist social milieu. Name the enslaving ill, Nnu Ego suffers it: infertililty, polygamy, sex-preferential treatment, enslavement to male-ego and to superstitious myths, lack of free choice in marriage, in short, all the themes that conduce to keep women in chains and enslaved, thus making marital happiness a mirage are deftly woven into a complex storyline. The curious rigor with which Emecheta treats Nnu Ego and some protagonists of her novels has given rise to a charge of antipathy and ambivalence towards her female fictional creations since only in her autobiographical works does her persona emerge triumphantly self-realized from an oppressive patriarchal universe. However, that Emecheta is concerned with these gender-constructed, politico-cultural norms which make of women, a beleaguered species, is well-attested to by the very encompassing sweep of her feminist perspective. In an interview with Marie Tioye, she reiterates:

> *the main themes of my novels are African society and family: the historical, social and political life as seen by a woman through events. I always try to show that the African male is oppressed and he*

too oppresses the African woman . . . (Unwinding Threads, 49).

This obviously bears out Ogundipe-Leslie's clearly defined second and fourth mountains on the woman's back, viz: "heritage of tradition and her men, weaned on centuries of male [colonial] domination who will not willingly relinquish their power and privilege -- [over women] (cited in *Ngambika* 7). The story of Nnu Ego spans a life-time and the author uses this *bildungsroman* as a medium of social commentary, presented from a feminist perspective. In this chapter, we are concerned with the young Nnu Ego as she experiences barrenness and abandonment at the hands of her first husband, Amatokwu.

Nwokocha Agbadi, exercising the right of *pater Romanus*[1] arranges for his beloved daughter, Nnu Ego to marry Amatokwu amidst great pomp. She is acquiescent and well-satisfied with the choice of Amatokwu - "long, wiry... lean legs and very dark skin" (*The Joys of Motherhood* 43). The very next day, Amatokwu's kinsmen, in gratitude, bring six-full kegs of palm wine because Nnu Ego has been confirmed a virgin[2]. Agbadi remarks to his life-long friend Obi Idayi: "when a woman is virtuous, it is easy for her to conceive. You shall soon see her children coming to play" (31). Characteristic of Emecheta's style are mordant ironies, lightened by, flashes of humor. Nnu Ego, though virtuous and a virgin, fails to conceive while married to Amtokwu. But the union does, at least, start off as a love union for "Nnu Ego and her new husband Amatokwu were very-happy" (31), a fact validated by her later plaint when matters have gone awry:

> *Remember, Amatokwu, when I first came to* your *house? Remember how you used to want me here*

with only the sky for our shelter? (32).

In the traditional worldview, of what use is an open-field love revelry when Nnu Ego cannot produce children to ensure the bloodline? Amatokwu hastens to inform her that his manhood is in doubt, "'my father is beginning to look at me in a strange way." As the months speed by without a visible change in her anatomy, Nnu Ego proves that she is a thoroughly socialized child of tradition for she accepts sole culpability for the. couple's childless state and thereafter embarks on the merry-go-round of the native medicine men *(dibias)*. Infertility, she believes, has become "her problem and hers alone" (31).

The verdict of the *dibias* attribute her infertility to her *chi*, the slave woman (buried with Agbadi's first wife), who while dying, vowed to torment Agbadi's household. The myth of the slave woman is centrally interwoven into the fabric of the life of Nnu Ego, who thus becomes the victim of antenatal misfortune or as Judith Fryer would say of Oliver Wendell Holmes' Elsie Venner "an unfortunate victim who received a moral poison from a remote ancestor [even] before [she] drew her first breath" (*The Faces of Eve* 29). Emecheta's recourse to the supernatural myth of reincarnation is often cited as further evidence of her ambivalence because this contradicts her stance of feminist realism and Western sophistication. This slave woman, who first plagues the protagonist with barrenness and later with ungrateful, selfish children is however regarded by Eustace Palmer as a literary artifact used to "enhance plot rather than a means of demonstrating the beliefs of the people as Amadi and Achebe do (*ALT 13*, 51). But it is our conviction that Emecheta deliberately is out to expose, as part of her slave *leitmotif* (evident in works like *The Slave Girl, The Bride* Price), how the patriarchal cultural universe bends and uses superstition to oppress the woman. When she suffers childlessness in Amatokwu's household, only Nnu Ego, through her personal *chi,* is culpable and when later she fills Nnaife's home with a litter of children who refuse to conform to traditional expectations, it is still Nnu Ego who is to blame, still through her *chi* who supposedly is intent on blighting her existence with "dirty children."

As all appeasement sacrifices prove futile, Nnu Ego finds herself moved to a hut normally kept for older wives since a new wife has been found for Amatokwu. The new wife promptly becomes pregnant the very first month and Nnu Ego shrinks like a snail into her lonely shell. Then, during the first harvest, she is demoted to the rank of an unpaid farm hand. Furthermore, Amatokwu completely denies her basic sexual rights; when she complains, he brutally shrugs her off:

> *I am a busy man. I have no time to waste my precious seed on a woman who is infertile. I have to raise children for my line (The Joys of Motherhood* 32).

Thus, abandonment sets in as polygamy is introduced into the marital home. The alienation is total for Amatokwu since finding her "a nervy female who is all bones" abstains from future sexual contact with her while concentrating exclusively on the new wife whether she is nursing or not. Agbadi himself observes that at the rate Amatokwu is going, he will kill his present wife. Thus Amatokwu, in his over-sexuality, immaturity, rabid male arrogance and, insensitivity, fails to empathize with Nnu Ego during a phase of infertility, which as later events prove, is only temporary; a little loving consideration, companionship and less pressure from him could have solved the problem. The contrast between him and Pokuwaa's husband in Asare Konadu's *A Woman in her Prime* is only too apparent. As Anita Kern, observes,

Pokuwaa's husband

> is a most perceptive man who has another wife but tries to spend more time with Pokuwaa because he senses that she needs his reassuring presence ... Pokuwaa tires of living in tense expectations .... That is when in her new, relaxed mood, she becomes pregnant at last. ("Women in West African Fiction" 13)

Furthermore, Amatokwu upsets the traditional hierarchical family order because his callous treatment of Nnu Ego ensures the erosion of all rights and respect to her as a first Wife. As Palmer observes, Buchi Emecheta adopting the female viewpoint, "makes us feel Nnu Ego's misery very strongly from her early frustration and emotional sterility caused by her barrenness in Amatokwu's household to her patient stoicism as he later degrades her" (Palmer 52). The character closest to Amatokwu in his overt sensuality, unrepentant male intransigence, immaturity and lack of humaneness is Bienvenu Delarumba (*La Nouvelle Romance*), who metes out to Wali, analogous ill-treatment and battering.

For the most part, Emecheta uses Nnu Ego as the central consciousness through which matters are perceived. Palmer, in this regard, commends the skill with which the author keeps us close to Nnu Ego's consciousness. Having traveled all along with Nnu Ego and come to share her point of view, we are in almost total sympathy with her. Certainly, the reader sorely needs this sympathy in order to understand Nnu Ego's subsequent actions when she degenerates into a state of near psychosis as, unaware that she is being watched, she puts her co-wife's child to her breasts. The next thing she feels is a double blow from behind. She almost dies of shock to see her husband there" (*The Joys of Motherhood* 35). Of course, this irrational act signals the end of the marriage as Nnu Ego promptly finds herself back in her father's compound. When Agbadi chooses another husband for her and she leaves for Lagos, the bride price is refunded to Amatokwu with a live goat added as an insult - a gesture whose significance is all lost on the greedy and sensuous Amatokwu. He rationalizes, "let her go, she is as barren as a desert" (39). In *Efuru*, Nwapa highlights the fact that Oguta society considers it a "curse not to have children. ... It was regarded as a failure" (207). Likewise, for the equally patriarchal cultural community of Ibusa, "a woman without a child for her husband was a failed woman" (*Efuru* 62).

Emecheta has received kudos for her great attention to detail; the diverse strings of narration are tightly held in place and the total effect is one of cohesion. Moreover, she infuses life with the breadth of her artistry and imaginative vision. Her characters come alive and achieve verisimilitude. Nnu Ego's character is very well delineated. She, unfortunately, lacks the robust arrogance and confidence which was the hallmark of her mother, Ona's personality and for which Agbadi was so enamored of Ona. Agbadi notes Nnu Ego's "singleness of purpose, wanting one thing at a time and wanting it badly" (*The Joys of Motherhood* 36). This trait, in a protagonist as emotionally fragile as Nnu Ego, can degenerate into a neurotic obsession. For Nnu Ego, fertility and pride in children become her *Achilles heel*, the flaw in her character. Thus, childlessness becomes an enslaving chain, robbing her of conjugal serenity and leading to her being abandoned. The paradox of her life which a subsequent chapter treats, is that even when the floodgate of fecundity is thrown wide open, those same children, the lack of which marked her first abandonment, become the final cause of her alienation from Nnaife, her second husband. Is the slave woman (who denies her children for

Amatokwu "because she had been dedicated to a river goddess" only to turn around to give her a litter for Nnaife) still to be blamed? We shall find out.

III

While Nnu Ego's first experience of abandonment occurs in a rural setting with the protagonist, a docile, pliable object of patriarchal indoctrination in the various superstitious myths, cultural mores and practices, Amaka's *(One is Enough)* marital travails have for background, urban Onitsha but which is still rooted in the traditional strictures that negate the woman's quest for a compassionate marriage. However, both Nnu Ego and Amaka (during the latter's pre-divorce stage), have an emotional dependency complex shown by actively desiring the man's love and approval. Their perspective is nurturant, their consciousness entirely female. Both end up as victims of oppression and abandonment owing to their failure at biological reproduction. However, Amaka transcends this stage as she turns radically feminist while Nnu Ego does not succeed in overcoming the myriad difficulties that make her a *woman in chains*. From Amaka to Nnu Ego, we shall see both spatial and ideological progression.

One is Enough significantly opens with Amaka groveling in submission before an iron-hearted mother-in-law and begging not to be "thrown away" for failing to produce a son for Obiora, after six years of marriage. Katherine Frank has pertinently observed that

> *in traditional society for a woman to lack reproductive power is to lack all power, indeed* to *be deprived of her very identity and "raison* d'être" *in life*. -- ("Women without Men: The Feminist Novel in Africa" 20)

To drive home the fact of Amaka's lack of all power and identity, Obiora's mother venomously spits at her:

> *You are barren. That's all, barren ... My son has two sons and tomorrow the mother of these sons will come and live in this house with her sons* (*One is Enough* 14).

This brutal imposition of polygamy signals also Amaka's awareness of betrayal - *une prise de conscience* - and an awakening from a state of self-deluding bliss. Anita Kern again aptly sums up the situation:

> *It is something like the classic case of the women who think that their husband's view of their union is the same as theirs, whereas in reality, what the man sees is not a companion but "only a woman," which to him means simply a servant or a monetary object of pleasure to be discarded at will.* ("Women in West African Fiction" 165)

And yet, Amaka had thought that their marriage was a compassionate union. Like all Nwapa's female heroes, Amaka is peerless - an enterprising, business woman, economically independent, yet supportive of Obiora even to the point of buying him a Peugeot 504 car. Oladele Taiwo opines of her: "she obviously possesses the sterling qualities which should ordinarily endear her to a man" (*Female Novelists of Modern Africa* 65). She had thought that Obiora was so proud of her because he used to flaunt her before his friends, saying: "if you want to know a good wife and how a man should be treated, just consult my wife" (*One is Enough* 17). Amaka had believed in marriage as a tradition to be treasured: "a home she can call her own, a man she would love and cherish and children to the marriage (20). Marriage, she confesses "had sobered her, had made her tolerant and peaceful". In all, it had seemed a happy union. And now this nightmare! Obiora had seemed like "such a wonderful lover, so considerate, so understanding." Like all her fictive sisters - Ramatoulaye, Aissatou, Mireille, Wali, Ije, Efuru - Amaka wonders out loud in confused bewilderment at this betrayal:

> *a wife, even a barren one, should have been taken into confidence. It beats me how you should do all this behind my back, be involved with a woman, have sons by her, marry her without breathing a word to your wife. You have changed* a good deal, *my husband* (26).

Obiora's betrayal brings home to Amaka the fact of the inequality of the sexes, a consciousness of the injustices that dehumanize and brutalize a woman's psyche, reducing her to the status of the "other," a second class citizen. Amaka now re-evaluates her worth as an existential being. It is a moment when every individual confronted with an intractable problem, wonders about life and one's place in it. Amaka now asks questions:

> *Was she* useless to *the world because she was childless? Was she unfulfilled because she had no child?... Was* a *woman nothing because she was unmarried or barren?* (22).

Sadly, Amaka accepts the hard fact of the mutual exclusiveness of barrenness and a monogamous love union: "a childless marriage cannot last in the Nigeria of today" (34). Traditional mores and strictures as well as excessive interference from relatives spell doom to an infertile marriage. Taiwo reinforces this point in observing that "the marriage between Obiora and Amaka might have succeeded if the villagers had not held a childless woman to such merciless ridicule." (Taiwo 65)

Nwabunor, Nnu Ego, Efuru, Wali and countless other women, fictive or real, have felt the sting of the derision that is the excruciating torment of the childless. The claustrophobic love Obiora's mother shows him is evidenced in the manipulative control she has over his life, seriously emasculating him and stifling the basic qualities of love he has formerly shown Amaka. Amaka now openly revolts against an unjust and inequitable social system; she opts out of marriage and journeys to Lagos to achieve wealth, rediscover her identity and force life to yield its sweet juices to her. From a nurturant female consciousness, Amaka swings into a radical feminist mood and turns victmizer rather than remain the victim; she next embarks on the "total annihilation of man, using all that her mother taught her" (*One is Enough* 74). Helen Chukwuma ideologically rationalizes Amaka's conversion from traditionalism to radical feminism:

> *We must not lose track of what brought about feminism in the first place. The female moves from an individual experience to fight a system. She suffers humiliation, neglect, brutality, disgrace and she may win sympathy from persons but none is ready to fight her cause by challenging the system.* ("Voices and Choices." In *Literature and Black Aesthetics* 139).

The quest motif clearly delineated in this novel conforms both metaphorically and literally to Katherine Frank's neat description of the feminist pilgrim, an erstwhile Woolfian angel in the house, who now "slams the door on her domestic prison, journeys out into the great world, slays the dragons of patriarchal society and triumphantly discovers the grail of feminism by finding herself" ("Women without Men" in *ALT 15*, 15) As Amaka jettisons her marriage and sets out on her quest of self-discovery and actualization, urban Lagos represents the great, wide, wicked world while the "grail" is economic wealth, achievement of motherhood and unqualified auto-dependence.

Baffling in their extremism are the character traits exhibited by older women in this work. That he later threatens to kill her for ruining his marriage is proof that Obiora resents his mother's excessive domination and manipulation. Likewise, Amaka's mother, aunt and sister, Ayo can all be classified as rabid feminists with galloping concepts of morality. They represent a reversed moral order as men become, in their opinion, mere instruments of procreation to enable the woman achieve motherhood. Amaka's mother had earlier counseled her "to go to other men and get pregnant." With utter lack of moral sense and in a reckless manner unbecoming of a mother, she blames her daughter for her failed marriage:

> But you refused to take my advice. You were being a good wife; chastity, faithfulness my foot. You can go ahead and eat virtue ((One is Enough 32).

In the same vein, Amaka's aunt advises her not to bottle herself up: "You are not going to be in a nunnery. What is important is not marriage as such but children, being able to have children, being a mother." Amaka's sister consequently introduces her to a racy crowd of females of "appalling behavior" among whom corruption is rife and prostitution... the order of the day (Taiwo 66), their ultimate goal being financial gain. Such depraved views held by both literate and illiterate older women who should form the moral bulwark of society would destroy homes as well as introduce chaotic social values. In fact, Amaka, hitherto convent-trained and conformist, protests in amazement at her mother's intemperate views,

> mother wait. Why are you not patient? I used to think

that the blood of the young burns in their *veins and they act rashly. I am discovering that the young are even more tolerant than the* old (*One is Enough* 88).

With all the brainwashing she gets, Amaka consequently turns into a female dragon, ready to batten on the fat proceeds of immorality. Lagos with its high level of social decadence and corruption rife in both public and private life becomes her appropriate theater of operation and soon, she becomes an embodiment of this corruption. Amaka secures contracts and pays with her body because "no man can do anything for a woman, even if the woman is wife of a head of state without asking her for her most precious possession -- herself (*One is Enough* 68). Next, she sallies forth into forbidden territory with a priest of God, Rev. Fr. Mclaid, "Izu," who is well-placed to secure contracts for her. Calculatingly, she decides "to put into practice what her mother had been teaching her. She was not going to wait, she was going for the kill. A priest was also a man, capable of manly feelings" (54). Her material success, Chukwuma summarizes "rose in correspondence with her moral-depravity" (Chukwuma 305). She is able to pay off her dowry, "build a house in Lagos, buy a car. She comes home to show off and becomes desirable again to Obiora, her erstwhile husband, who had abandoned her as a "barren and senseless woman" (*One is Enough* 19). Because of her wealth, both he and his mother scheme to get Amaka back. But, Amaka's amazon of a mother outwits both in a fitting act of poetic justice.

A most unexpected but infinitely gratifying (to Amaka and her mother) result of her liaison with Fr. Mclaid is that she gives birth to twin boys, thereby attaining that status of motherhood which had eluded her. Amaka's cup of happiness is full. She thus fulfills her mother's earlier injunction to say goodbye to husbands, not, to men (because) "they are two different things." Now, she has not only achieved great financial and emotional independence through men but motherhood as well. The prospect of single parenthood, "playing the role of father and mother . . . excited her" (120). One wonders if author Nwapa, is using Amaka to redress all the wrongs meted out to Efuru by fate? Amaka's mother calls her "lucky" because

> *women who made great fortunes . . . were childless. Wealth came first and blocked the chances of having children. According to their belief, the two did not go together. You either had children or you had wealth. Her own daughter had disproved this belief. She now had **two lovely sons and wealth**_*(116, Emphases mine).

So now, the myth of Uhamiri - she who "gave women, beauty and wealth . . . but no child" *(Efuru 2)* is effectively debunked. Amaka, now in a position of strength, proves obdurate when Fr. Mclaid derobes and is ready to fulfil all his obligations as husband and father. What she wants is "a man, just a man and she wanted to be independent of this man, pure and simple" (100). Izu is now a commissioner and her mother, bent on acquiring him as a son-in-law, tries to force Amaka to yield to the marriage. In a powerfully radical feminist speech, a far cry from the likes of Nnu Ego, Amaka explains to Ayo her antipathy:

> *I don't want to be a wife anymore,- a mistress yes, with a lover, yes of course, but not a wife. There is something in that word that does not suit me. As a wife, I am never free. I am a shadow of myself. As a wife, I am impotent. I am in prison,, unable to advance in body and soul. something gets hold of me as a wife and destroys me. When I rid myself of Obiora, things started working for me. I don't want to go back to my*

"wifely" days. No, I am through with husbands.

Amaka, though selfishly-motivated in her dealings with Izu, is right in rejecting his offer of marriage. Taiwo again agrees:

> there is no genuine love between the two. The attempt to forge a union comes only with the arrival of twin boys. Izu expresses a wish to marry Amaka, not because he loves her but because he is already a father (65).

Thus, Nwapa's ideology seems to be that self-realization and marriage are non-complementary since marriage is fraught with problems and provides limited opportunity for the ambitious woman. This radical stance directly contradicts Betty Friedan's liberal, bourgeois feminist position that defines the family as

> the last symbol of the last area where one has any hope of individual control over one's destiny, of meeting one's most basic human needs, of nourishing that core of personhood threatened now by vast, impersonal institutions . . . I've spelt out a personal truth: that the assumption of your own identity, equality and even political power does not mean you stop needing to love, be loved by a man or that you stop caring for your kids (*The Feminine Mystique* 394-5).

Realizing the importance of the family as a symbol of togetherness and meaning to society itself, Li *(The Stillborn)*, self-actualized, generously forgives her hurt and gives marriage another chance. Contrariwise, Amaka appears incapable of loving "anybody except her twins and her relations. In that way, she reasoned, one avoided being hurt" (*One is Enough* 120) whereas Ramatoulaye, a fictive sister-in-suffering, undeterred by her own hurts -

deceptions et humiliations - still determines to continue her search for happiness within the concept of the couple:

> *[I warn you, I have not given up wanting to refashion my life ... hope still lives on within me ... it is from the dirty and nauseating humus that the green plant sprouts into life and I can feel new buds springing up in me]* (*So Long a Letter* 89).

So, if as Filomena Steady believes, "true feminism is an abnegation of male protection and a determination to be resourceful and self-reliant" (In *Ngambika* 7), then, Nwapa's Amaka represents the apotheosis of the feminist goal. All along, Nwapa's concept of feminism has been following a diachronic progression culminating in this female protagonist who dispenses altogether with the inconvenient feature that a husband represents. She achieves financial autonomy, motherhood and embarks on a course of single parenting with its concomitance of unqualified ethical independence. Such intemperateness, unrestrained and behavioral, does not augur well for the stability of the family, the unit cell of society. As postulated by Chikwenye Okonjo Ogunyemi, feminism as an ideology

> *smacks of rebelliousness, fearlessness, political awareness of sexism and an unpardonable (from the male viewpoint) drive for equality between the sexes* ("Women and Nigerian Literature" 65).

To be deplored is this streak of extremism that smacks of irrational radicalism. And Chukwuma wonders with justification:

> *must female assertion be immoral? Can not a woman state her claim without sacrificing her body? Can not protest be legitimate or is it in the nature of change*

itself to be different? (33)

At issue is Nwapa's reiterated emphasis on financial autonomy *at all costs*. She considers unhampered financial prosperity as the key to success and happiness for woman. The crux of the matter is the method used to achieve financial independence. Certainly, not *at all costs* like Amaka "using her bottom power, as they say in Nigeria" (*One is Enough* 121). The end cannot justify the means. No matter how convenient, women must seek means of acquiring wealth other than the sexual such as "brain power"- ingenuity, resourcefulness, industry that go with education. There are literary examples: Li (*The Stillborn*), Agom (*High Life for Lizards*) and though rural and illiterate, Agom is intelligent, shrewd and resourceful. These not only overcome all obstacles impeding marital happiness but in the end, like Amaka, they achieve not only motherhood but wealth and prestige as fulfilled individuals to be reckoned with - all effected through a subtle and positive accommodationism that is in itself quite subversive. It will be a literary feat for Nwapa and other writers to create modern and robustly dynamic female characters who achieve a happy symbiosis of all these desiderata.

Another facet of Flora Nwapa's feminist ideology that appears to require modification is the over-preoccupation with childbearing. Critics like Ogundipe-Leslie believe the theme of childlessness is over-flogged. But the response seems obvious: infertility is still a nagging problem and to date no acceptable solution has been proffered to guide affected couples to help them adapt to a child-hungry society or to cope with the scorn and ridicule meted out by unkind neighbors and relatives. Laudable literary portraits have been made of the solidarity of a couple faced with this problem such as in John Munoye's *Obi* in which Joe and Anna survive as a couple despite great odds. Asare Konadu's *A Woman in Her Prime* is another example. Consequently, although Nwapa has ably delineated in her works the threat to marital happiness that infertility poses, in *One is Enough,* at least, the issue is over-flogged. In this story, the older women, especially, counsel Amaka to achieve motherhood at all costs. Convinced at last, Amaka herself expounds to Fr. Mclaid / Izu, "I would have gone to a beggar in the street if he could make me pregnant" (104). Haba! With that show of ethical irresponsibility, one wonders at the quality of moral concepts Amaka would inculcate in her children. We therefore lend ouvert support to Friedan's thesis that motherhood is "an essential part of life, but not the whole of it" (*The Feminine Mystique* 395).

The fore-going arguments have attempted to point the way out for a childless woman desirous of self-support within or outside marriage. When Nwapa asks as in *Idu,* "what else do we want if we have children?" she unwittingly entices her women, as Nnolim sagely observes, "into biological, cultural, psychologic traps ... that bind them with iron-hooks to patriarchy" ("A House divided: Feminism in African Literature" 5). Besides, even Nwapa's Idu, Ojiugo and Emecheta's Nnu Ego discover to their fatal chagrin that there is more to life than just producing children. Paradoxically, Nwapa's posture creates perpetual ambiguities even in her radical feminist ideology which critics like Nnolim understandably label "janus-faced, confusion-ridden feminist ideology" (6).

Finally, by advocating complete separation of the warring male and female, Nwapa encourages separatist tendencies, a "lack of commitment to the survival and unity of men and women brought together in marriage" (Nnolim 5). Besides, she also infringes on the central thesis of this study which seeks to encourage creative, visionary artists to search for and point the way out of such intractable, cultural problems as infertility in order that a couple can reconcile their differences and thus survive within marriage for the stability of home and society - a solution which will rid women of the chains of immanence in abandonment.

IV

This need for a harmonious, familial environment conducive to the proper care and training of a child is well-appreciated by Wali, the female protagonist of Henri Lopes' *La Nouvelle Romance*. She, similarly, goes through the stresses, neglect and outright abandonment which are the unenviable lot of the barren woman. Though she fails in her effort to keep her marriage afloat, both she and the reader, nonetheless, have the satisfaction of knowing that she does try her best. The storyline follows a linear progression and the spatial canvas encompasses Africa and Europe within a twelve month timespan well beyond the rural and traditional society of Nnu Ego or the urban environment of Amaka. The story unfolds against the background of a patriarchal culture in which men have all the rights, leisure and benefits while women are chained to all the responsibilities of the "other." Lopes charts the agonies and traumas suffered by the childless Wali which culminate in her abandoning her marriage. Her gradual awareness of the lot of the woman as the "ou," her contact with feminism and commitment to Marxism as an ideology which lead to a largely intellectual revolt and a revaluation of *l'ordre des choses* are traced in a later chapter dealing with feminism.

Lopes adopts the intriguing title of his novel from a paragraph of the French Marxist, Louis Aragon's *Les*

Cloches de Bâle:
>Maintenant, ici commence la nouvelle romance. Ici, finit le roman de chevalerie. Ici, pour la première fois dans le monde, la place est faite au véritable amour. Celui qui n,est pas souillée par la hiérarchie de l'homme et de la femme, par la sordide histoire des robes et des baisers, par la domination d'argent de l'homme sur la femme ou de la femme sur l'lhomme. La femme des temps modernes est née, et c'est elle que je chante. Et c'est elle que je chanterai.
>(In Anita Kern's "Women in West African Fiction" 144)

>[*Now, here begins the new romance. Here ends the novel of chilvalry. Here, for the first time in the world, room is made for real love. That love unsoiled by the hierarchy between men and women, by the sordid story of wardrobes and kisses, the domination through money of man over woman or woman over man. The woman of modern times is born and it is of her that I sing. And it is of her I will sing.]*

That woman of today of whom Lopes sings is Wali, a young woman of twenty-five, married to Bienvenu N'Kama alias Delarumba (Emperor of football), semi-literate, irresponsible but a charismatic football hero. Building up an image of himself as a playboy, he spends his days cruising about the town, showing off in his Mercedes amidst the praise chants of his adoring fans. He spends the nights whoring around, neglecting his wife to her chagrin and resentful discontentment. To add to her troubles, she is infertile.

Most francophone authors generally do not lay that much stress on the problem of childlessness as it bedevils the African woman. Rather, they concentrate on such woman questions as the complications of polygamy which destroy the familial structure (see Sembène, Seydou Badian, Mariam Bâ, Aminata Sow Fall). There are a few exceptions: Guy Menga's *La Palabre stérile* (*The Sterile Palavar*) which competently presents the comic story of a man who believes himself sterile only to be confronted with three pregnancies from three women each ascribing the paternity to him. But this story rather panders to man's ego as the virile, conquering hero, scattering around his fertile seeds. Sembène, in his well-known encompassing portraiture of the African woman as part of the exploited masses, sallies into the area of infertility with a touching account in *0 pays, mon beau Peuple* of Oumar Faye's mother, Rokhaya's agonizing efforts to conceive and nurse children who keep dying at birth. Her misfortune is ascribed to an evil eye or fetishistic bewitchment. Therefore, as soon as Rokhaya conceives Oumar, she determines to have and to hold this child and so scours the countryside in search of witch doctors whose treatments she stoically undergoes:

Elle avait absorbé toutes sortes de breuvages, s'è tait entourée de gris-gris, de cornes, d'amulettes et deracines pour se préserver de mauvais oeil. (*0, pays. . . 23*)

[*she had imbibed all sorts of drinks, had surrounded herself with bric-a-brac - horns, amulets and roots to protect herself from bewitchment.*]

This fertility fixation recalls Nnu Ego's (*(The Joys of Motherhood)*), or even Pokuwaa's situation in Konadu's (*A Woman in Her Prime*) in which she is enmeshed in the sacrifice of black hens and ritual ablutions so as to appease the god of fertility until finally, nauseated by this irrational enslavement to ritualistic lores, she rebels against tradition with: "I can't spend my whole life bathing in herbs." Ignorance, it can be seen, is at the root of the persecution suffered by women because of childlessness. In *Les Soleiis des Indépendances*, Salimata similarly adheres to both religious and traditional practices in order to get pregnant and ward off despair. Ironically, all her efforts prove futile since it is Fama, the husband, who is the sterile one.

So, although few francophone authors dwell on the theme of infecundity as directly leading to the dissolution of marriage, evidence abounds that it is culturally abhorred in both Christian and Muslim francophone territories as well as in the Anglophone areas. Sembène testifies to the true situation in Senegal:

> Dans un pays où la sterilité est bannie, une femme ne peut vivre sans rejeton parmi sea rivales. Dans plusieurs cas, le divorce est exigé, la dot rendue et la honte rejaillit sur la famille... (23)

> [In a country where barrenness is abhorred, a woman can not live amongst her peers without offspring. In many cases, divorce is demanded, the dowry refunded and scorn cast on the family...

And once a woman produces even one child, all her caprices and even infidelities are overlooked. Therefore, to salvage her marriage, Wali undergoes all these prescribed ritualistic ceremonies to no avail. As Lopes summarily states it:

> malgré l,argent, les sacrifices aux mânes ancestraux et les soins, medecins et féticheurs sont formels: elle n'aura pas d'enfant. Vingt-cinq ans et déjà un gout

d'amertume à la bouche (Lopes 15).

[Despite money, sacrifices to ancestral shrines, the care of doctors and native medicine men alike: she is still without a child. Twenty-five years and already there is a taste of bitterness in the mouth].

Bienvenu, on the other hand, vainglorious and compulsively unfaithful, has several children outside wedlock, caring little for his wife's sensibilities, his "scandales" are the talk of the town. For Wali, therefore, Bienvenu has become "un bon à rien" and "le mariage ne fut qu'escroquerie" [marriage was only a cheat] (*La Nouvelle Romance* 14). And yet, their marriage had started off well. It may not have been the fairy-tale romance she had with Kwala, her first love, who had jilted her to marry a white woman in France, but they had been happy together, for Bienvenu "aimait la sortir, la présenter et la montrer avant le manage" [loved to take her out and show her off before marriage.] But once married, Bienvenu reverts to the archetypic, patriarchal chauvinist male. He stops her education:

Je veux une femme à moi, qui m'appartient entiè rement et qui reste à la maison pour slen occuper, me prèparer à manger et accueillir mes amis comme je le dèsire à toute heure de la journèe (16).

[I want my own wife to belong entirely to me, stay in the house to look after me solely, prepare my meals, welcome my friends just as I wish at any time of the day.]

But for Wali, housekeeping, the kitchen, dishwashing seem an eternal drudgery, "un perpétuel recommencement" (16). She who had sought in marriage, gaiety, love and companionship, marriage to Bienvenu left bitter ashes in the mouth for "tandis qu'elle pile, Bienvenu, là-bas, bavarde dans le salon" [as she pounds, Bienvenu, over there, gossips in the salon] (16).

An excerpt from the early English feminist writer, Mary Astell's *Some Reflections Upon Marriage* (1700) reads as if tailor-made to fit what Africans like Bienvenu desire from marriage:

> A husband wants someone to manage his family. . . One who may breed his children taking all the care and trouble of their education, to preserve his name and family. One ... who will ... soothe his pride and flatter his vanity. . . who will not be blind to his merit nor contradict his will and pleasure but make it her business, her very ambition to content him...In a word, one whom he can entirely govern, and consequently may form her to his will and liking, who must be his for life, and therefore cannot quit his service, let him treat her how he will.(Cited by Catherine Belsey in *The Subject of Tragedy* 142)

And Bienvenu does ill-treat Wali atrociously, changing mistresses at will; he is often the object of verbal and physical combat by jealous, warring females in the nightclub, Le *Démocratique*. The seventeenth-century Bathsua Makin anticipates Bienvenu and his ilk in his belief that women "are bred low, not imbued with as much sense as men nor capable of being improved by education as men are" (142). Expressing similar sentiments, Bienvenu explains to his uncle:

> les femmes ne sont pas de la même espèce que les hommes. Il ne faut pas trop chercher à raisonner avec elles. Il est inutile de vouloir leur expliquer quoi que ce soit. On perd son temps. Il faut les battre. Oui. Les battre . . . ca les soulage (20).

[Women are not of the same sort as men. it is unnecessary to reason much with them ... it is usless bothering to explain whatever to them. it is a waste of time. Better to beat them. Yes, beat them ... that brings them relief.]

This study has maintained that violence and wife-battering, insensitivity and lack of respect are antithetical to the concept of a couple. Similarly, in Lopes' ideological framework, Bienvenu and his ilk lack depth, energy and serious commitment in their relationships with women, in their inability to grasp the essence and implications of the concept of the couple which Lopes holds up as a touchstone. The men clearly need to learn, evolve and be re-socialized to change from their sexist attitudes since a compassionate marriage has no room for hegemonic intransigence.

Wali's situation is especially delicate because she has no children. After an abortion, her husband taunts her with "même pas capable de lui faire un enfant" [not even capable of giving him a child] (19). To Wali's complaints comes this unfeeling rejoinder from Bienvenu - as reported by Wali:

Si je ne pouvais lui assurer sa descendance, il avait le devoir de se l'assurer. Que d'ailleurs, il ne tarderait pas à me rendre à mes parents qui l'avaient tromper en lui donnant une femme stérile et qu'il faudrait bien qu'on lui rembourse sa dot.

[If I could not assure his lineage, he owed himself the duty to make sure of it himself. That besides, he would not hesitate to send me back to my parents who had deceived him by giving him a barren woman and he would equally demand a repayment of the dowry [19].

A barren wife has little worth apart from perhaps the domestic for as Amatokwu bluntly puts it to Nnu Ego, "if you can't produce sons, at least you can help harvest yams" (*The Joys of Motherhood* 33). In Mongo Beti's *Mission Terminée,* Naim organizes a campaign to bring back his barren but errant wife for reason of her domestic indispensability. Wali's utility to Bienvenu is similarly limited to cooking to satiate his voracious appetite, washing his clothes, entertaining his friends and generally being a convenient outlet for his sexual appetite - all of which constitute woman's unpaid labor.

As normally happens, the corruption of the individual self permeates from the private to the public realm. Bienvenu brings to his job as a bank clerk, the same attitude of profligacy and tardiness that mark his homelife and this earns him the sack. Consequently, Lopes uses this novel as a medium of attack against prevailing social ills such as corruption, debauchery, hypocrisy and tribalism by which a corrupt ruling elite despoil the masses. Bienvenu, making recourse to these ills secures a diplomatic position in the embassy in Brussels and is thus catapulted to a lifestyle previously undreamt of. Wali follows shortly, desperately hoping for a rapprochement between her and her husband since they will be all alone in a cold, alien environment. But, this hope proves delusory. In a letter to her childhood friend, the courtesan Elise, Wali despairs:

> Mon epoux ne s'en améliore pas pour autant. J'en suis désespérée. Depuis un mois, il se conduit comme en Afrique . . . C'est te dire ma déception: moi qui pensais qu'au milieu de coutumes étrangeres, il reviendrait à moi (*La Nouvelle Romance* 116).
>
> [*my husband has not changed at all. I am in despair about it. Since a month, he's been behaving as he used*

to in Africa . . . This is to confess to you my disappointment: I who thought that in this strange land, he would come back to me.]

From Wali comes this "véritable cri du coeur" - a haunting lament of the barren. In despair, she indicts Bienvenu: "*Tu es l'égoisme personifié*" [you are selfishness personified] (137). Wali is only rescued from complete isolation and perhaps death through her friendship with the Impanis, a couple she meets in Brussels who teach her what it really means to live as a couple, a relationship in which husband and wife in partnership face life's vicissitudes, challenges, difficulties and pleasures. From the husband, Wali learns with astonishment that a man can cook and serve at home and "avait rien d'éfféminé" (122). From Jeanne Impanis, she learns the value of education and that it is possible to combine educational pursuit with a worthwhile existence under a stable, warmly loving, familial relationship. As she confesses in a letter to Elise, "mon séjour chez les Européens m'a ouvert les yeux" (192). She therefore, longs for a child in whom to inculcate values different from what she has received. Consulting specialists, she ascertains that her condition is remediable but at great, expense. Choosing an appropriately intimate moment, she broaches the matter to Bienvenu who brutally replies: "on n'a pas d'argent à foutre en l'air. On voit bien que tu ne sais pas ce que c'est, toi, que de gagner sa vie" (133). [I have no money to waste. One can see that you do not know what it means to make a living.] And as usual, when Bienvenu loses an argument, he resorts to physical brute assault -- "d'abord, des gifles, puis des coups de poing . . . mais il n'était plus un homme. Il frappait, frappait, pour se décharger d'un trop d'énergie" (138); [at first, slaps, then blows from his fists ... But he was no longer a man. He hit, hit in order to release excess energy.] According to Wali, "c'en était trop!" [it was too much.]

Male brutality appears to be a common phenomenon since many writers depict gruesome scenes of wife-battering. In Elechi Amadi's *Estrangement*, Ibekwe engages in a near-fatal (to both) brawl with Alekiri whom he accuses of infidelity; Obiora (*One is Enough*) resorts to brute force towards Amaka with dire consequences to himself, while in *Perpétue*, Edouard similarly batters Perpetua to death. Totally lacking in these relationships are "love, care, responsibility, respect . . . active concern for the life and growth of that which we love" - basic qualities without which as Erich Fromm posits, a being regresses to an undesirable state of loneliness and abandonment fraught with dire psychological results (*The Art of Loving* 20). To save her sanity and life, Wali, apparently, realizes that a woman, must herself, determine the terms of her own emancipation from centuries of interiorized crippling ideologies of patriarchy and gender hierarchy; that she must herself overcome her dependency complexes and attitudes to please and submit for more self-assertive actions. The means Wali chooses to self-emancipate is through education. She, therefore, enrolls for courses in the *Universitaire Populaire*, writes to her childhood friend Awa in Paris to try and secure a job for her. Still pursuing his undisciplined lifestyle, Bienvenu gets enmeshed in a drug-oriented scandal, squandering Embassy finances. He is finally deported from Belgium back home as *persona-non-grata*. Yet, his luck holds true; instead of being disciplined, he is reposted as a counselor to the Embassy in Washington D.C. An astonished admirer, Damba recounts Bienvenu's incredible escapades and promotions to an unimpressed colleague who, doubling as persona for the omniscient narrator /author, remarks with cynicism and *sangfroid*

Cette crapule? Mais ca ne m'étonne pas. Puisque ce sont les bandits qui sont au pouvoir. Entre les gens de la mafia, on s,appuie toujours (*La Nouvelle Romance* 182).

[*That scoundrel? But that does not surpriseme. But those in* power *are bandits. Amongst the mafia, there is always mutual support.*]

Not surprisingly, Wali's marriage breaks down irretrievably as she initiates the separation in a loveless union that has become a trap, a *cul-de-sac;* but she is not embittered. Her feminist suasion (this angle will be developed in a later chapter dealing with feminism as an ideology) is not strident, negative or destructive. The crux of the matter is not that women should stop loving or should stop being feminine but simply that they should be their authentic selves and no longer agree to be or remain slaves and *women in chains.*

La Nouvelle Romance is a straight-forward, readable narrative with no rhetorical flourishes nor any pretensions about bending the French language to reflect local dialects through transliteration or similar efforts. Lopes makes copious use of the epistolary style as a means of furthering the already tripartite, intimate relationship between Wali, Elise and Awa. They keep one another informed of current developments in each of their lives as well as make judgemental observations about events and social practices. This "familiar letter-writing" as Lovelace observes in Samuel Richardson's *Clarissa,* "is writing from the heart . . as the very word, 'correspondence,' implied, not the heart only, the soul was in it." Through Wali's and Awa's letters, the reader covers a large spatial expanse as the action moves to and from Africa back to Europe. The reader remains close to Wali's inner consciousness as she goes through, in Ojo-

Ade's words, life in a "psychological ghetto of mental torture and social disorder, where the woman is a slave and a beast of prey" ("Still a Victim . . .?" 73) for as Mme de Stael maintains, the epistolary method "always presupposes more sentiment than action" (quoted in Watt's *The Rise of the Novel*).

Wali, in spite of all handicaps, survives, evolves and emerges self-realized. This is because she has outlets for the release of tension which a character like Nnu Ego lacks entirely. Henri Lopes, in the feminist tradition, advocates bonding with other human beings for mutual encouragement and as a means of assuaging pain and loneliness. In the dying embers of her twilight years, Nnu Ego sadly observes that "she would have been better off had she had time (*The Joys of Motherhood* 219) to cultivate those women who had offered her hands of friendship" - Adaku, Cordelia, Ato (her childhood playmate), Mama Abby, Iyawo Itsekiri or the Ibusa women group in Lagos. In life as in death, she was a-lonely woman. In contradistinction, Amaka (*One is Enough*) survives her marital travails because she has the firm solidarity of relatives and friends. Meeting and conversing with her friends as well as writing to them provide her with a tension-release valve - "une évasion de son enfer domestique" [an escape route from her domestic hell.] Awa is a diligently studious, lofty-minded, intellectual, with little time for men and who achieves a brilliant academic feat and stands as a lodestar for Wali's tentative venture into academia. Elise, the seamstress courtesan, sensual yet "pathetically dependent in her very independence" (Okafor 130) is a reminder to Wali as to what may not be. These provide the brutalized Wali with affection and solace. When she leaves Bienvenu and decides to join Awa to pursue her studies in Paris, it is to the uncomprehending Elise that she explains her actions and motivation, ideas and dreams.

Wali's decision to stay in Europe is a momentous one, arrived at after mature soul-searching, self-knowledge and education, the kind advocated by Friedan (*The Feminine Mystique* 344). The reader is left with the enduring feeling that when she finds the ideal love partner, Wali will not shy away from marriage like Amaka or Efuru; rather, she will bring to it proven integrity, fidelity, courage and enlightenment arising from a solid, liberal education and mature self-knowledge. Self-actualized and a responsible mother, she will train out children who will carry on the mantle of emancipating Africa from the restrictive cultural chains that destroy homelife and make of the woman "de *mule uh de world*" (*Their Eyes Were Watching God* 14). As this tale of abandonment and the lament of the barren Wali ends, the feeling lingers that if Bienvenu Nkama had not been the unmitigated and profligate cad that he is, had he only met Wali half-way, just as Dozie Apia more than does in the work that follows, the marriage between Wali and Bienvenu may have been rescued.

V

The story of Ije and Dozie Apia in Ifeoma Okoye's *Behind the Clouds* deepens the thesis that childlessness is a principal cause of the disunity of a couple whose marriage is built on love and mutual appreciation. Infertility wields tyrannic power over women and wreaks havoc on love relationships. What then is societal attitude when a man is the identified culprit? R.S.Easmon deals with it in the *Burnt-Out Marriage.* Ahmadou Kourouma broaches it in *Les Soleil des indépendances* and in each case, it is the woman who is unfairly indicted and ostracized. In *Idu*, Flora Nwapa, deciding to call a spade a spade, lays the blame squarely on the man. Ojiugo leaves Amarajeme for the fertile Obukodi for whom she conceives and bears a son, proving incontestably the fact of Amarajeme's impotence. Amarajeme is even willing to claim the resulting son, "I am going to claim that child . . . In the sight of God, that boy is my son, my blood and my strength" (*Idu* 132). Such is the mystical fascination of a son in a child-centered society with high sex-role traditionalism that a man is even ready to claim another man's child. It therefore follows that any man publicly proclaimed impotent feels acutely this public loss of virility. Hence, Amarajeme acknowledges: "I am not a man" and hangs himself. Any wonder that society (especially mothers and relations of the man), by an unspoken conspiracy of patriarchy, cleverly prefers to ascribe this anathema to the woman rather than to the man.

Now, recent writings herald a revision of values. Ifeoma Okoye, donning the mantle of the artist as an instrument of social change, through creating a new consciousness of stagnant cultural beliefs, makes male infertility the central theme of *Behind the Clouds*. It is a unique perspective of the problem of childlessness. Critic Nnolim focuses attention on the fictional landscape of this moral fable which, he says, traces "a storyline conceived in irony and ended in irony" (31). The story opens with Ije patiently sitting in the waiting room of Blest Clinic to see Dr. Melie in an effort to conceive a child. She has already been to so many:

> *She remembered vividly all the doctors who had treated her - the tests, the minor operations and the major ones that had almost killed her . . . the herbalist* (*Behind the Clouds* 2)

One had treated her for *ogbanie*; the other had

attributed her problem to the evil machinations of her enemies, extorting a large sum from her "to buy what [the doctor] needed for his battle with the powers of evil" (2). She had narrowly escaped death at the hands of one of the herbalists. An operation for Fibroids had turned septic after she had lost so much blood that she had to be transfused only to discover afterwards that she had no Fibroids and that the operation had been a mistake. All this torture, in an effort to have a baby. Now, this latest specialist, Dr. Melie sees her through a series of tests and x-rays that reveal nothing; even he fails to suggest a check-up for the husband also. Beatrice, a former school mate she meets at the clinic opines the author's all-round indictment of society:

> *I don't know why in this country of ours it is always the women who take all the blame when a couple is childless* (5).

Beatrice determines her next line of action: to turn to the faith-healers because "my husband is worried to death. His parents, his relations, his friends all keep telling him to get himself another wife to bear him an heir"(4).

The specter of polygamy looms large in every childless woman's marital horizon as the months come and go with no significant news. Ije, like all women socialized into believing herself the sole cause of infertility, bemoans to Dozie, "I have failed you . . . I know I have" (15) and Dozie tries to comfort her and cheer her up.

Ije and Dozie's conjugal life is an idealized union of a compatible couple whose personality differences the author deftly balances to yield a harvest of complementarity. Ije is the touchstone around which the debased image of African womanhood as a "second class citizen" is rehabilitated to become a dignified, capable being - humane, compassionate yet capable of withstanding the turbulent storms of marriage and also prepared to chart a new, independent course if the need arises. Therefore, to underscore the changing position of the woman in Nigerian society, Okoye unfurls the banner of the "new marriage contract" between man and woman of which the hallmark are mutual respect, reciprocal "confidence in both public and private matters uncommon in Nigerian literature" (Marie Umeh 264):

> *She (Ije) had given her whole life to her husband, always taking him into her confidence. . . . Reciprocally, Dozie's love for his wife was noteworthy; a love that had been ennobled by the fact that Ije had married him when he had no material wealth to offer her* (50).

Dozie's inability to take decisions easily and stick to them is counteracted by Ije's promptness to act shown by her "giving him the courage to take the plunge, as when he left the government service to begin his own business" (70). Theirs is a marriage in which the couple "had learnt to understand each other . . . to communicate even without speaking . . . had grown to be as much as one flesh" (8). Therefore, at the climactic moment of betrayal, when Ije's trust and love are shattered by Dozie's adventitious infidelity, she would plumb the depths of despair, her faith in the ideal of love sinking to its nadir.

In *Behind the Clouds,* Okoye does not exclude even the female hero from the general indictment of society and its attitude to the problem of childlessness, which she posits, is rooted in ignorance, patriarchal chauvinism, traditionalism, cruelty, insensitivity of older women and the inquisitiveness of neighbors. The Igbo man, pampered by motherlove, shielded by doting sisters and kindred, consequently thinks himself a demi-god and develops a bloated ego. Ije, whose "only obsession was to have a child" (21) becomes the scapegoat of tradition as she, like Nnu Ego before her, regards her unfruitful marriage as a female concern, thereby making herself a willing victim, sacrificed on the altar of unreasoning societal hysteria. Mama Dozie, contravening the tenets of sisterly bonding, treats Ije with unrelenting hatred as she strives to uphold tradition and have grandsons by pressurizing her son into what turns out to be a hoax of a marriage. Ije, who incarnates fidelity, bravely withstands even the amorous onslaughts of a hypocritical purveyor of a sham religion of lust, Apostle Joseph; "to hell with you and your church," she upbraids him.

Thus, unlike Flora Nwapa, Ifeoma Okoye advocates marital fidelity even at the expense of remaining childless. Aniebo's Janet (*The Journey Within*) also is an embodiment of marital fidelity. Not motherhood at all costs, these writers seem to be preaching. Okoye, however, still falls into the traditional trap of viewing children as a sort of old-age insurance policy, a fact deduced from another character, Beatrice's rationalization of her duplicity

> *I don't regret my action . . . If my marriage breaks down, at least I'll have a child who will look after my old age. A childless woman in our society does not realise the extent of her handicap until she grows old* (*Behind the Clouds* 62).

Thus, Nwapa and Okoye, despite their progressive feminism, show themselves incapable of rising above certain cultural and traditional beliefs. Perhaps, Charlotte Bruner is right after all when she maintains that in some circumstances, these female writers "do not necessarily desire change; some also defend traditional securities" (Bruner xiv).

Since the logical consequence of sterility is the advent

of a new wife, Dozie is forced to accept pregnant Virginia who holds out the hope of paternity. Employing the artistic technique of scathing dramatic irony, Ifeoma Okoye uses this saucy adventuress to demystify the halo of reverence with which the Igbo society has shrouded motherhood and paternity. Thus in a child-crazed society in which male virility is equated with fertility, an impostor like Virginia, cleverly exploiting male sexual vulnerability, succeeds in foisting on Dozie and his deluded mother a pregnancy for which he is not responsible. Polygamy is thus introduced and Ije's and Dozie's formerly happy conjugal bliss is shattered. There ensues the agony, pains and humiliation a woman presumed barren suffers as she competes with a younger, fertile and wily woman for a husband's favor. The proverbial adage that women are their own worst enemies becomes a reality once more. This estrangement strips Ije of her notions of romantic love as the weak, indecisive Dozie cannot maintain familial serenity in such a volcanic situation. Both suffer. Ije succumbs to stress and is hospitalized for a raised blood pressure while Dozie in Ugo Ushie's eyes "had lost weight and bags were forming under his eyes. She could even spot some strands of grey hair in his head and beard - a sign of stress" (*Behind the Clouds* 104). His home, a former haven of peace and contentment now becomes a battlefield. Becoming a fugitive, he would escape into his office for peace of mind since that peace which seemed so stable a part of his home was shattered" (85). At last, Ije decides to leave and replan her life. She, normally dependent emotionally, now initiates the process of abandonment and finds salvation in her ability to secure employment and achieve financial autonomy. Ugo Ushie and her husband, the ideal couple, prove loyal to their friend. Ije confesses to Ugo her discouragement and disillusionment:

I've lost Dozie to Virginia because I can't have his baby. In this situation, love is second-rate (86).

This is so reminiscent of (*One is Enough*) Amaka's bitter observation that "a childless marriage can not last in Nigeria of today" (34). Amaka, Wali and many a childless woman real or fictional have experienced this feeling of helplessness when faced with this intractable problem. Ije's rumination about the durability of love also calls to mind Alekiri's verdict that "people only love themselves not their spouses. Love is beyond human beings ... Men only love themselves...Marriage is a sham, a make-believe" (*Estrangement* 56). Deciding, like Amaka, that a barren woman is considered useless in Nigeria, Ije determines that one such marriage experience is enough for her: "one thing I am sure of, I am not going to marry again, (*One is Enough* 114).

The irony, moving in a circular form, closes up as Dozie, stung to the quick by Virginia's incautious and witless taunt of impotence, undergoes a quick overseas check-up that lays the burden of sterility at his door. In this lies the author's entire thesis declared at the beginning by Beatrice, "*I don't know why in this country of ours it is always the woman who takes the blame when a couple is childless*" (5).

Repentant, Dozie pleads with Ije for forgiveness, "*I am sorry you've subjected yourself to all kinds of treatment, unpleasant ones and dangerous ones, when I have all along been the cause of our childlessness*" (118).

Thus the story ends where it should have started. In Nnolim's words, "it takes two to have a childless marriage. The man should also submit himself to a cure" (33). Ije had earlier vowed not to forgive Dozie. She now undergoes a change of heart since Dozie ejects the wretched intruder Virginia from the marital home. The marriage, shorn of excessive romanticism and viewed with more realism by a more mature couple, has a better chance of surviving. Marie Umeh sums it up:

> *The message is clear; Ifeoma Okoye aims at cementing matrimonial ties by presenting the couple's reconciliatory gestures towards the end of the novel. Whereas feminist plots end with the separation of the man and woman . . . womanist novels are committed to the survival and unity of males and females* (Marie Umeh 264).

The forces of light overcome the forces of darkness and the sunlight of marital happiness steals out again from *Behind the Clouds* of betrayal, tears and pains of abandonment. Abandonment is temporary as one more link in the chain binding the woman to immanence is broken. Thus, Ifeoma Okoye, this votary of accommodationism, now joins forces with her radical female compeers: Nwapa, Emecheta and with gynandrists - Okpewho, Sembène, Lopes *et al* in seeking to extirpate the ignorance, superstition and prejudices that complicate unfortunate factors such as infertility, which rob the human family of peace and leave the African woman a victim of suffering and abandonment. In a recent discussion about her feminist suasion, ifeoma okoye confesses to espousing an ideology which ensures the *wholeness and survival of both man and woman.* In her own words: *I am a humanist*[3].

    In concluding this chapter, it is pertinent to point out once again that infertility, with the havoc it causes in the home, is a common thread running through the fabric of these culture-bound anglophone and francophone African societies. Of the four novels studied, three of the marriages - Nnu Ego/Amatokwu, Amaka/Obiora, Wali/Bienvenu - end in permanent separation and abandonment; only one, Ije/Dozie, is redeemed from the edge of the precipice because of the mature, compassionate characters of the couple concerned. Of significance is the uniformly crude insensitivity, irresponsibility and lack of enlightenment and accommodation that characterize the husbands in the first three marriages listed above. These men - Amatokwu, Obiora, and Bienvenu - bully their wives and prove incapable of putting themselves in their wives' shoes, believing it is their masculine prerogative to misbehave and the woman's lot to bear it all. That may have happened in the past, these revisionist authors seem to be saying; but now, with better education, employment opportunities and financial autonomy (which all the writers insist on as necessary to survival), a woman does have a choice and a chance to survive even abandonment occasioned by childlessness. She now knows she has a lot more to offer to society besides children.

Evidently, childlessness can truly be a problem for any couple; and either partner can be responsible for it. In a love union in which tolerance, mutual understanding and easy communication exist, the couple can join forces and solve the problem of childlessness. The awareness writers are out to create is that the tragedy compounding the issue of infertility has more to do with ignorance arising from superstition, cultural chauvinism, masculine hubris, and general societal intransigence. A consciousness of these factors, less interference from ill-motivated, overbearing relatives and inquisitive neighbors, and a readiness by the couple to give and take - do as you will like to be done to – otherwise called "accommodationism" - will go a long way to ensure peace and serenity in a conjugal construct. Thus will be obviated the resort to polygamy (the subject of the next chapter) which leads equally to abandonment of the woman, creating disunity and rancor in the human family.

Notes:

1. By the patriarchal concept of Roman Law, the father, who was *sui juris,* was the only legal entity in the household. He had power of life and death over wife and children, who, as his property, could be disposed of as he wished. He thus could arrange marriages for his daughters without consideration for their feelings on the matter. Richardson's eponymous Clarissa ends tragically for choosing to rebel against her father's imposition of Solmes as a husband

2. The issue of virginity remains a vexed issue which feminists criticize as symbolizing both male double stand and an assertion of male dominance. Emecheta takes it up later in the novel when she uses the technique of doubles - the twins, Kehinde and Taiwo - the one to symbolize the assertive and asocial and the other the docile conformist. The issue features in the *Bride Price* as well as in *Double Yoke.*

3. Ifeoma Okoye. Interview with Rose Ure Mezu on the occasion of the Conference of the *West African Association of Commonwealth Literature and Language Studies* (WAACLAS) holden at Alvan Ikoku college of Education, Owerri, Nigeria, June 29 - July 2, 1993.

Works Cited:

Achebe, Christie C. "Continuities, Change and Challenges: Women's Role in Nigerian Society." In *Présence Africaine,* 120, 4th Quart.
Amadi, Elechi. *Estrangement.* London: Heinemann. 1986.
Aragon, Louis. *Les Cloches de Bâles.* Paris: Editions Denoel, 1935.
Bello, Eniola. "The Pains of the Childless." In [*Nigerian*] *Sunday Vanguard,* April 4, 1991.

Belsey, Catherine. *The Subject of Tragedy.* In *Modern Literary Theory.* Ed. Philip Rice and Patricia Waugh. London: Edward Arnold, 1989.

Beti, Mongo. *Mission Terminée.* Paris: Correa, 1957.

Bruner, Charlotte. *Unwinding Threads: Writing by Women in Africa.* London: Heinemann, 1983.

Chinweizu. *Anatomy of Female Power.* Lagos, Nigeria: Pero Press, 1990.

Chukwuma, Helen. "Voices and Choices: The Feminist Dilemma in Four African Novels." In *Literature and Black Aesthetics.* Ed. Ernest Emenyonu. Ibadan: Heinemann Educational Books Ltd., 1990.

Davies, Boyce Carole and Anne Adam Graves, eds. *Ngambika: Studies of Women in African Literature.* New Jersey: Africa World Press.

de Beauvoir, Simone. *Le Deuxième sexe* I & 11. Paris: Gallimard, 1976.

Emecheta, Buchi. *The Joys of Motherhood.* London: Heinemann, 1980.

Frank, Katherine. "Women Without Men: The Feminist Novel in Africa" in *African Literature Today* 15. London: James Curry, 1987.

Friedan, Betty. *The Feminine Mystique.* New York: Norton and Co., 1963.

Fromm, Erich. *The Art of Loving.* London: Unwin Books, 1972.

Fryer, Judith. *The Faces of Eve.* Now York: Oxford University Press, 1976.

Kern, Anita. *Women in West African Fiction.* An unpublished doctoral dissertation of the University of Toronto (1978).

Kourouma, Ahmadou. *Les Soleils des Indépendances.* Montreal: Presses de L'Université, 1968.

Lopes, Henri. *La Nouvelle Romance.* Yaounde: Editions CLE, 1976.

Mengan, Guy. *La Palabre Stérile.* Yaounde: Editions.

CLE, 1968, 1970. 21.
Mme de Stael, *De l'Allemagne* in *Oeuvres Complètes,* XII, 86-70. Quoted in *The Rise of the Novel* (Great Britain: Peregrine Books, 1957).
Nnolim, Charles. "A House Divided: Feminism in African Literature." In *Feminism in African Literature.* Ed. Helen Chukwuma, University of Port Harcourt. Unpublished essay collection.
_____. "The writings of Ifeoma Okoye." In *Nigerian Writers: A Critical Perspective.* Ed. Henrietta C. Otokunefor and Obiageli C. Nwodo. Ikeja: Malthouse Press Ltd. 1987.
Nwapa, Flora. *Idu.* London: Heinemann, 1970.
_____. *One is Enough.* Enugu: Tana Press, 1981.
Nzekwu, Onuora. *Highlife for Lizards.* London: Hutchinson & Co. Ltd., 1965.
Ogunyemi, Chikwenye Okonjo. "Women and Nigerian Literature." In *Perspectives on Nigerian Literature,* vol. 3. Lagos: Guardian Books Publications, 1988.
Ojo-Ade, Femi. "Still a Victim?" Mariama Bâ's *Une Si Longue Lettre.* In *ALT* 12 1982.
Okafor, Raymond N. "Feminism on the Congo: A Critique of *La Nouvelle Romance* by Henri Lopes." In *Kiabara: Journal of the Humanities,* volume II. P.H., Nigeria: University of Port Harcourt, 1979.
Okoye, Ifeoma. *Behind the Clouds.* London: Heinemann, 1982.
Ousmane, Sembène. *0 Pays, mon beau peuple.* Paris: Le livre contemporain Amoit-Dumond, 1957.
Palmer, Eustace."The Feminine Point of View: Buchi Emecheta's *The Joys of Motherhood."* In *African Literature Today* 13. London: Heinemann, 1983.
Steady, Filomena Chioma. *The Black woman Cross-culturally.* Cambridge, Mass: Schenkman, 1981.
Taiwo, Oladele. *Female Novelists of Modern Africa.*

London and Basingstoke: Macmillan Publishers, 1984.

Umeh, Marie A. "Ifeoma Okoye." In *Perspectives on Nigerian Literature,* Vol. II.

Watt, Ian. *The Rise of the Novel.* Middlesex: Penguin Books, 1957.

CHAPTER THREE

POLYGAMY AND ABANDONMENT

The excesses of polygamy which most offend women include the man's prerogative to be catered to by several women, the fact that he usually has the choice, the rejection of women and the competition between them his choices generate.[1]

"C'est une pratique qui ne se justifie de.nos jours"[2] (Aminata Sow Fall 9).
 [It is a practice that can no longer be justified these days.]

C'est de l'harmonie du couple que nait la reussite familiale.... Ce sont toutes les familles... qui constituent la Nation. La reussite d'une nation passe donc irremediablement par la famille[3] (Sow Fall, 43).

[The success of the family is born of a couple's harmony. ...The nation is made up of all the families.... Therefore, the success of a nation depends inevitably on the family.]

This chapter will critically examine polygamy as a factor that causes the disintegration of the unity of a couple with abandonment as a consequence. It will consider, among other things, the victim's awareness of the import of her situation, her management of the crisis - submission or radicalization, survival or death. It will examine whether the victims resign themselves to their fate or take control of their lives and achieve self-realization, become feminist in the end or settle for a realistic accommodationism. The chapter will also examine the different attitudes and reactions of the male practitioners of polygamy; the differences between male and female authorial viewpoints and the writers' recommendations for eradicating abandonment and polygamy. In the process, an attempt will be made to show why and how polygamy causes abandonment and the levels of abandonment within a traditionally polygamous family and within an originally monogamous marriage between two educated couples or with a liberated woman.

In non-muslim Africa, polygamy - the practice of having more than one wife at a time - is traditional and socially accepted. As a literary theme, polygamy has received very wide treatment in African literature. But recently, its utility and relevance to harmonious living are more and more being called into question. And polygamy, Katherine Frank declares "is the most glaringly inequitable and sexist feature of traditional African society"[4] (Frank, 15). In life, as in literature, polygamy has very often, proved the bane of marital bliss, leading to rejection and abandonment. Harmonious conjugal living, which is the very health and essence of any corporate group, demands a good measure of happiness and stability as its essential ingredients. On the other hand, destabilization of familial and communal peace and unity, acute unhappiness, a final parting of ways and sometimes death can be some of the unfortunate fruits of this practice that is so asymmetrical genderwise. Polygamy has pandered and still panders to the vanity of the sex whose fortunate lot it is to exercise the choice while it has a deleterious effect on the bond of fellowship of the members of the "other" sex on the receiving end - it puts a wedge between women and pitches them one against the other. Therefore, today's woman bravely opposes polygamy because for her, it represents a nightmare.

In earlier times (illustrations abound in the Bible for instance), polygamy served a useful purpose at times when a nation is establishing itself or loses part of its male population or when conditions of life are harsh and life expectancy short. Similar exigencies must have informed the establishment of polygamy in traditional Africa since it had always been an integral feature of African patriarchy. In the anglophone sector, early African novels of cultural nationalism depicted polygamy as a matter of custom and without apology: that was how things were and were supposed to be. Men were supposed to marry multiple wives; it was not to be questioned. *Homo faber* has the traditional society made to his measure; he is the warrior - (*Things Fall* Apart[5], *The Great Ponds*) - upholding clan and communal prestige; he is the prosperous farmer, needing wives and children (sons mainly) to work his farms and build up unrivalled yam barns, all of which will yield him the greatest gains, and entry into the highest cults. Nwakibie (*Things Fall Apart*) for instance, "had three huge yam barns, nine wives and thirty children ... he had taken the highest title but one which a man could take in the clan ..." (21). And besides, the patrilineage needed to be secured. Polygamy was thus the rule rather than the exception and the concept of multiple wives was viewed with complacent pride.

Thus, reasons of lineage, wealth and prestige so necessary to man's ego informed the existence and continuance of polygamy which feminist writers and critics alike denounce as a vehicle of female enslavement and debasement. The practice of polygamy which reduces women to chattels is a purveyor of acrimony and disharmony in the marital construct and leads directly to abandonment, misery and sometimes death (*The*

Victims)[6]. Yet, some notable exponents of African feminism like Buchi Emecheta personally believe that polygamy as an African institution has actual utilitarian aspects, possessing features which worked in many ways to women's benefit with respect to childcare and the sharing of household responsibility. And still some others, like Elechi Amadi, perceive among its other advantages, that of minimizing the problems of prostitution and unmarried women.

But even in the traditional set-up (*Arrow of God*), the crack in the façade of polygamy is discernible, demonstrating the flaws in the system though the crack was not portrayed sufficiently to conduce to abandonment simply because expediency demanded that the image of the *pater familias* be maintained - life in a polygamous homestead must be under the tight control of a patriarchal figure, the father. Nevertheless the crack is visible enough to allow a spectacle of wives bickering as they compete for their husband's favor as jealousy and squabbles become rife.

In *Things Fall Apart*, Achebe had posited that "any man who was unable to rule his women and children (especially women)...was not really a man" (52). The objective of Achebe or that of the authors of cultural nationalism would not be to expose the weakness of their macho characters such as Okonkwo or Ezeulu in domiciliary matters since polygamy was considered to be a revered and time-honoured traditional practice. Hence any resulting familial discordance would be contained by the man to show strength; Okonkwo and Ezeulu are cases in point. It would, however, take the authors of literary revisionism such as Emecheta or Okpewho to present a different angle of vision; instead of turning a blind eye, these revisionist writers shatter its traditional showcase image and affirm that polygamy, practised under certain circumstances does definitely conduce to the incidence of abandonment. The turning point is brought about by the education of women in Christian societies, enabling both female writers and qynandrists to view the practice of polygamy in a new feminist perspective. Emecheta's Nnu Ego, for instance, remains the most oppressed and powerless of all her characters because she is denied the illumination conferred by education which enables Ojebeta (*The Slave Girl*) and Akunna (*The Bride Price*) to enjoy a measure of autonomy in the choice of marriage partners, or Adah (*Second Class Citizen*) to emerge triumphant from her ordeals.

Early Francophone literary writings reveal an identical situation. Novelists like Abdoulaye Sadji dealt with the issues of racial and cultural alienation (*Nini: mulâtresse du Sénégal*) as well as with the corrupting influence of the big city on young, country girls (Maïmouna). Others, like Ferdinand Oyono (*Une Vie de Boy*), and the early Mongo Beti (*Mission Terminée, Le Pauvre Christ de Bomba*) treated issues of colonialism and cultural assimilation respectively. The early Beti depicted women as *un troupeau des femmes* and certainly did not experience any dissatisfaction with the practice of polygamy nor with the situation of women in Africa. Neither in his early works nor in the works of other Francophone writers did the African woman find relief from circumscriptive social mores like polygamy and the calamities it unleashes on the family. An exception is Joseph Owono, who in *Tante Bella* (1959), makes a vigorous plea for female emancipation. But Beti would undergo a transformation with *Perpétue* (1974), and begin to see more clearly the necessity for female emancipation from restrictive cultural forces.

Paradoxically, much of the challenge to polygamy is to come from a significant quarter - of all places - Muslim areas deeply steeped in the religio-cultural ethos of a harem of four wives. Ousmane Sembène, Mariama Bâ,

Aminata Sow Fall from Senegal, Seydou Badian (*Sous l'Orage*) from Mali, are at the forefront. In Muslim areas, polygamy is religiously-sanctioned, with strict stipulations to treat all the wives equitably. The situational nature of pre-islamic society was utopian in its practice of monogamy. Leila Ahmad records the fact that the marriage contracted between Mohammed and his first wife Khadija, who employed him, was monogamous. Following Khadija's death, Mohammed married much younger wives and instituted polygamy, veiling[10] and seclusion of his wives. But Badawi observes that polygamy in Islamic areas served to positively protect the weaker sex and since women outnumber men, the incidence of prostitution is further reduced. However on this issue, Charlotte Bruner wonders rhetorically:

> *Is Muslim polygamy protection for multiple wives who would otherwise have only the rights of concubines or prostitutes or is it a mockery of the woman and her subservience?* *(Unwinding Threads: Writing by Women in Africa, xv).*

Little wonder that even in these *milieux* where questioning the norm was hitherto unheard of, radical voices are now being heard of women seeking "to lift their veils to emerge from the enforced domesticity and female servitude religiously defined and defended" (Bruner, xv). Vitiating the workability of the practice of polygamy is the phenomenon of philandering *nouveaux riches* husbands who set out to marry younger girls, set them up in luxurious villas and abandon their loyal, middle-aged wives. Ousmane Sembène had, in a short story (*Ses Trois Jours*), painted a touching portrait of abandonment with the loutish husband flouting an injunction established to protect women in a multiple wife situation. The four wives allowed every Muslim husband are expected to receive equal attention - "un partage equitable selon L'Islam" (*Une Si Longue Lettre* 69) - the husband visits each wife when it is her "*moomé*" -- her entitled days and nights. This practice, naturally, is subject to abuses as evidenced also in *Xala*[7], and *Une Si Longue Lettre* where the favoured wife appropriates the husband thus exceeding her stated period. In *La Femme Dans L'Inconscient Musulman*, Fatna Ait Sabbah tells of an Eastern potentate who had four wives and three hundred and sixty concubines and consequently found himself unable to meet up with the demands of the rotatory rights of each woman according to Islam. What happens to the unsatisfied ones is better left to the imagination. These very loud verbal and literary questioning and repudiation of an established normative or religious practice evidently reflect the conmplexities of a changing African continent out to demonstrate the dehumanizing effect of polygamy on her female population.

The question is sometimes asked whether the African wife places much premium on romantic love. Sylvia Leith-Ross has expressed grave doubts as to the amount of premium placed by the traditional African woman on emotional relationship:

> *a woman's satisfaction does not have to be solely as a result of her husband's affection for she does not care very much about the value attached to love* (*African Women* 124).

Arguably, to the traditional African, the concept of romantic love is inseparable from the issues of procreation. Love in the traditional African marriage is said not to have much of the magic, fantasy and courtliness characteristic of the European concept of love primarily because of the practice of polygamy which robs a woman of much-needed privacy with her husband. But this writer posits here that the African woman does indeed care about the emotional content of her husband's love. Phanuel Egejuru buttresses this viewpoint when she aptly observes in "The Absence of the Passionate Love Theme in African Literature," that "the expressions of it [love] are more complex than a non-African would care to analyze," (*Design and Intent in African Literature* 85) since, beseiged by a plethora of socio-cultural problems such as infertility, male child fixation and other concomitant complications centred on polygamy, the African woman barely manages to survive. Yet, when she suffers abandonment within polygamy, she is aware of it even if her reaction to it and the measures she adopts may be strictly personal and different from another woman's.

Therefore, this chapter will explore in depth, each woman's reaction to polygamy and to the incidence of abandonment. The texts to be considered here are Aminata Sow Fall's *La Grève des Battus*, Marjama Bâ's *Une Si Longue Lettre*, Ousmane Sembène's *Xala*, Isidore Okpewho's *The Victims*, and Ifeoma Okoye's *Behind the Clouds*[8]. The central thesis unifying the five books to be discussed is that polygamy inevitably leads to abandonment: (1) when a husband with philandering propensities mismanages it; (2) when an improvident and irresponsible husband such as Obanua engages in the practice of polygamy, and (3) when, as is sometimes the case, a loving but weak husband such as Dozie proves incapable of the quick, decisive action (characteristic of an Ezeulu, for instance) necessary for familial harmony. The books are accordingly arranged - the first three falling into the first category, the fourth- *The Victims* - under the second while the fifth book, Okoye's *Behind the Clouds* comes under the third category.

II

Aminata Sow Fall[9], Senegalese Muslim novelist, publishing even before Mariama Bâ, is a writer whose inspiration is original. In *La Grève des Battus*, she engineers the total embarrassment of the powers that be when even beggars organize a strike and refuse to be pushed around. The story also explores the theme of abandonment brought about by the practice of polygamy. It is the story of Lolli Badiane and her husband of twenty-four years, Mour Ndiaye, who after eight children abandons Lolli for a younger wife. Their eldest child Raabi, an emancipated young woman and a law student at a university is conscious of the changing times, national and world problems, dehumanization of society (49) and the struggle by women for emancipation. Lolli would listen with complacency as Raabi explains her views on polygamy which she insists

> *on devrait supprimer . . . c'est une pratique qui ne se justifie plus de nos jours (43)*
> [must be-eradicated . . . it is a practice without relevance these days].

Raabi, young Muslim "évoluée" is the prototype of Daba (*Une Si Longue Lettre*), Rama (*Xala*) and Tioumbe (*L'Harmattan*) who represent the younger generation. To borrow Ortova's terms, they possess "cette sureté d'elle-même, cette prise de conscience." Lolli and Mour Ndiaye had started out poor and Lolli had made many sacrifices which once left her with only one "boubou" - an item of clothing that became synonymous with her being since neighbours would jeer: "*le boubou là-bas, c'est Lolli Badiane*" (44) [that boubou over there, that's Lolli Badiane.] She had gone the rounds of the marabouts in quest of prosperity for her husband. And finally, prosperity came with a chance of Mour being offered the country's vice-Presidency. Lolli has this scintillating vision of herself as the wife of the vice-President of the Republic, taking precedence over the wives of Ministers, even before the ministers themselves - "*Quel honneur!...*" (37) [What honor!]

Like Sembène's technique in *Xala,* the irony In *La Grève des Battus* is mordant, for at the height of these intoxicating dreams, there comes a sudden reversal. One cold, murky night, Mour Ndiaye wakes up Lolli to inform her: "On me donne une femme demain" (40) [I'm being given a wife tomorrow.] The reader feels the full impact of Lolli's shock by the writer's technique of juxtaposing this anticlimactic news item with the euphoric anticipation of being the wife of the Vice-President. At this news, Lolli "a senti un courant glacial courir à travers son corps; elle a senti ses machoires s'entrochoquer et une épaisse couche de brouillard assombrir sa vue . . ." (40) [felt an icy shiver run through her whole body; she felt her teeth chatter and a thick mist clouded her eyes]. The new wife in question is Sine, a deliciously fresh, young girl of seventeen, secretary in a tourist agency, emancipated, "élégante et très moderne" (45). Lolli explodes, and temporarily deranged, hurls insults at Mour. Lolli's temporary derangement may accord with the definition given in *Mad Women in Romantic Writing* that

> *a disruption of the familiar values (makes) the mind vulnerable to the disturbances caused by an obsession with past happiness or promises (Martin 1-8).*

The mad woman motif is found abundantly in nineteenth century European literature. In African literature, characters like Ramatoulaye, Jacqueline (*Une Si Longue Lettre*), Mireille (*Un Chant écarlate*), Nnu Ego (*The Joys of Motherhood*), Nwabunor (*The Victims*) experience similar derangement in varying degrees.[10]

The character of Mour Ndiaye is very well realised. Like El Hadji Abdou Bèye (*Xala*), or Modou Fall (*Une Si Longue Lettre*), Ndiaye becomes the archetype of polygamists who, through wanton display of wealth, seduce greedy young girls. He sets up Sine, the new young wife in a sumptuous villa. Unable to bear Lolli's imprecations and reproaches, he arrogantly asks Lolli: "dis-moi quel est le contrat qui me lie et qui m'empêche de prendre une seconde *é*pouse si je le désire" (44) - [tell me by what contract I am tied that stops me from taking a second wife if I so desire?] Lolli reminds him of the contract of "honesty and gratitude." But she is talking to a stone wall.

Like Adja Awa (*Xala*) and Ramatoulaye (*Une Si Longue Lettre*), Lolli has the warm friendship of her daughter Raabi, who urges her mother to separate, and not give in to pressures from the older generation out of touch with modern realities. Raabi like Daba (*Une Si Longue Lettre*) and Rama (*Xala*), stands up to her father, carrying on a cold war with him. From a Freudian viewpoint, one could correctly assert that these young women exhibit an Electra complex. Each girl clearly empathizes with her respective mother's state of helplessness (Freudian castration and **a type of mirroring relationship that Lacan calls "the Imaginary"**). Therefore, perceiving that she could later in life be placed in a similar state of powerlessness, each empathizes and identifies with her mother rather than the father, and thus urges the mother towards a path of independent existence that appears too radically modern for each of the older women. It is also worth noticing, the striking similarities in the various portraitures and tropes found in the works of these Senegalese writers - the philandering older husbands, their doting but deserted, older wives, the rebellious eldest daughters who oppose their fathers and champion their mothers' causes. However, it is safe to assume, since he published first, that Ousmane Sembène set the pace and provided inspiration for both Mariama Bâ and Aminata Sow Fall.

But Lolli is unable to rise above her environment or withstand pressures from her old parents. Together, her parents spell out to her the social stigma attached to divorce. The old father's view-point is the voice of patriarchy vaunting centuries of masculine superiority and dominance: "Mour est ton mari. Il est libre. Il ne t'appartient pas"[11] (46) [Mour is your husband. He is free; he does not belong to you.] This is so reminiscent of Ajanupu telling the eponymous Efuru that "only a bad woman would like to be married alone to her husband." Evidently, centuries of socialisation in the patriarchal tenets of sex-role differentiation and "lord of the manor" attitude have produced this world-view internalized, promoted and perpetuated by by older women. This exercise of an oppressive power over women resulting in a lopsided, power-structured, gender relationship, "the entire arrangement whereby one group of people is governed by another, one group is dominant and the other subordinate" is what Kate Millet regards as *Sexual Politics*.
<http://www.marxists.org/subject/women/authors/millett-kate/sexual-politics.htm>.

In this specific Senegalese cultural context, Aminata Sow Fall is asserting that men have succeeded in brainwashing women into not only espousing, but actively promoting male rights and privileges to maintain the status quo favorable to men only, and for the power that accrues to older women only.

The madness over, Lolli confesses wearily to her daughter just like her fictive Senegalese sisters in a similar predicament:

> *Raabi ma fille . . . si je quittais ce menage aujourd'hui, père et mère me maudiraient, ainsi que tous les membres de la famille . . . Réflechi bien, ma fille, sans travail, toute seule, que ferais-je de vous si je vous emmenais? (47)*
>
> [*Raabi, my daughter . . . if I leave this household today, father and mother would curse me as well as other members of the family . . . Think carefully, my daughter, without work, all alone, what would I do with you if I take you all with me.*] (My translation)

Lacking education, occupation or financial support, Lolli is unable to act in the same manner as Ije (*Behind the Clouds*), and is thus reduced to an object of prey. Ogundipe's sixth mountain on a woman's back which places any woman's emancipation and self-perception on the woman's ability to decide on a course of action fits Lolli's personality like a glove, for she "react[s] with fear, dependency complexes and attitudes to please and cajole where more self-assertive actions are needed..." ("Feminist Consciousness" 7).[12] Helpless and impecunious, Lolli at middle-age, enters into competition with a fresh young girl for her husband's favor. Thus is illustrated one of feminist critics' objection to polygamy: man's prerogative to be catered to by several women and the competition arising therefrom. Aminata Sow Fall, "Nwapa's daughter," creatively paints this picture of female debasement and abandonment due to polygamy for the benefit, enlightenment and instruction of fellow women. Mour Ndiaye's punishment does come when young Sine proves a handful, refusing to become the doting "mouton" (126) [sheep] that first wife Lolli has been. Sine balks at Mour Ndiaye's commands and refuses to be remade to his male specifications. Mour Ndiaye comes to regret his new marriage. His cup of humiliation brims over as the post of the Vice-Presidency is given to another. The irony is complete. It would be mere speculation to wonder whether he would sensibly, like El Hadji Abdou Kader Bèye (*Xala*), go back to his true but long-suffering wife, or continue living in his fool's paradise. Possibly, Sine[13] like Oumi N'Doye did to El Hadji, will desert Mour Ndiaye. If Lolli (*La Grève des Battus*), browbeaten by patriarchy into passively acquiescing to abandonment within polygamy, has no options, Aminata Sow Fall's young heroine does; she is Raabi poised to transcend this state of immanence by virtue of her education, financial autonomy and female bonding.

III

Mariama Bâ was the first significant Francophone African woman of letters to attract international attention with *Une Si Longue Lettre*, a novel in epistolary form. It is an unmailed diary letter of a woman to her childhood friend, Aissatou, resident abroad, written during four months and ten days of mourning her late, traitorous husband. It is a confession of sorrow, a record of love betrayed and of abandonment occasioned by the cultural feature of polygamy. Modou Fall, Ramatoulaye's husband of thirty years, suddenly and secretly marries Binetou, their daughter's classmate and then totally abandons Ramatoulaye. Then, Modou dies suddenly and the customary, lengthy, mourning period becomes the occasion of "a long lament and meditation on the pain, anger and despair she suffers as a result of the brutal imposition of polygamy" (Katherine Frank, 18). Ramatoulaye's remembrances of a love won and then lost constitute the body of the story.

In this critical chapter of Bâ's *Une Si Longue Lettre*,

following Mour Ndiaye (*La Grève des Battus*), Modou Fall is the second in the chain of philandering *nouveaux riches* Senegalese husbands who, at middle age, suddenly jettison their doting first wives to search for the elixir of youth with girls young enough to be their daughters. Together with El Hadji in *Xala*, they constitute a new cultural pattern. Thus, Ramatoulaye's souvenirs "ont le goût de l'amertume" (19) [smack of bitterness] as she recalls Modou's early efforts to win her love. A member of the first generation of educated African women, Ramatoulaye had a destiny "hors du commun" (27). She becomes an iconoclast as she rejects Daouda Dieng, flouting traditional conventions to marry tall, athletic Modou against the wishes of her father, mother and sister "sans dot, sans faste . . . dans notre ville muette de surprise" (29) [without dowry, without pomp . . . in our town dumb with astonishment].

Sandwiched within Ramatoulaye's story is another story dealing with the same subject of polygamy concerning her friend Aissatou and Mawdo, Modou's friend. Aissatou likewise marries Mawdo amidst "angry rumours" and controversy. If Ramatoulaye's family accepted her marriage with resignation, Mawdo's mother, Tante Nabou, opposes his son's union with Aissatou. Stiff with caste pride, she "looks down a long 'geer' (noble) nose on this upstart" blacksmith's daughter, Aissatou. Her vengeance, coolly subtle, shatters her son's marriage. Meanwhile, undeterred by familial opposition, Ramatoulaye and Modou, Aissatou and Mawdo lead their young married lives, luminous with blissful happiness. Bâ's reiterative, lyrical style creates an almost frienzied idyll such that the abandonment, when it comes, finds Ramatoulaye plunged into the depths of despair.

But what forces conduce to the process of infidelity and abandonment in the male? Bâ makes Ramatoulaye wonder equally: "Folie? Veulerie? Manque de coeur ou amour irresistible?" (230) [was it madness, weakness, heartlessness or irresistible love?] Mbye B. Cham, remarking pertinently that abandonment in Bâ's novels is both "physical and psychological" (90) attributes it to the whim or accidental fancy of the male. For her part, Bâ indicts male hypocrisy, egotism or weakness as the greatest obstacle to the achievement of marital love. In a study of *Une Si Longue Lettre*, Marie Grésillon posits that

L'homme detruit plus vite l'amour qu'il ne le construit a cause d'une certaine hypocrisie, de son egoïsme, de sa faiblesse. (51)
[Man destroys love quicker than he builds it because of a certain hypocrisy, egotism, weakness.]

Euphoric and idyllic early love dies as the pampered husbands at middle age turn into oppressors instead of protectors. And so, polygamy is introduced into the lives of Bâ's women. Ramatoulaye resents the patent injustice of a system that transforms the jaunty traitor, Modou into "defenseur de l'opprimé" (12) [defender of the oppressed]. Ba, through the judgments, observations and meditations of her persona (Ramatoulaye) unequivocally condemns polygamy which Dele Momodu regards as "the biggest devil harassing the Senegalese woman today since the wife becomes a disused commodity once her husband brings in another woman" (*Guardian Newspaper,* July 8, 1989, 5). Oladele Taiwo has questioned the reasonableness of her antipathy towards polygamy since Bâ is a fervent Muslim. But herein lies Bâ's radical and subtly subversive departure from her conventional Muslim religion and society in so far as she condemns polygamy which she regards as the vehicle of female enslavement and abandonment. She unequivocally restates her strong belief in the family as a unit and a woman's right to happiness in marriage which polygamy nullifies. Bâ postulates:

> *C'est de l'harmonia du couple que naït la réussite familiale...la réussite d'une nation passe irremédia- blement par la famille (130)*
> *(The success of the family is born of a couple's harmony... The success of a nation therefore depends on the family.)*

And so, when both Ramatoulaye and Aïssatou are confronted with the reality of polygamy, they feel betrayed, but their reactions are interesting contrasts. Aissatou vehemently rejects the polygamous set-up. Unable to dissociate sentimental love from the physical, she opts out: "Je me dépouille de ton amour, de ton nom. Vêtue du seul habit valable de la dignité, je poursuis ma route" (50). [I am stripping myself of your love, your name. Clothed in my dignity, the only worthy garment, I go my way.] Apostle of family togetherness, Bâ seems to advocate separatism in Aissatou, hence, critics' charge of ambivalence. Education, again, becomes *le mot-clef* to the survival of the female suffering abandonment. Through assiduous studies, Aissatou secures a good job as an interpreter in New York. Thus, she joins the rank of the quitessential new African womanhood of international relevance. Ramatoulaye, on the other hand, chooses to remain faithful "à l'immense tendrease que je vouais à Modou Fall" (69) [to the immense tenderness I felt towards Modou Fall]. Her decision, no doubt, accords with the author's belief in the woman's right to choose, and in the concept of the couple, defined as an association between two equals, and their sharing of pains, joys, hopes, disappointments and successes. Ramatoulaye herself sums it up to Aissatou as she restates her commitment to harmony in marriage and to accommodationism:

Je suis de celles qui ne peuvent se réaliser et s'épanouir que dans le couple . . . Je n'ai jamais conçu le bonheur hors du couple, tout en te comprenant, tout en respectant le choix des femmes libres (82).

(I am one of those who can realize themselves fully and bloom only when they form part of a couple ...I have never conceived of happiness outside of marriage. Even though I understand your stand, even though I respect the choice of liberated women.]

Mbye Cham regards the issue of abandonment as "a social disease:

It is the gradual opening and enlargement of the emotional / sexual circle that originally binds two partners [a husband and a wife] to introduce and accommodate a third partner [a second wife] in a manner so devious and deceptive that a new process is set in motion. (92)

"Why did he put Binetou between us?" Bâ's wondering question encapsulates all the encompassing pain of lost intimacy, of the misery of betrayal and abandonment. Ramatoulaye remembers all the women known to her, who are either abandoned or divorced. She remembers Jacqueline, the Ivorian girl, who temporarily lost her mind because of her husband's neglect and betrayal. And realistically, Ramatoulaye takes stock of her person and sees the physical ruin of her middle aged figure, sacrificed to twelve pregnancies. An so, intimidated at the prospect of starting life all over again at middle age, she bows to tradition to the chagrin of her daughter, Daba and the rest of the family who urge her to a clean break. "Tu n'es pas au bout de tes peines" (69), predicts Daba, the "évoluée" who like the rest of her fictive Francophone peers does not compromise on strict monogamy. Both Daba and her husband Abou thus represent the ideal couple who identify with each other, discuss everything so as to arrive at a compromise whereas, barring polygamy, life to Ramatoulaye, is "l'éternel compromis" (105).

And once more, we find the feminist advocacy of female bonding. In her battle to survive, her friend Aissatou stands her in good stead. She sends Ramatoulaye a car to make living easier for the Fall children. Bâ makes-her persona, Ramatoulaye laud in lyrical terms the concept of friendship:

> *L'amitié a des grandeurs inconnues de l'amour. Elle se fortifie dans les difficultés, alors que les contraintes massacrent l'amour ... Elle a des élevations incnnues de l'amour (79).*
>
> *[Friendship has splendors that love knows not. It grows stronger when crossed whereas obstacles kill love ... It has heights unknown to love.]*

Later in chapter twenty-two, Ramatoulaye reiterates: "tu m'as souvent prouvé la superiorité de l'amitié sur l'amour" [you have often proved to me the superiority of friendship over love.] Ije (*Behind the Clouds*) testifies to this in her friendship with Ugo Ushie. It is the tragedy of NnuEgo (*The Joys of Motherhood*) that she was too busy sacrificing herself to her children to cultivate friendship with fellow women, so consoling in times of marital travails. Yet, the joys derivable from good children which the Ramas, Adja Awas, Lollis (equally good mothers) enjoy, ironically elude NnuEgo. The concept of female bonding, as perceived by the feminist authors, is devoid of the power play and attempt to subordinate implicit in male / female relationships. Rather, female bonding as conceptualized by Bâ is a beautiful trope by which the stronger seeks to uplift the weaker sister. For this reason, Ramatoulaye like Adja Awa in *Xala* is large-hearted towards Binetou, her co-spouse whom she believes is a victim, sacrificed on the parental altar of materialism and cupidity by older women. Ramatoulaye questions wonderingly how one woman can willingly rob another of happiness. Binetou is nothing less than her own mother's victim (103).

Thus the family as an institution is threatened when elders lose their position as moral arbiters on account of their immoral actions. There ensues, a reversal of values with the young lecturing the elders: Naba to Dame Belle-Mère, Soukeyna to Yaye Khady (*Un Chant Ecarlate*), Rama (*Xala*) to her father, and Raabi (*La Grève*) to her parents while these elders bristle in unrighteous indignation. This anomalous situation, in Bâ's opinion, is another negative end result of the process of abandonment occasioned in this instance by polygamy.

Ramatoulaye's freedom, at first, is neither willed nor chosen, rather, she is forced to cope under a destructive institution and her instincts for survival call forth a courage of which she has hitherto been unaware, thus liberating herself from all the patriarchal strictures that repress female individuation. And then, with Modou's sudden death, she achieves true emancipation as she frees herself from a number of traditional beliefs: she extends sympathy, understanding and solidarity to her young daughter Aissatou in this girl's unplanned pregnancy, indicting a society that condemns the victim while leaving the man unpunished; next, she deals with her suitors, those "greedy hounds" one by one, starting with her brother-in-law Tamsir, whose offer of marriage she rejects: "Tu oublies que j'ai un coeur, une raison, que je ne suis pas un objet que l'on passe de main en main."

(85) [You forget that I have a heart, a mind, and that I am not an object to be passed from hand to hand]. And as she breaks "thirty years of silence," she contravenes the ultimate in Islamic tenets: that of female silence, immobility and acquiescence. In La *Femme Dans L'Inconscient Musulman*, Fatna Ait Sabbah questions:

> *Pourquoi le silence, l'immobilité et l'obéissance sont-ils les critères clefs de la beauté feminine dans la société musulmane? . . . Qu'est-ce que la beauté a avoir avec le droit à l'expresaion?*
>
> *[Why are silence, immobility and obedience the chief criteria of feminine beauty in the Muslim society? . . . What has beauty to do with the right to self-expression?]*

Thus, Ramatoulaye sloughs off the sexist costume of the incomparable angel in the house and dons the mantle of the quintessential new mother and independent African woman who is no longer a drudge and so escapes patriarchal tyranny. When her old suitor, Daouda Dieng, proposes, she will not desecrate the sacred tenets of sisterhood. She, who has been the victim of polygamy would not occasion another woman's misery. She rejects polygamy in its entirety. Thus, Ramatoulaye trascends her state of abandonment within polygamy. Neither Mariama Bâ's rejection of polygamy nor her advocacy for female bonding in any way signifies a repudiation of men for a separate female sub-culture for Bâ uses her persona Ramatoulaye to restate her stance: "Je reste persuadée à l'inévitable et nécessaire complémentarité de l'homme et de la femme" (129). [I remain persuaded of the inevitable and necessary complementarity of men and women] (88). Apostle of married love, Bâ is an accommodationist par excelllence. In the musings of her persona Ramatoulaye lie the essential qualities needed to combat abandonment, to promote conjugal love and family unity: sincerity, fellow feeling and acceptance (130). Tolerance, understanding, self-knowledge, humanism in both partners will solidify love within the union of a couple. Thus, *Une Si Longue Lettre*, sung in lyrical language, remains a powerful study of women lonely in abandonment and their efforts at survival.

IV

Ousmane Sembène is acknowledged as both.a precursor and an advocate of woman consciousness in African literature. In his utopian Marxist vision, the differences between rich and poor, powerful and downtrodden, men and women, constitute geniune challenges. We are concerned here with Sembène's Marxist-feminist stance as it applies to the study of abandonment in polygamy. As an institution-alized practice, he has isolated and indicted polygamy as a feature of patriarchy responsible for marital and familial unhappiness and which conduces ultimately to abandonment. *Xala* is therefore, a pungent fictional satire against a cultural society in which Islam as a religion functions to entrench more firmly male domination and oppression of females in its practice of polygamy. Sembène's obvious disaffection with Islam may be summarized in Hamideh Sedghi's contention (and it accords with de Beauvoir's theory of the **"other"**) that

> *Islamic marriages serve to guarantee male hegemony: men were not only providers of economic support, they were preferred by God in the context, as a woman's role is always defined in relation to a man not to herself as an independent being. ("Women in Iran," in Women in the World . . . 221)*

Thus, the Islamic dogma of multiple wives vitiates

female individuation as it cudgels the ordinary Senegalese woman into passivity as a sexual object. Fatna Ait Sabbah concurs as she insists that

> sur le plan idéologique, la culture musulmane a une nécessité structurelle envers la dimension économique de la femme qui est souvent perçue, conçue et définie comme un objet exclusivement sexuel. (33)
>
> (on the ideological plane, Muslim culture has a structural necessity with regard to the economic dimension of the woman who is often seen, thought of, and defined exclusively as a sex object].

Because to the Muslim husband, a woman has relevance only as a sexual object, he, understandably, lacks those qualities of respect, love and consideration necessary for harmonious conjugal living; he can, in addition, marry up to four wives and keep as many concubines as he can afford. Thus, stability and peace in the family are sacrificed because women become classified as property and the unfortunate wives who do not find favor with the husband are neglected or abandoned. This moral reflection forms part of the many themes treated in Sembène's *Xala*.

Sembène, in *Xala*, was the first to add a new dimension to the theme of abandonment in polygamy. He set the pace and Sow Fall and Mariama Bâ further extended his hypothesis that Senegalese Muslim nouveaux riches, adhering spuriously to a convenient Muslim Law systematically and callously sacrifice their doting older wives for younger, trendy girls whom they set up in luxurious suburban villas. Thus, El Hadji (*Xala*), Moudou Fall (*Une si Longue Lettre*), and Mour Ndiaye (*La Grève*) become cultural archetypes of polygamists who wantonly seduce young, parasitic girls who are egged on by their yet greedier relatives. When the story opens, El Hadji, a "nouveau riche" agent of a redistributive trade, has just married his third wife, nineteen year old Ngone Babacar, "une victim" sacrificed to help extricate her family from wretched poverty. In his inordinate self-conceit, despite his fifty years, two wives and eleven children, he allows himself to be cajoled by Ya Bineta, Ngone's aunt (a superb schemer and manipulator) into this disastrous third marriage that leads to his downfall.

Sembène has drawn a fine psychological portrait of this first wife, Adja Awa Astou, who is the only female character that suffers abandonment. She continually strives to sublimate her natural feelings of jealousy and bitterness and accommodate herself to living the life of a neglected first wife. Adja Awa's marriage of twenty-four years led to her estrangement from her Catholic family; she had renounced both faith and family for love of E Hadji, then a primary school teacher, "pour mieux partager les féicités d'une vie conjugale" (*Xala* 24) [so as to enjoy more fully, the pleasures of a married life]. Adja Awa incarnates virtues which Jarmila Ortova regards as "les éléments, les plus 'stables' de l'ordre social traditionnel" - " the most stable elements of the traditional social order" (Fatna Ait Sabbah 33). But Awa's intention to attend her husband's nuptial festivity encounters stiff opposition from Rama, the eldest of her six children. Rama is a university student, intelligent and fearlessly bold, "une évoluée," a grown-up prototype of young Ad'jibid'ji (Sembène's *Les Bouts de Bois de Dieu*), primed as the quintessential new African woman to be the author's mouthpiece against polygamy and to act as foil to the virtuous Awa. She remonstrates with her mother for countenancing this third marriage:

Jamais je ne partagerai mon mari avec une autre

femme. Plutôt divorcer. . . . (25)

*[I will never share my husband with another woman.
I'd rather divorce him. . . .)*

Without equivocation, Rama confronts her selfish father: "Je suis contre ce marriage. Un polygame n'est jamais un homme franc" (27) - (I am against this marriage. A polygamist is never honest). The family as an institution is threatened when elders lose their position as moral arbiters on account of their immoral actions. There ensues a reversal of values with the young lecturing the elders. Similar incidents occur in *Une Si Longue Lettre* between Daba and Dame Belle-Mère, between Soukeyna and her mother, Yaye Khady (*Un Chant Écarlate*), between Raabi and her father, Mour Ndiaye in (La Grève). In the novelists' opinions, this anomalous situation is one end result of the process of abandonment occasioned, in this instance, by polygamy. Teshone H. Gabriel has aptly observed that in *Xala*, Rama "acts as her father's conscience . . . She is represented as the hope of liberated Africa so that all progressive statements . . . are from her" *(Xala: A Cinema of Wax and Gold* 206). To Pathe, her fiance, the unyielding Rama restates her antipathy: "sache que je suis contre la polygamie" (*Xala* 77) - [You should know that I'm against polygamy]. Sembène very nearly idealizes her. Obviously, Rama is meant to agree with Agnes in *O, Pays Mon Beau Peuple!* that:

*Il n'y a pas de plus puissant obstacle que la polygamie
en ce qui concerne l'évolution. (98)*
[*There is no obstacle more insurmountable to progress
than polygamy*].

Evidently also, Sembène believes that women must

themselves define the terms of their own emancipation as he insists:

> *De toute façon, je crois fermement que la solution des problèmes posés par les femmes ne pourra venir que des femmes elles-mêmes. Le jour où les femmes auront le courage de dire à leurs maris: "Si tu prends une autre épouse, je m'en vais alors;" et alors seulement, la polygamie disparaïtra. (Paulin Vieyra, "Sembène Ousmane: Cineaste" 184).*
>
> *[In any case, I firmly believe that the solution to the problems imposed by polygamy can only come from the women themselves. The day when women will summon up courage and tell their husbands: "if you take another wife. I will leave you;" then and only then will polygamy be eradicated.]*

And the key to this gate of emancipation is education as Sembène once again states through Agnes, his mouthpiece in O, Pays Mon Beau Peuple! that once women "ont acquis le moindre bagage intellectuel, il . . . est impossible de les faire entrer dans la ronde de la polygamie" [have acquired the least semblance of education, it becomes impossible to get them involved in the round-around of polygamy]. In Rama and her prototypes, Sembène's prophecy receives literary fulfilment. However, much as we concur with Sembène as to the efficacy of education towards eradicating retrogressive sexist, cultural norms, divorce as the only effective solution sounds rather simplistic since it has obvious limitations. For example, *Xala*'s Adja Awa is equipped neither with sufficient education, financial autonomy nor moral conviction to resort to divorce as an option for independent living.

Firinne Ni Chreachain-Adelugba argues pertinently

that "in *Xala*, hardly a character escapes ironic treatment" ("Self and Other in Sembène's *Xala* "21). One illustration is the fact that polygamy which objectifies women is now shown as also having a detrimental effect on man's potential to become a human being in the fullest sense. El Hadji Bèye erroneously assumes that "la virilité dans la société musulmane patriarcale est définie en terme de puissance économique" - [virility in a patriarchal Muslim society is defined by economic power]. Having installed his wives in villas, he now flits like a "butterfly from one to the other" *(Xala* 42). While rotating wives, the man himself equally suffers by losing an enriching part of his selfhood. As Firinne Ni Chreachain further points out, "one's sense of self, one's whole identity, is inseparable from the other and the group. Separation is quite simply death" (93). In El Hadji's case, the death is both spiritual as well as psychological. When he has a problem to think out, he lacks "a room of [his] own" and he does not know where to go; in fact, he lives nowhere:

mais où éait réellement le "chez lui?"
Chez chacune il n'était que de passage. (Xala 115).

[but where was his real home? In each one's house, he was merely "passing through".]

Rootless as a bird of passage, it dawns on El Hadji that living no where, he actually has no choice but to go to a hotel room which sets his chauffeur, Modou, wondering "comment peut-on aller dormir à l'hôtel, lorsqu'on a trois villas, trois femmes?" [How does a man go and sleep in a hotel when he has three villas and three wives?]. The tension generated by the real consequences of polygamy in a familial construct is effectively apprehended by Sembène in *Xala*. As El Hadji rides with

Awa to the party, their hearts are far apart: "l'homme et sa première femme, chacun le regard ailleurs, gardent le silence; l'ésprit soucieux" (28) - [the man and his first wife, each looking in opposite direction, maintain silence with worried mind]. El Hadji's family, lacking a strong central authority, has its share of competition; ill-will and jealousy are always rife among co-wives. Oumi N'Doye is saucy, arrogant and vain. Culturally alienated like N'Doye Touti *(Les Bouts de bois de Dieu)*, she is preoccupied with the tinsels of the West. Adja Awa, despite surface fragility and an immense capacity to bear ill-treatment, yet possesses great strength of will and a determination to preserve her self-pride and honour, hence her blunt refusal to enter Oumi N'Doye's villa. Her portraiture is the complete antithesis of that of her co-spouse. And so, Bestman compares them:

La simplicité touchante de la première épouse constraste fortement avec la sophistication et l'ardeur sensuelle volcanlque de la deuxième. . . . *(Bestman 334)*

[The touching simplicity of the first wife contrasts strongly with the sophistication, sensual and volcanic ardour of the second.]

As summed up by Kenneth Little, "relations between the two women are at best polite and formal. There is no warmth or friendliness whatever" (*The Sociology of Urban Women's Image in African Literature* 69). Even when amour-propre throws them together in opposition to N'Gone's family, the union is shortlived as Awa brings home to Oumi the fact of the latter's animosity.

In seventeen years of sharing the same man, they had only seen each other seven times with Awa doing the visiting and Oumi never reciprocating. Materialistic, coquettish as she is bellicose, Oumi has always exploited El Hadji to pander to her lust for money. Her consciousness is as feminine as Awa's is female. Insensitive to her husband's condition, Oumi threatens El Hadji when he fails to perform in bed: "Je ne suis pas de bois . . . je peux aller ailleurs" (*Xala* 103). [I am not made of wood . . . I can go somewhere else.] El Hadji accepts that she is sexually insatiable; he also acknowledges the constant partiality he has always shown in her favor: "Je la gate plus que la Awa" (53) [I spoil her more than the Awa.] Now, no longer the youngest or the favoured wife, Oumi is eaten up with jealousy and she therefore becomes intractable. The corruption of polygamy permeates from the individual to the family. As is usual with dysfyunctional estates, the children are the first casualties. When, as to be expected bankruptcy results and indigence sets in, Rama herself opposes giving shelter to Oumi's children. Thus, Sembène relentlessly details the evils and the excruciating torment of living in a polygamous home and the incalculable miseducation imparted to the children.

Readers' sympathy lies entirely with the gentle, long-suffering Adja Awa Astou, who confesses herself incapable "of fighting and rivalry," but who, in the privacy of her villa, feels the loneliness of the rejected wife, and hides this from her children. She had thought she had mastered jealous emotions. When Rama urges her to divorce her father, Adja Awa answers, "Où irai-je, à mon âge? où trouverais-je un mari? Un homme de mon âge encore celibataire? . . . Et vous, qu'est-ce que vous deviendrez?" (26) [Where would I go at my age? Where would I find another husband? A man of my own age and still a bachelor? . . . And what would become of you?]

Similar reactions emanate from Ramatoulaye (*Une Si Longue Lettre*) and Lolli (*La Grève des battus*) who like Awa cannot conceive of life outside of the couple. Amaka of *One Is Enough* had also wondered what would become of her "if she decided to leave her husband? How was she going to cope?" Equitable sharing according to Islam works only in principle. As Awa chooses to stay in her marriage, Rama may as well be predicting to Awa as Daba does to Ramatoulaye: "tu n'est pas au bout de tes peines" (69) [you have not finished suffering). Jarmila Ortova calls these older women "les femmes résignées, passives, prenant leur sort comme fatal et inchangeable" [resigned, passive women accepting their lot as fatal and unchangeable.]

But can the purveyor of so much pervasive unhappiness be allowed to go scott-free? A revisionist author, Sembène's genius is more creatively prescriptive than merely presentational or expository. He always provides a solution. His women must move from a dystopia to a utopian ideal. To achieve this in *Xala*, Sembène adopts a system of poetic justice as unique as it is original in African literature. In a milieu where virility presumably equates masculinity, he castrates the philandrous and sybaritic husband. El Hadji is stricken with **xala** - impotence. His colleagues hurry him to deflower his virgin. But this "stallion" suddenly cannot "pierce" his young bride - a sacrificial offering who now turns out to be "a femme fatale . . . incarnation de la persécution morale et physique" (101) [. . . the embodiment of mental and physical torture.] So it is that this former "victorious bird of prey" is robbed of his victims – N'Gone as well as the sacrificial cock. His lack of libido drives home the reality of his impotence while it is never confirmed whether N'Gone is actually a virgin or not.[13] El Hadji is a "slowly sinking ship." As his family disintegrates, he is finally reduced to a "cipher." One calamity follows on the heel of another: he is expelled from membership of the National Grain Board as his colleagues desert him; his property is sold off; his third wife, young N'Gone regains her freedom; Oumi N'Doye takes to prostitution. Fatna Ait Sabbah aptly summarizes El Hadji's position when she observes that:

> la défaite économique serait vécue par la mâle comme une castration, comme une pertubation de la virilité, comme une impuissance.
>
> *[the male views financial failure as a form of castration, as trouble to his virility; as powerlesaness.]*

Elaine Showalter describes the punitive techniques adopted by nineteenth century female novelists as literary transvestism - "symbolic immersions of the hero in feminine experience. Men ... must learn how it feels to be helpless and to be forced unwillingly into dependency. Only then can they understand that women need love but hate to be weak. If he is to be redeemed and to rediscover his humanity, the 'woman's man' must find out how it feels to be a woman." As Ebie Tinuma confesses to his daughter, the eponymous, illegitimate Chimere, "Now I know what it feels like to be abandoned: Your mother must have suffered so much when I deserted her and I made her bear alone the burden of our joint sins" (*Chimere* 174). El Hadji, like Dozie Apia and Mour Ndiaye, experiences these feelings of helplessness and dependency to the utmost as he now turns to the erstwhile abandoned Adja Awa for succor.

The Latin aphorism goes thus: "bonum est diffusivium sui" (goodness manifests itself). Adja Awa Astou provides the needed shelter and place of refuge from the storm engulfing El Hadji. Her character has the enduring solidity of the oak tree and the luminence of goodness. The words of Ortova once more apply to Adja Awa: that she belongs to the class of women who represent *une certaine guarantie de la stabilité de la societé aficaine, un élément de calme; de paix, source d'amour sans limite et absolument désinteréssé.*

[a kind of guarantee for the stability of African society, an element of calm, of peace, source of unlimited, absolutely disinterested love].

El Hadji now remembers his early love and yearns for her silence and serenity; Awa becomes his "retour aux sources" (152). Characteristically uncomplaining, she shelters him. But his cup is not yet full. Sembène links El Hadji with his class of bourgeois nouveaux riches exploiters of the poor and the women. The beggar's denunciation and indictment demystify the halo of grandeur surrounding him and his ilk. The beggar had given him the xala and can only relieve El Hadji of his impotence if he would strip and be spat at. In an incredibly dramatic and gruesome scene, El Hadji Abdou -Kader Bèye stands naked as object of gaze. As he divests himself of his clothes, he symbolically strips himself of his egotism, hedonism and of all his past vices as well as, hopefully, of future exploitative tendencies. He must as Showalter maintains, learn "how it is to be helpless and to be forced unwillingly into dependency." The irony is complete. El Hadji is, hopefully, awakened to a new consciousness of the beast he has been, of the sterling qualities of Awa, of the supportive love and warmth which family represents. Sembène, advocate of divorce, radical gynandrist, surprisingly appears to tilt towards accommo-dationism at the end of the novel, *Xala*. The story ends in a reconciliation, placing Sembène in the same league as his female compatriots, Mariama Bâ and Aminata Sow Fall, as advocates of the concept of the couple.

V

In the first three novels considered in this chapter, the female protagonists - Lolli Badiane, Ramatoulaye Fall (though she later transcends her state) and Adja Awa Astou are seen to resign themselves to their state of abandonment, licking their wounds with resignation. However, Nwabunor, the abandoned protagonist of Okpewho's *The Victims*, falls into a class of her own. Oppressed and rendered as powerless as NnuEgo, or Lolli, Nwabunor takes dramatic measures to relieve herself of the cause of her angst, according to her perception. Abandonment in the story ensues because of the irresponsible and improvident nature of a weak, drinksodden husband, incapable of handling the many problems of a polygamous homestead. In this story, abandonment takes a peculiar twist as not only the wives become victims of material, physical and emotional abandonment, but the husband equally abandons himself, and gives up on both himself and on life.

A Francophone parallel would be Ake Loba's *Les Dépossédés* (The Dispossessed) - a polygamous household headed by the uncaring and partial husband, Païs. As described by Anita Kern, the same pettiness and squabbles existing among the co-wives in *The Victims* precipitate a final tragedy in which the third wife's small child dies and Akrébié, the muchwronged first wife finally leaves the marital construct for her paternal home like Nwabunor, cursing as she goes along. In both stories, there is loss of life - that of children. Contrastingly, although the same turbulent, potentially tragic emotions are found in Onuora Nzekwu's *Highlife for Lizards*, but Udezue's timely and decisive act of sending away the unmanageable Nwadi complements Agom's mature, enlightened efforts to ensure for the couple, a happy, lifelong co-existence.

Ideally, the family is considered the matrix of harmony and peaceful co-existence where children are trained to be productive members of society. In contrast, *The Victims* paints a gruesome picture of faanily life in a polygamous set-up, sombrely tracing the disintegration of this polygamous home mismanaged by an ineffectual Obanua Ozoma. In *The Victims*, the gynandrist Okpewho bears out the claim that woman is the negative "**ou**" in society. As he explains:

It is not so difficult to sympathise with women if you are familiar with the traditional society that gives so little power to a woman. It is a man's world. (Cited in Chioma Opara dissertation 66)

Just like Chinua Achebe's treatment of the issue of polygamly, Isidore Okpewho's depiction of polygamy proves antithetical and V.U.Ola remarks:

The theme of polygamy is a recurrent one in African Literature. Chinua Achebe and Isidore Okpewho have both treated this theme from its two extremes, that is, as a success or a failure respectively. (In *Okike*, no. 21 78)

Both *Things Fall Apart* and *Arrow of God* contain a fair amount of female squabbling, petty jealousies, and wife-battering. The difference lies in Achebe's and Okpewho's portraiture of the personalities of the male characters - Obanua is no Okonkwo neither is he an Ezeulu nor yet a Nwakibie, and so, when he goes on to bring in Ogugua as second wife, Obanua sowed the seeds of familial disharmony. Where Okonkwo maintains discipline amongst his wrangling wives through a process of intimidation exploiting his predictably violent temper, and where Ezeulu keeps peace because of his imposing

153

personality, Obanua is a risible puppet whose heart is apt to melt in despair (*The Victims* 11) as he makes "few last weary attempts to reassert an authority he knew was now slipping completely away from him" (144). Ogugua further debunks the myth of his being the paterfamilias when she challenges his complaint over her immoral lifestyle: "I think one day you will have to tell me when you became man enough to worry about my looks" (46). Of course, Obanua indeed was "not man enough" to challenge his wife's lover, Odafe Gwam (101). Supporting this view, Little observes pertinently that such is Obanua's pusillanimity that instead of his dominating the domestic scene, the struggle for power is between the two wives. It is the more intense because Obanua himself is too drinksodden to intervene.

Contrasting, Okonkwo's fear-inspiring handling of his wives with Nwakibie's firm, impartial method of administering the affairs of his hierarchically respect-filled multiple wife family, V.U. Ola concludes (and this pertinently applies to Obanua) that "Achebe sees polygamy as a system of relationships which works or fails according to the character of each person involved." ("Aspects of Development in Chinua Achebe's Treatment of Women" 94). Obanua is thus too weak to handle the tensions in his family. Perhaps had he had the gumption to promptly send away Ogugua in the manner Udezue dealt with Nwadi (*High Life for Lizards*), he would have averted an imminent domestic catastrophe. Kenneth Little provides a further clue to this tragic drama when he observes that both of Obanua's wives share the same house. Our sympathies lie entirely with Nwabunor. She is sickly, older and less emancipated than Ogugua and is the character who suffers abandonment in the real, abject sense of it whereas Ogugua has no claim on readers' sympathies as she is relatively emancipated, healthy, young, pretty and possesses professional skill swhich, with industry, she can develop into a flourishing level. But she chooses to be greedy, immoral and egotistical, allowing need to propel her into adultery with Gwam. On the other hand, Aku's adultery in Okpewho's *The Last Duty* is dictated by near starvation and loneliness emanating from her state of social ostracism. Adisa's act of adultery in Iyayi's *Violence* may even be seen as an act of self-immolation in order to save a loved husband. Perpétue allows Edoaurd to push her into adultery in order to obtain her brother's release from prison. For the wayward Ogugua with a roving eye, we evince no sympathy.

The tragedy of Obanua's life stems from utter irresponsibility as, perpetually somnolent, he "pours his wages down his throat." This earns him from Okpewho, a portraiture as one of the most despicable, caricatured and emasculated characters in West African fiction. Nwanze, his drinking companion, ironically drives home the point that "a man sleeps on his mat according as he spreads it on the floor" (18). His mother, Ma Nwojide evidently thinks similarly.

The "very serious emotional and psychological" dimensions of *The Victims* are well-appreciated by V.U.Ola who sees the fundamental problem of Nwabunor as one of human identity. Nwabunor is an object of derision to her foes and neighbours; her life has been blighted by the intractable problem of infertility; she is frustrated and harassed by a feckless husband and an unsympathetic, more alluring, younger co-wife, who at first, receives all of their husband's attention and who besides, is blessed with fecundity. Nwabunor is understandably eaten up by fear, jealousy and resentment; she yet receives sympathy from writer and readers because she is abandoned and isolated. Mentally challenged, Nwabunor resorts to poisoning as an act calculated to solve all her problems thus leaving the

Ozoma home littered with the dead bodies of the poisoned inmates. The main "victims" are the children. That the children unjustly share the same fate underscores the supreme irony contained in the novel that polygamy which usually increases the numerical strength of a family now becomes the root-cause of the near-extirpation of the Obanua family.

Thus, it can be understood why Okpewho's *The Victims* has been compared to a living hell in which both conjugal serenity and self-individuation are blighted by the practice of polygamy. Okpewho lucidly indicts polygamy as the harbinger of doom that strikes a death-blow to marital bliss especially as practised under conditions of economic constraints. Interestingly, another female compatriot, Ifeoma Okoye, representing a female view point and from the same cultural, linguistic and geographical milieu, still takes a swipe at polygamy as a direct cause of marital strife, disunity and abandonment in her novel, *Behind the Clouds*.

VI

Ifeoma Okoye's *Behind the Clouds*, a compact novelette of domestic realism, considers the factor of polygamy which the novel treats as it graphically delineates the tensions, abrasive clashes and misery that form almost a normal routine in polygamous living. Abandonment in this novel results from a character flaw - mindless infideity aggravated by Dozie's inability to take quick and decisive action as Udezue (*Highlife for Lizards*) does when disaster threatens.

To Dozie, Ije was a trustworthy wife and companion, a perfect "Angel in the house" whose consciousness is entirely female. Together, they had built up a compatible, companionate marriage. They had one mind just like the love story of Ndulue and Ozoemena in *Things Fall Apart* until a casual, one-day affair between Dozie and an opportunist called Virginia triggers off unexpected events which culminate in the imposition of polygamy on the household. With Virginia, a living reality, Ije feels Dozie had violated his marriage vows. She would be held up to ridicule and shame as an abandoned wife. Like every betrayed woman in African fiction (the eponymous Efuru, Ramatoulaye (*Une Si Longue Lettre*), Mireille (*Un Chant Écarlate*), Amaka (*One is Enough*), or Wali (*Une Nouvelle Romance*), Adah (*Second Class Citizen*), or Perpétue, etc., "tears of anger, hurt disappointment, regret and uncertainty flowed copiously down her cheeks" (*Behind the Clouds* 77).

Ije falls within the class of urban, emancipated, career-trained women who yet are emotionally and economically dependent on their husbands; these are women who choose to give up all for love and yet appear to have lost all - husband, home and career. Radical feminist, Germaine Greer, apparently has these "love victims" in mind when she denounces "love" as being one of the myths by which men and society have castrated women into becoming **female eunuchs.**" Denouncing the irrationality of women who give up their careers for "love, love, love - all the wretched cant of it, masking egotism, lust, masochism, fantasy under a mythology of sentimental postures of courtship, in the kissing and the dating and the desire, the compliments and the quarrels which vivify its barrenness" (*The Female Eunuch* 165). Ije, a considerate and sensitive woman, tries to accommodate herself to living in a polygamous household but, of course, she is no match for the calculating Virginia, who appears "as unexcited and implacable as the sphinx" (77). And so the battle for man's favour begins. Ije proves unequal to it all. Like Adja Awa Astou (*Xala*), Ije is incapable of fighting and rivalry. At last, a charge by Virginia that Ije sprinkled some poison into their food becomes the last straw. "Why did you do such a thing, Ije?" the now servile Dozie, who has become like potter's clay in Virginia's "dexterous hands" (105) questions Ije. The formerly loved first wife wonders in amazed and puzzled sorrow as Dozie doubts her integrity. Lonely, "sick with stress-induced hypertension, Ije struggles" to go on living. She gets a job and an apartment and moves out of the home she helped to build. The man becomes no longer "**my** husband" but "**our**" husband; three have become a crowd and the sense of commitment is gone.

Ije, like Ramatoulaye (*Une Si Longue Lettre*), transcends her state of emotional abandonment only because she rises from her passive position of dependency to an active one of economic autonomy, thanks to her education and profession. Ije's capacity to bounce back accords with the ideology of dynamic agency preached by every feminist and gynandrist writer. Nwapa, preaches economic independence; and so does Betty Friedan who believes that women who depend entirely on their husbands "have forfeited themselves." Women facing marital difficulties, Friedan insists, must adopt a new life plan. At the base of it all is education, which Friedan insists is the matrix of human evolution. In the thinking of writers/ideologues such as Virginia Woolf (*A Room of One's Own*), Mariama Bâ, Lopes, Emecheta, Sembène, *et al*, education leads to financial autonomy and it is the tool which enables woman to survive and live meaningfully, irrespective of marital travails. Like Amaka (*One is Enough*), Ije can confidently (from the economic standpoint) assure her friend, Ugo Ushie, "one thing I am sure, I am not going to marry again."

Abandonment in *Behind the Clouds* occurs on an emotional plane. Ije, as an act of self-protection, spatially relocates herself as she leaves a home that has now become alien to her. Like Aïssatou (*Une Si Longue*

Lettre), Ije may thus be seen as initiating the act of physical abandonment as it is she who leaves the marital home of her own accord even if on an emotional level, yet she is the one who stands abandoned because Dozie brings in a new woman into their lives. She stands alienated by the fact of his infidelity for as Aïssatou insists in *Une Si Longue Lettre*, "la communion charnelle ne peut être sans l'acceptation du coeur, si minime soit-il" (51) - [there can be no union of bodies without the heart's acceptance, however little that may be.] A normally indecisive man, Dozie who would never have embarked on polygamy that easily, now becomes an easy prey for the more dominating, bossy and voraciously money-hungry Virginia: "I've made up your mind for you," (*Behind the Clouds* 77), Virginia informs him. From Dozie's angle of vision, polygamy is an entrapment, for he realises that "from this point forward, his life was going to be complicated; that the peace which had seemed a stable part of his home was shattered" (85), and like El Hadji (*Xala*), Obanua (*The Victims*) and many a man before him who self-creates his own hellfire, "Dozie became a fugitive from his own house, taking refuge in his office and not in his club where his friends would ask him embarrassing questions" (*Behind the Clouds*). Unlike Obanua, of course, Dozie, at least, has an office to go to. Nwanze may as well have had him in mind when he tells Obanua that a man sleeps on his mat "according as he spread it on the floor" (*The Victims* 17).

This novel like other feminist works treated earlier advocates female bonding and denounces women who undermine sisterhood. Feminist writers like Mary Daly (*Gyn/Ecology: The Metaethics of Radical Feminism*) and Bell Hooks (*Feminist Theory: From Margin to Center*) consider female bonding as the "essence of sisterhood." Showalter credits early nineteenth-century English women novelists with initiating the advocacy of sisterhood amongst their female audience with Sarah Ellis wondering, "what should we think of a community of slaves, who betrayed each other's interests?" (*A Literature of Their Own: British Women Novelists from Brontë to Lessing* 16). Okoye depicts the attitudes of Mama Apia (Dozie's mother) and Virginia as opposing this concept. In the portraiture of these characters, she probes "the disturbing phenomenon of victims victimizing victims," or women, themselves prisoners of canons of tradition inimical to their socio-economic progress or marital peace, yet who "deliberately and maliciously sabotage the happiness of others" (Mbye B. Cham 98). Mentally castrated, Mary Daly opines, "these women participate in the destruction of their own kind - of womankind - and in the destruction of strength and bonding among women" (Daly 163-4). The sassy Virginia finds easy identification with Ouleymatou (*Un Chant Écarlate*) in her scheming viciousness and sphinx-like implacability, while Mama Apia finds congenial company with Tante Nabou (*Une Si Longue Lettre*), Yaye Khady (*Un Chant Écarlate*), Amaka's mother-in-law (*One is Enough*) and Gikere's mother (*Ripples in the Pool*) in their unrelenting hatefulnese to their respective daughters-in-law. These mothers-in-law are total opposites to Ma Nwojide (*The Victims*) whose sense of fairness and lack of interference are only equalled by her desire to keep peace in the home.

Expectedly, for his act of betrayal and wilful destruction of conjugal peace, Okoye employs the novelistic technique of masculine reductionism to ordain that Dozie passes through the furnace of ego battering and emasculation as Virginia finally, unable to wrest money from him, tactlessly blurts out the truth:

> *The baby is not yours. I chose you as its father because you're the richest of the lot and because you wanted a*

child so badly. Do you call yourself a man? (Behind the Clouds 111).

The hitherto placid and indecisive Dozie, now humiliated, is finally stung to quick action when Virginia uses a derogatory vernacular word to accuse him of sterility and he can not bear the putdown. This incident pitches him in the rank of Joe in John Munonye's *Obi* and Amarajeme in Nwapa's *Idu* whom similar taunts sting respectively either to attempted murder, or to suicide. Dozie's imbroglio with Virginia and the latter's disgrace on being thrown out of Dozie's house are considered acts of poetic justice. Now a chastised new African man, resocialised into a new consciousness of fairness, Dozie makes a supreme sacrifice to salvage his battered marriage by apologising to Ije: "I've wronged you in every way. All I ask of you is to forgive me . . . I've learnt my lesson and I've learnt it the hard way" (*Behind the Clouds* 118). Dozie has indeed learnt to value love in a union, based on tolerance, understanding and compassion. Ije's misery ends in an accommodationist act of reconciliation with Dozie. Okoye, like Mariama Bâ, the highpriestess of family love, upholds this positive ideal. The same glove fits these two female writers when Elaine Showalter proclaims that women writers were the annointed priestesses of their sex, "Recording Angels exposing society's vice with careful and loving concern . . . in women writers' hands lies the regeneration of the world" (*A Literature of Their Own* 183)

Finally, the symbolism of *Behind the Clouds* lies in the name. It was taken from Longfellow's poem "**The Rainy Day**": "Be still, sad heart and cease repining. Behind the clouds is the sun still shining." Indeed, every adversity carries with it the seed of success; **Patience** is a much sung and sorely needed virtue. *Behind the Clouds* preaches the message of compromise, forgiveness and maturity that come with the successful facing together of the harsh realities of life. Together, Ije and Dozie have come through the furnace' refined like silver, or gold. Thus, this story of estrangement and abandonment in polygamy ends on a forward-looking note of reunification in monogamy.

The works treated in this chapter are all novels of domestic realism in which polygamy leads to abandonment which is regarded as a symbol of the debasement of the woman, for she is robbed of the care, respect and affection which constitute the integral qualities of conjugal love. The writers uniformly anchor their poetic discourse on the asymmetry that exists in West African societies where sexist cultural and religious mores help to create conditions that favour the entrenchment of polygamy. In polygamy, innocent children also suffer as they are forced to take sides with one parent or the other. As in *The Victims*, their lives can be sacrificed to polygamy, when mismanaged. What unites the women of these stories is the phenomenon of abandonment? All the female protagnists possess a female consciousness that is nurturant and accommodationist; and the hallmark of the ideology of accommodationism is reconciliation. This study has underscored this feature while also highlighting the marked contrast between the husbands - Dozie Apia and the Senegalese cultural archetypes such as El Hadji *(Xala)*, Mour Ndiaye *(La Grève)*, Modou Fall *(Une Si Longue Lettre)*, the former weak and indecisive, the others, hedonistic profligates who deliberately embark on polygamy as a matter of pleasure. For the women, education and financial autonomy confer the will to change a state of abandonment to Woolf's prescribed one of transcendence.

It can safely be assumed that despite their disparate ethnic groupings, the writers treated here agree that the tide of polygamy must be stemmed if Africa is to know real progress.

NOTES:

1. Carole Boyce Davies, "Introduction: Feminist Consciousness and African Literary Criticism" in *Ngambika: Studies of Women in African Literature*. Eds. Carole Boyce Davies and Anne Adams Graves (Trenton, New Jersey: Africa World Press, Inc., 1986). All further references to this edition will be incorporated within the text.
2. Aminata Sow Fall, *La Greve des battus*. Hereinafter to be referred to in the text as La Gr&ve. (Dakar: Lea Nouvelles Editions Africaines, 1979. All further references to this edition will be incorporated within the text. Translations are mine.
3. Mariama Ha, *Une Si Longue Lettre* (Dakar: Les Nouvelles Éditions Africaines, 1981 - (English Trans.by Moudupe Bode-Thomas. *So Long a Letter*. New Horn Press, 1981). All references are to these editions and are incorporated within the text.
4. Katherine Frank, "Women without Men: The Feminist Novel in Africa in *African Literature Today* 15 (Trenton, New Jersey: Africa World Press, 1987). Further references to this edition will be incorporated in the text.
5. Chinua Achebe, *Things Fall Apart* (New York: Fawcett crest, 1990), p. 21. Further references are to this edition and will be incorporated within the text.
6. Isidore Okpewho. *The Victims*. (Nigeria:-Longman Drumbeat, 1979). All further refeences will be incorporated within the texts..
7. Ousmane Sembcne, *Xala* (Paris: Editions Présence Africaine,. 1973). Translated by Olive Wake (London: Heinemann, 1976). Further references are to this edition and.will be incorporated within the text.
8. Ifeoma Okoye, *Behind the Clouds*. (Essex, England: Longman Group Ltd., 1982). All references are to this edition and are incorporated within the text.
9. It must be pointed out that Aminata Sow Fall practises discretionary sexual politics and has in newspaper interviews insisted that the Muslim religion in no way hampers her literary

creative efforts.

10. Gamal A. Badawi, "Woman in Islam." In Islam *its Meaning and Message*, ed. Khurshid Ahmad (Lagos Islamic Publications Bureau, 1976), 131-145.

11. Ogundipe's outlined sixth mountain places the burden of a woman's emancipation on her own self-perception and on her ability to decide on a course of action. See Davies, "Feminist Consciousness," p. 7.

12. In Nuruddin Farah's *From a Crooked Rib*, the widow explains to Ebla that her Arab husband made her cover herself with a veil because "he was as jealous as a monkey," p. 57). Conjectures that jealousy is a reason for Mohammed's action seem valid given the youth of his subsequent wives.

13. This is an example of the asymmetrics in gender politics.While African men practically vaunt their sexual prowess, virginity remains a highly-prized virtue for women. A young wife found to be "at home" on her bridal night is a source of joy and reward for her family. Compare Agbadi's exaltation at receiving "**six full kegs of palm wine** because my daughter has been found an unspoiled virgin. Nu Ego has not shamed us" (*Joys of Motherhood,* 31) and Okuata, who was "found at home," and for that "goat and other presents will be sent to her mother" (*Arrow of God*) to Ogbanje Omenyi "whose husband was said to have sent to her parents for a matchet to cut the bush on either side of the highway she carried between her thighs" (ibid). The rumpus about **virginity** reminds readers of Isak Dinesen's short story - "**The Blank Page**" in which blood-splattered bridal sheets are hung on the balcony and a chamberlain proclaims sonorously "*virginem eam tenemus*" [We declare her to be a virgin.] ("Feminist Scholarship" in *Ngambika: Studies of Women in African Literature*). Eds. Carole.Boyce Daivies and Anne Adam Graves. Trenbton, New Jersey.

Works Cited:

Ahmad, Leila. "Women and the Advent of Islam." In *Signs*, 11: 4 (Summer 1986).

Bestman, Martin T. *Sembène.Ousmane et l'Ésthétique du Roman Negro-Africain*. Quebec: Edition Naaman de

Sherbroke, 1981.
Bruner. Charlotte H. (ed.), *Unwinding Threads: Writing by Women in Africa.* (London: Heinemann; 1983.
Cham, Mbye S. "Contemporary Society and the Female Imagination: A Study of the Novels of Mariama Bâ" in *ALT* 15. (Trenton, New Jersey: Africa World Press), 1987.
Chreachain-Adelugba, Firinne Ni. "Self and Other in Sembène Ousmane's *Xala*," in *New West African Literature*. Ed. Kolawole Ogungbesan, London: Heinemann Education Books Ltd., 1979.
Daly, Mary. *Gyn/Ecology: The Metaethics of Radical Feminisn.* (Boston: Beacon press, 1978.
Egejuru, Phanuel. "The Absence of the Passionate Love Theme in African Literature," *Design and Intent in African Literature*, eds. David Dorsey, Phanuei Egejuru and Stephen Arnold (Washington D.C.: Three Continent Press, Inc.), 1979.
Friedan, Betty. *The Feminine Mystique.* New York: W. W. Norton & Co., Inc. 1974.
Gabriel, Teshone H.. "Xala: A Cinema of Wax and Gold" *Presence Africaine*: Paris, no.116, 1980.
Greer, Germaine. *The Female Eunuch.* New York: McGraw-Hill Book Co., 1971.
Grésillon, Marie. *Une Si Longue Lettre* de Marlama Bâ, (Paris: Les Classiques Africaines), 1986.
Hooks, Bell. *Feminist,Theory: From Margin to Center.* Boston: South End Press, 1984.
Kern, Anita. "Women-in West African Fiction." (unpublished Ph.D. dissertation, University of Toronto, 1978). 163-166.
Leith-Ross, Sylvia. *African Women.* (London: Routledge and Kegan Paul), 1965.
Little, Kenneth. *A Sociology of Urban Women's Image in African Literature.* London: Macmillan Press. 1980.
Martin, Philip W. *Mad Women in Romantic Writing* (Great Britain: Harvester Press), 1987, 1-8.
Momodu, Dele. "Mariama Bâ" in Guardian Newspaper (Lagos: Nigeria), July 8, 1989.
Nwapa, Flora. Efuru (London: Heinemann), 1966.
_____. *One is Enough.* Enugu: Tana Press, 1981.

Okoye, Ifeoma. *Chimere*. Ikeja: Longman Nigeria, 1992
Ola, V.U. "The Novels of Isidore Okpewho" in *ALT*, 13 (1983).
_____. "The Christian Wives of John Munonye's Novels," *Okike*, no. 21 (July, 1982).
_____. "Aspects of Development in Chinua Achebe's Treatment of Women," University of Benin, Nigeria.
Oladele, Taiwo. *Female Novelists of Modern Africa*. London: Macmillan, 1984.
Ortova, Jarmila. "Les Femmes dans l'Oeuvre Littéraire d'Ousmane Sembène.° Présence Africaine, v. 71 (3rd Quarter), 1969.
Ousmane, Sembène. *O Pay!: Mon Beau Peuple*. Paris: Le Livre Contemporain,1957.
Reohane, Nannerl O., Michelle Z. Rosaldo and Barbara Guelpi, eds. Feminist *Theory: A Critique of Ideology*. Great Britain: The Harvester Press, Ltd., 1982.
Sabbah, Fatna Ait. *La Femme dana L'Inconscient musulman: Désir et Pouvoir*. (Paris: Le Sycomore, 1982.
Sedghi, Hamideh. "Women in Iran," in *Women in the World: A Comparative Study*. Eds. Lynne B. Iglitzin and Ruth Ross (Oxford: Clio Books), 1976.
Showalter, Elaine. *A Literature of Their Own: British Women Novelists from Brontë to Lesstng*. Princeton, New Jersey: Princeton University Press, 1977.
Thomas, Thomas. *Review of African Arts*: Vl'(Autumn 1972. 83-84.
Vieyra, Paulin. *Sembène Ousmane Cineaste*. Paris: Presence Africaine 1972.

CHAPTER FOUR

INFIDELITY, INCEST AND ABANDONMENT

Familial harmony is anchored on mutual trust and fidelity. When men and women understand and trust one another, the family flourishes because children are brought up by loving parents to grow up into stable, well-balanced and morally upright citizens. Society therefore benefits because its unit cells – the families – are stable. But in marriages where trust and fidelity become rare qualities, the reverse is the case. This chapter introduces infidelity as a factor that causes familial disunity that keeps the women in chains of neglect which brings about the abandonment of the women who regard marital infidelity as an act of treachery – an infringement of mutual trust. In the books under discussion, abandonment results when

(a) a husband's self-indulgence turns destructively inward, becoming incestrous as in Sembène's *Véhi-Ciosane*[1];

(b) over-sensuality, hypocrisy and egocentrism coalesce to lead the husbands into infidelity as in Mariama Bâ's *Un Chant Écarlate*[2], or in I.N.C. Aniebo's *The Journey Within*[3];

(c) an immoral, syphilitic, child-hating husband with overblown philandering propensities decides deliberately to make life hell on earth for his wife;

(d) a weak, degenerate husband is unable to resist the immoral enticements of city life as in Zaynab Alkali's *The Stillborn*[4].

As has been pointed out in the preceding chapter,

infidelity, as it turns incestuous, transcends normal boundary even in a rural traditional Muslim society as happens in Ousmane Sembène's *Véhi-Ciosane*, a social milieu where the concept of multiple wives and concubinage receives religious sanction. When a family wars against itself, it cannot survive. The act is beyond pardon and the result is that a whole family is literally and figuratively obliterated. Bâ's *Un Chant Écarlate* introduces into this Muslim environment, an interracial marriage, miscegenation and a conflict of cultural values. In Mireille's socio-cultural viewpoint, marriage is a monogamous concept and introducing a third partner is considered an act of treacherous betrayal which results in neglect and abandonment. A maddened wife avenges this betrayal by seeking to extirpate patriarchy. The last two works treated in this chapter, Aniebo's *The Journey Within* and Alkali's *The Stillborn* portray marital infidelity as producing varying consequences. In Aniebo's pessimistic philosophy, life is problematic and living is an individualistic affair. The operating principle is grounded on masculinist morality: women are faithful, men are not. Christian's inveterate immorality receives commensurate moral punishment while Ejiaka's practical commonsense saves a marriage. Alkali's female hero Li receives a rough deal in the marriage game but her humanity and large-hearted forgiveness of Habu's cruel neglect upholds the principle of accommodationism as the hub around which a love union can thrive. Self-actualized and self-reclaimed, she stoops from a position of strength to offer a helping hand to a chastised husband and by so doing redeems her marriage.

In sum, the female protagonists of the four novels considered in this chapter show interesting contrasts in their reactions to the reality of abandonment, occasioned by infidelity: in the Francophone novels, Ngoné War Thiandum (*Véhi-Ciosane*) and Mireille (*Un Chant*

Écarlate), neither resign themselves to their fate nor turn feminists; rather, they radically take charge of their lives in an extreme fashion with telling consequences on the family as a social institution. On the other hand, while for Janet (*The Journey Within*), marriage is a battlefield where the superior partner is determined, both Ejiaka and Li, despite the disparity in education, offer a similar solution to the fact of infidelity and abandonment - large-hearted forgiveness and realistic accommodationism. Mireille, Li and Janet are financially autonomous but only Li, from the feminist viewpoint, can be considered self-actualized, acceding to accommodation from a vantage point, not out of necessity but out of love.

In *Véhi-Ciosane*, Sembène, critic of cultural colonialism, now speaks up for humanity as he veers off to denounce those aspects of cultural nationalism that dehumanize not just women but human beings, pose a real threat to a meaningful conjugal life and constitute a slur on Africa as a whole. Infidelity can destabilize marriages but incest must be considered the lowest form of infidelity - an aberration, a self-destructive act and a betrayal of familial love. Tragedies such as the one in *Véhi- Ciosane* are a result of over-dependence on features of the cultural past like the excessive caste system which produces weak, degenerate men and which equally debilitates the Africans' strength, promoting an in-grown thwarted type of love and adding to general social oppression. The symbolism is striking as Ousmane Sembène depicts the village of Santhiu-Niaye as literally dying out; it is gradually being swallowed up by the sands of the *"niaye,"* a region of dunes and undulating sands. A merciless sun and a torrid atmosphere worsen the harsh, climatic conditions, forcing man, beasts and insects to retreat and take cover within the immense, silent loneliness of the niaye. This strange, sterile, surrealistic background presages the ingrown nature of this act of moral degeneracy which itself confirms the dying out of family as well as village. The storyline is short and starkly tragic. Guibril Guedj Diob, of a noble family and chief of the village, with a polygamous household, gets his own daughter, Khar Madigua Diob, pregnant. The son, back from a war in Indochina is already mad. The mother, Ngoné War Thiandum commits suicide while Tanor Ngoné Diob, the mad son, instigated by the uncle (who has ambition to supersede his brother as village chief), kills his own father.

As is already seen in *Xala*, in Sembène's philosophical framework, female oppression forms an aspect of class oppression and nowhere is woman more exploited as in the family which normally should provide warmth and space, shelter and comfort in times of distress. His disenchantment with Islam stems, therefore, from the Religion's sanctioning of polygamy – a practice that accentuates the strength of a family but debases womanhood because it objectifies it. The image of the fearful, naked girl at the beginning of the story is a germane simile, a presage of the incestuous rape of womanhood within its own home by a morally-bankrupt patriarchy:

> *Les maisons se couchaient comme une fille frileuse, peureuse, nue, les mains jointes entre les cuisses* (*Véhi-Ciosane* 25)
>
> *[The house lay like a young girl shivering, frightened, naked, her hands clasped between her thighs]* (11).

The cowering girl will grow up to become a passive woman, bludgeoned into domesticity as the inessential "ou" by a social system receiving moral sanction from a masculine-biased religion. The passive mother, Ngoné

War Thiandum, faced with this inexplicable problem of her daughter's incestuous pregnancy is now forced to think as an independent being and to question precepts to which she had hitherto given passive acquiescence. The incestuous behavior of her husband marks her moment of betrayal as this act subverts and indeed destroys all ideals as well as the ethical reasons that constitute the base structure of family and society alike. Her awareness of betrayal becomes also her awakening to new and more lucid perceptions. Her position has gone beyond betrayal and abandonment into unimagined realms of bestial behavior. Like Adah (Emecheta's *Second Class Citizen*), her insurrection starts from the bed, as she ruminates over the nightmare that is keeping her awake. Her whole life flashes like a film before her mental screen. She reviews her conformity to the dictates of her religion: her docility to "mon maître après toi, Yallah, mon guide dans ce monde, mon plaideur dans l'autre selon tes dictées, Yallah..." (*Véhi-Ciosane* 30) [my master after you, Yallah, my guide in this world, my advocate in the next, according to your teaching]. Ngoné plucks up courage to withdraw her foot, interlocked with her husband's as an act of protest and gets out of the bed and the room. The author heightens the pathos around Ngoné as she prays fervently in anguish, to be rid of destructive thoughts:

Yallah, pardonne-moi, mais pourquoi cet act? Pourquoi?. . . Yallah ait pitié de moi, simple femme. Qu'il éloigne de moi les sombres et tenaces pensées vengeuresses (30)

[Yallah, forgive me, but why this act? Why?. . . Yallah, have pity on me, a simple woman. Drive from me dark, stubborn thoughts of vengeance].

The author really puts himself under the woman's skin

as Ngoné feels that her whole life has been a lie. We can not but deplore the bestiality of a father capable of such an annihilating act against his own daughter. Contrastingly, Sembène celebrates the immense capacity of a woman's love for her children in these lines:

> *Je vous salue femmes d'ici, d'ailleurs. Profondeur océane...Vous êtes terre, si profonde, si large est la mer; vous êtes le dessus et le dessous et l'autre rive* (24).

> [*I salute you, women, here and everywhere. Deep as the sea: You are the earth, so deep, so wide is the sea, you are the sky above, the sea-bed beneath and the other bank* (11).

Guibril Diob's act certainly does not indicate a vast love, profound as the sea, for his daughter. In Sembène's opinion, it is because the father is incapable of the symbiotic, child/mother affection, or what Julia Kristeva calls the semiotic, pre-oedipal relationship (*Women's Review* no.12, 19-21) between mother and child that he can perpetrate this mindless act of sexual expoitation and cruelty. Clearly Sembène would agree with Mary O'Brien's view that paternity

> *is not like motherhood an experienced relation to the natural world mediated in labour, but an idea dependent upon the development of human mental powers to a level that can adduce the notion of cause and effect. Fatherhood cannot be confined by immediate "experience"* ("*Feminist Theory and Dialetical Logic;*" *in Feminist Theory. . .* 109).

Put in more simple terms, Janet (*The Journey Within)* would say of Nelson, a new father: "he had had little to do with the birth of the baby. He experienced little of the pain and the weariness of bringing forth new life" (24), or as Li (*The Stillborn*) reminds Habu, there is more to being a father than lying between a woman's thighs. Evidently, paternity is not an experiential reality. Therefore, some fathers can callously exploit their children. Guibril Diob feels neither guilt nor remorse as he deliberately plans to live down his act just like the husband in Ralph Ellison's *Invisible Man*. At least, Cholly Breedlove in Toni Morrison's *The Bluest Eye* had the grace to walk out on his family after his act of incestuous rape. But when Guibril Diob's perturbed wife informs him of their daughter's condition, he replies with brazen audacity, "Si tu surveillais mieux ta fille, rien ne serait arrivé" (45) - [If you watched over your daughter better, nothing would have happened] (26).

Feminists find hypocritical, this sexist double standard of parenthood where the mother is charged with the responsibility for inculcating good moral upbringing while even the token nature of fatherhood gives a man rights and privileges over children toward whom he assumes minimal responsibility. The author uses this occasion to awaken our consciousness to the exploitation of womanhood. At last, worn down by the mother's persistent questioning, Khar Mandiagua Diob confesses to her mother: "C'est mon père." In fury, Ngonè, the mother, curses men and decides that at the Last Judgement, she will definitely have things to say. And this from a woman who only a few days ago defined her existence only by her husband's, who outside her domestic tasks was never given the opportunity to express her point of view! Emotionally and psychologically, Ngoné grows up overnight. So what punishment is meted out to an incestuous father? In cases of adultery, a double moral standard exists. And Brenda F. Berrain acknowledges:

In Moslem societies, attitudes toward adultery are one-

sided. *Traditional customs tend to endorse the fact that married men, engaged in extra-marital affairs, can not commit adultery, only* women ("Through the Prism of Social and Political Justice: Sembène's Female Characters in *Tribal Scars*;" in *Ngambika*... 198).

The men of Santhieu-Niaye debate the matter. The penalty for incest is death as stated in the Koran. But it is a moribund law since the sanction has never so far been applied to any known case. They only end up ostracizing Guibril Guedj Diob. For Ngoné War Thiandum of an ancient family whose boundless pride thrives on this motto: "plutôt mourir mille fois de mille manniéres plus affreuses l'une que l'autre, que de supporter un jour un affront" (23) - [Rather die a thousand deaths in a thousand ways each more terrible than the other rather than endure an insult for a single day]. For Ngoné, the only way to redeem the slur on the family honour is death. She is in a horrible mental state:

Elle se demandait comment se réagir son mari. Pourra-t-il vivre avec cet enfant? Avec la fille-mère de cet enfant dans la même maison? Même village? Même pays? Vivre avec eux? Avec les co-épouses? Et elle, mère, grand-mère, comment accomplira-t-elle ses devoirs conjugaux?

[She wondered what her husband's reaction would be? Would he be able to live with this child? With the daughter-mother in the same house? In the same village? In the same country? Live with them? With his other wives? And herself, mother and grandmother, how would she carry out her conjugal duties?]

Such are the unanswerable questions tormenting the poor woman's mind. Thinking and judging every act from a female subjective viewpoint proves an overwhelming responsibility for a woman whose opinion had hitherto been decided for her by others. At the end, she commits suicide. From one perspective, the suicide is perhaps the only way out of an intolerable situation. Certainly, to accord with the Ceddo spirit, Sembène appears to consider it an act of open rebellion, completing the revolt started in bed a few days earlier. In death, Ngoné, like Nnu Ego (*The Joys of Motherhood*), eludes those who render life unlivable for her.

However, the death of Ngoné, considered from another perspective, is an act of selfishness and pusillanimity similar to Idu's because the concern of these women does not extend in both cases to other people, or their children. The same egocentricism informs the action of most of the characters in the story: the father's libidinous compulsion that wreaks so much havoc, the brother's instigation of Tanor Ngoné to kill his father so that he, Medioune Diob, would become chief.

Again, as in most of the texts considered so far, women bond together when confronted with male treachery and exploitation. Ngoné's childhood friend of a lower cast, the griot, Gnagna Guisse provides loving comfort to soothe her friend's bruised and battered psyche. When she finds Ngoné dead, she readies her friend for burial. She also delivers Khar Madiagua Diob's baby daughter and when the villagers banish Khar, she sees the young girl off to the cross-roads - a turning point in Khar's life - and to a new life in Dakar. The young baby is christened Véhi-Ciosane (White Genesis) by her grandmother to symbolize a new, perhaps, purer generation "car c'est des tares d'un vieux monde, condamné, que naîtra ce monde noveau tant attendu, tant revé" (6) [for out of the defects of an old, condemned world will be born this new world that has been so long awaited and for so long part of our dreams] (6).

The old polluted world of the village of Santhieu-

Niaye is dying out; its moral and physical degeneration prove too unhealthy for both young and old. Young men desert the village for other cities. Tanor Ngoné Diob kills his father and Medioune Diob takes over his brother's chieftaincy stool. It's a sorry state of affairs and Amath exclaims:

> *La mère qui se suicide, un fils parricide, un enfant incestueux. Maintenant, il ne reste de doute sur l'état de Tanor Ngoné Diob - c'est la fin de notre village. Yallah, merci que je parte vite.*
>
> [A mother who commits suicide, a son who kills his father, a child born of incest. Now, there is no doubt about Tanor Ngoné Diob's madness. It is the end of our village. Thanks Yallah, I am leaving soon].

Santhieu-Niaye is a veritable hamlet of abomination and desolation. Consequently, it is deserted and abandoned. As Gnagna Guisse escorts the young mother and the infant, Véhi-Ciosane Ngoné War Thiandum, out of the village, she counsels the young girl thus: "Ta vie sera ce que tu feras" [Your life will be what you make of it]. Khar Madiagua Diob sets off on her lonely journey to a new life; she successfully overcomes a temptation to kill the inconvienent baby and hen she puts the baby to the breast, her hitherto shadowy and undefined, passive figure, assumes a definite individuality as the progenitor of a new generation of, hopefully, self-actualized men and women. As Jonathan Peters puts it, Khar "ceases to be a child and becomes a woman." ("Sembène Ousmane as Griot: *The Money Order with White Genesis*," in *ALT* 12, 198). The old patriarchal and repressive order must give way to a healthier, more progressive one in which marriage will be a more equal, monogamous partnership, marked by mutual respect and fidelity, in which children will be properly brought up to put into practice, the ideals of social justice. "Your life will be what you make of it": Gnagna Guisse's advice to the young Khar sums up Sembéne's philosophy of self-determinism akin to that espoused by Zaynab Alkali in *The Stillborn*. Seeds, roots, ancestry, pride of family or caste - these are of no consequence since no person can determine his ancestry or choose his parents himself. What matters is what one makes of one's life. According to the feminist ideology, only a woman (and man too) can determine the terms of one's personal freedom. One's success or failure in life is auto-determined. As Grange Copeland in Alice Walker's *The Third Life of Grange Copeland* reminds his son, Brownstone, "We own our souls." Though Ngoné's abandonment triggers off familial tragedy, there is still hope for the future generation. Clearly, Sembène, not only inaugurates the tradition of Senegalese social novels, he is also at the vanguard of African "feminist" literature.

III

Marital infidelity continues to set off a chain of reactions culminating in another tragedy. This time, the setting, rather than rural, is urban and involves an interracial marriage. Like Sembène's *Véhi-Ciosane,* Bâ's *Un Chant Écarlate* is a quiet but profound tragic tale of abandonment arising from infidelity. It has lyricism and a delicate sensibility with that well-drawn, psychological portraiture which has become the hallmark of Bâ's artistry. In *Une Si Longue Lettre,* Bâ comes down heavily on many aspects of culture (including caste pride similarly treated by Sembène in *Vèhi-Ciosane*) as contributory causes of abandonment.

Now, in *Un Chant Écarlate,* a case is made for the aspect of cultural heritage that should provide a solid anchor for conjugal living. However, what Bâ means by culture is a healthy heritage of traditions based on equality, respect for the dignity of personhood and regard for the well-being of individuals free from exploitative tendencies. These qualities would constitute the true culture, rooted in the meaningful and equitable traditions of a people. The irreverent flouting by Mireille and Ousmane, of the canons of their respective heritage, signals their mutual destruction, because, when trouble comes, there is nothing to cushion the certain fall. This is succinctly summarized by Djibri Guèye at the end when he quotes a Wolof proverb which equates abandonment of one's culture to destruction. To Mariama Bâ, for whom abandonment is, essentially, a universal female phenomenon transcending ethnicity, caste, or race, the inference does not mean that she repugns inter-racial marriages (indeed, she holds up the successful inter-racial marriage between Lamine and Pierrette as a foil to that of Mireille and Ousmane); rather, here she uses an inter-racial marriage as part of her consciousness-raising campaign to open the eyes of men and women to inequities in male/female relationships.

In *Un Chant Écarlate*, Ousmane's infidelity directly brings about the abandonment of Mireille and the destruction of their conjugal existence; it is infidelity overtly encouraged through greed and a deliberate seduction campaign by a fellow young woman[6]; the couple's alienation is further deepened by the antagonism of, and manipulation by a mother-in-law; it is ultimately brought about through the weakness and egocentricism of the husband, himself. These forces of destabilization, Bâ advocates, society must keep in check. She explains:

> *We have no illusions that we, by ourselves, can change the fate of Senegal's women. But what we can do is to help open their eyes* (*Unwinding Threads: Writing by*

Women in Africa 32).

Open their eyes to the place of woman in a society made largely for men; open their eyes to the fact that "in this man-made, man-governed world, a woman might still adhere to all the rules, behave with the utmost propriety and yet come to grief;" (Norah Lofts, *Women in the Old Testament*[7] 182), open their eyes to the fact that the pursuit of personal happiness within the concept of the couple, is being undermined by unsisterly, younger mistresses who subvert the tenets of female bonding. So, for Mariama Bâ, a daring pioneer for the promotion of African womanhood, her "mission émancipatrice" (*Une Si Longue Lettre*[8] - *USSL*) includes a fierce opposition to factors like infidelity which vitiate female individuation and conjugal happiness since she is irrevocably committed to the concept of the couple.

For the youthful couple, Ousmane and Mireille, the halcyon days of early love are euphoric and idyllic: "ils riaient, ivres de jeunesse, d'illusions et d'éspace" [They used to laugh, intoxicated with youth, illusions and space]. Golden-haired Mireille is the daughter of a French diplomat based in Dakar and her family is placed at the highest echelon of her country's bourgeoisie. An only child, accomplished and well educated, she is without racial prejudices and sincerely believes in the equality of all human beings, loving Ousmane with a love "sans patrie", only seeking in a partner' "l'intelligence et le charme". Rashly, she makes herself a willing victim for the sake of love: "ordonne et rien n'aura plus d'importance que toi" [command and nothing will be of more importance than you]. For the African, Ousmane, brought up in the slums of Usine Niari Talli, Mireille is a vision of grace and he confesses that "elle était devant moi, comme une flambeau, illuminant mon chemin [she

moved before me, like a torch, illumining my way].
Mireille, so privileged, so beautiful, Ousmane can be
pardoned when he ascertains from her:

> *M'aimes tu? Ne suis-je pas pour toi que le jouet
> original qui manqué à ta collection dans ton univers
> comblé?*
>
> [Do you love me? Am I not for you the original toy
> lacking in your already over-indulged universe?].

The irony is palpable when it is seen who turns out to be whose plaything. Jean de la vallée finds out about the relationship and Mireille is appalled by her father's violent reactions, by his deeply-ingrained repugnance for the Black race. But she puts up a spirited defence of her love, revolted by the hypocrisy of yesterday's colonizer, clothed in deceptive humanism. She taunts her father:

> *...grate ta peau. Tu verras le même sang rouge gicler,
> signe de ta resemblance avec tous les hommes de la
> terre. Ton Coeur n'est pas à droite. Il est à gauche,
> papa, comme le coeur de tout humain"* (44)
>
> [scratch your skin. You will see the same red blood
> flowing, a sign of your resemblance to all men on
> earth. Your heart is not on your right. It is very much
> on your left, papa, like that of every human].

For love of Ousmane, Mireille gives up everything- parents, social prestige, race and religion - and is ill- prepared by both her extreme youth and inexperience to appreciate the implications of her many renunciations. It is very tempting to credit Ousmane Guèye with sincerity. However, a closer examination reveals the nature of his love; it is tainted with a multiplicity of motives both conscious and unconscious: he has a wounded ego to salvage; his youthful worship of Ouleymatou, a childwood sweetheart, has been disdainfully scorned by the girl who "ne veut pas d'un garçon qui balaie, porte des seaux d'eau, et sent le poisson sec" (18) [does not want a boy who sweeps, carries buckets of water and smells of dry fish], for Ousmane normally helps his mother with some of her household chores, becoming her "legs and arms." Consequently, when Mireille, quintessence of wealth, beauty and culture falls madly in love with him, her adoration proves to be the much-needed balm to his wounded self-love and esteem. So flattered, so adulated by this lover so much above him, Ousmane, understandably "se sentait homme et comme tel, digne de tous les témoignages de l'amour" (33) - [felt himself a man and as such, worthy of all love]. This manifestation of latent "égoïsme" negates any speculation that Ousmane appreciates Mireille's self-abnegation. He does confess later:

Mireille? C'était pour moi prouver quoi? Ma virilité? Ma capacité de séduire si haut, si loin? La difficulté de l'entreprise m'éxcitait. Mon but atteint, j'ai senti le vide immense qui me sépare de Mireille. (205)

[Mireille? It was to prove what for me? My virility? My ability to seduce so high, so far away? The difficulty of the enterprise excited me. Once attained, I felt the immense void which separates me from Mireille.]

For men like Ousmane, the excitement lies only in the chase for once conquered, the prize loses its lustrous sheen. More than any other factor, Ourmane's betrayal destroys Mireille. His hypocrisy, egotism and cowardice, latent at the early stage, develops into definite obstacles to the happiness of the couple. He is well-aware that his parents' reaction (especially his mother's) will be equally as hostile as Mireille's parents'. Modified by the Muslim belief in fatality, his father may accept the marriage, but definitely not Yaye Khady. She had earlier warned him

> *Il paraît que les femmes blanches s'attachaient facilement aux noirs. Méfies-toi. Ne nous ramène pas l'une d'elles.*
>
> *[It seems that white women easily attach themselves to Blacks. Be careful. Do not bring back one of them].*

For Ousmane, knowing his mother's prejudice and still acking the requisite courage to keep her in her proper place, the act of bringing Mireille straight into a communal set-up proves ill-advised for she is ill-equipped to adapt successfully. Djibril Gueye, believing that the Billy-goat chooses its female for itself, counsels his wife to accept reality, like him, since "le marriage est une oeuvre divine" (102). But, Yaye Khady, despite her belief in free choice in marriage, defies her husband's advice and proceeds to choose a wife for her "Oussou." For reasons of financial gain, Mère Fatim and Ouleymatou's mother encourage their illiterate daughter in her archetypal role of Eve, the seductress. Distilled in Mariama Bâ's two novels is an unequivocal denunciation of older women who subvert their children's happiness because of crass materialism. Tante Nabou (*USLL*), out of caste pride, manipulates Mawdo into marrying her brother's daughter. Ousmane Sembène has already shown in *Véhi-Ciosane* that excessive pride in ancestry can become in-grown and dessicating, giving rise to a thwarted morality – incest. Dame Belle-Mère mortgages Binetou's happiness and education for material gains. These machinations trigger off undesirable consequences. Pandering to the lustful and vain posturings of their men, all these women undermine marital bliss as they constitute the social forces that bring about the process of abandonment. Consequently, they lose their position as elders and moral arbiters. What ensues is a reversal of values as their offsprings lecture and call them to order.

Bâ indicts Yaye Khady's behavior which smacks of over-possessive and self-interested motherlove. She had dreamed of a black daughter-in-law who would wash, iron and generally, relieve her of household drudgery. As seen through the eyes of her sister-in-law Coumba, Yaye Khady has herself become aged and faded under back-breaking labor, thus typifying the traditional beast of burden. She has sacrificed her selfhood in bringing up her children and like Nnu Ego (*The Joys*. . .), she has constructed all her future hopes of happiness around her son's progress and success; hence her rancorous detestation of this foreign daughter-in-law - "that she-devil whith the hair of a genie" (*Un Chant Écarlate* 113). She vows, "j'ai du travail à faire" (103). That self-imposed task is to chase away this foreign "usurper" whose beauty she has likened to that of a genie escaped from its own world. When the baptismal ceremony of Gorgui, Mireille's son does not yield her the expected rewards, she confronts Mireille: "Tue es assise sur l'argent de mon fils. Par n'importe quel moyen, je te délogerai un jour" (50). [You are sitting on my son's money. By whatever means, I will one day dislodge you].

At first, her ploy is subtle but encouraged by both Ousmane and Ouleymatou, it develops into full-scale aggression. Even when Mireille secures both employment and her own flat, things are no better for Yaye Khady would torment her whith surprise visits, behave intolerably and set her at odds with Ousmane, who condones his mother's behavior while labeling his wife "possessive." Ousmane shows incredible cruelty and insensitivity towards Mireille, even resuscitating primary school friends with whom he carouses in his home regardless of Mireille's disapproval. His gross disrespect to his wife earns him the dubious compliment of being "Un Nègre marié à une Toubab qui conserve des rapports avec père, mère, famille et ses amis" (132) [a Black married to a white woman who preserves links with father, mother, family and friends] – and all these at Mireille's expense. Just as Modou Fall (*USSL*) does with Ramatoulaye's, Ousmane uses their joint savings to set up Ouleymatou in a villa, hire maids and play at being the rich, successful "son of the soil" – a misguided "retour aux sources" (*Un Chant Écarlate* 158) practiced by a victim of cultural narcissism. One can easily comprehend why Mbye Cham asserts that in Modou Fall and Ousmane Guèye, Mariama Bâ "presents a comprehensive picture of the dynamics and nuances of abandonment" (Mbye B. Cham, "Contemporary Society and the Female Imagination: A Study of the Novels of Mariama Bâ" in *ALT*, 95).

Undoubtedly, Bâ injects into Ousmane, a huge feeling of inferiority complex. At Ouleymatou's where he plays the lord of the manor – "il se déshabillait où il voulait ... salissait ce qu'il voulait (*Un Chant Écarlate* 222) - [He would undress where he wished...dirtied whatever he wished]. At Mireille's, a certain standard is expected of him. Like Ramatoulaye, "angel in the house" Mireille turns her house into a haven of peace as she fusses over its tidiness: "pas de désordre!..chaque chose à sa place" (222) [no disorder!...Everything in its proper place]. But Sheila Rowbotham has deduced that by such obsessive tidiness, a wife aims at self-validation:

> ...proves that she is needed. This can turn into a kind of power which traps husband and children and makes them see home as a kind of prison. (*Women's Consciousness, Man's World* 80)

Loneliness crushes Mireille who oscillates between worry and jealousy as each evening, Ousmane is absent from the home. Mireille, though financially independent, yet falls into the class of emotionally-dependent women whose total absorption in husband and home render them easy prey to selfish men. This validates the theory of John Stuart Mill that every person requires a worthy outlet for strong human emotions in order to maintain psychological balance (*The Subjection of Women* 204). Certainly extra-domiciliary activities possess proven revivifying and tonic effects on the human psyche. Nnu Ego's fate proves the validity of this assertion. But for Bâ's female heroes, love is "all or nothing." Mireille has built her whole world on Ousmane's love. For him, she has forfeited everything on earth; has burnt all her bridges. The conjugal edifice, constructed with so much love and sacrifice has, alas, only sand for foundation for when the winds and storms of infidelity, injustice, and abandonment blow, it crumbles so easily. Already, culturally alienated, there is nothing to prop her up. Her despair reaches its nadir.

In her abandonment, Mireille resembles more closely *Une Si Longue Lettre's* Jacqueline than Ramatoulaye. Like Jacqueline, Mireille lacks a cultural base and a secondary family whereas Ramatoulaye, "issu d'une grande famille de cette ville" [child of a great family of this town] is on firm, familiar, social and cultural terrain; she maintains cordial relations with Modou's people, has her twelve children and friends like Aissatou and Farmata to comfort her. In her case, deprived of the love, comfort, respect and companionship – these well-known hallmarks of a companionate marriage, Mireille is totally forlorn. Bâ has her wondering about the transient nature of love: "Le moment où meurt un sentiment est aussi insaisissable que le moment où il naît..." [The moment when a feeling dies is as elusive as the moment when it is born...[238]. By this time, of course, Ousmane is lost to all reason and does not heed Lamine's remonstrance:

> *On ne peut allier deux conceptions de vies différentes. Si l'on est honnête, il y a un choix à faire. Tu veux être heureux sans rien sacrifier. Tu ne veux rien céder et tu exiges des concessions. La vie conjugale est plutôt humaine approche et tolerance* (*Un Chant Écarlate* 151)

> [You can not marry two different views of life. If one is honest, a choice has to be made. You want to be happy without sacrificing anything. You do not want to give in an inch yet you demand concessions. Conjugal living is rather one of human approach and tolerance.].

Lamine and Pierette's inter-racial marriage, built on these principles, is successful. But for Ousmane, "tout compromise est synonyme de capitulation." In this, he resembles Achebe's Okokwo to whom tenderness and compromise symbolize weakness. Ousmane proves incapable of appreciating his wife's double yoke- of conjugal living and learning to be a blackman's wife in Africa. Lamine points out to him: "tu ne veux pas une femme. Tu as besoin d'une esclave" [you do not want a wife, you need a slave]. Even Ali, his colleague, points out to him the injustice of it all:

> *Tu fais romper une femme avec sa famille et tu ne l'aides pas à intégrer dans un nouvel environnement, en créant les facteurs de son isolement...Tu sembles avoir liquidé tout vertu* (*Un Chant Écarlate* 204)

> [You make a woman break with her family and yet you do not help her integrate in a new environment, while creating conditions that bring about her isolation...You seem to be emptied of all virtue].

Ali further warns him to beware of God's avenging hand. But deaf to persuasion, impervious to all logic, Ourmane like all of Bâ's pampered men, lack the necessary courage and decency to pay their debt of love to their doting wives. And his friend reminds him of that obligation:

> *Tu es le seul fautif, le seul responsable...Cette femme ne t'a rien demandé, rien impose. Au contraire, elle t'a tout donné. Paie la dette. Aie le courage de payer la dette. Répudier Ouleymatou* (206)

[You alone are at fault, alone are guilty...This woman has demanded nothing from you, imposed nothing. On the contrary, she has given you everything. Pay your debt. Have the courage to pay. Repudiate Ouleymatou].

Bâ verbally flagellates young women like Ouleymatou and Binetou who betray the norms of sisterhood and in their roles as mistresses, become willing tools of male oppression. Greed informs her actions. Her scheming chicanery earns her the disgusted Rosalie's derision:

> *Elle attend que tu sois marié pour s'accrocher! Quel cinema! Son attitude est indigne de la femme de ce siècle. Les femmes doivent être solidaires* (205)

[She waits for you to marry in order to attach herself. What a display! Her attitude is unworthy of a woman of this century. Women must show solidarity to others].

Bâ intends the sisterly behavior of Rosalie and Soukeyna to contrast with those of these unfortunate traitors to female bonding. Soukeyna admires and comforts Mireille, her sister-in-law and as Daba does to Dame Belle-Mère, she bravely upbraids her mother for her perfidious hatred of Mireille:

> *Par ègoïsme, tu pousses Ousmane a la catastrophe et en même temps, tu "tues" une fille d'autrui...Pourquoi? Seule sa couleur motive ta haine* (229).

[Out of selfishness, you push Ousmane to catastrophe and at the same time, you "kill" another woman's daughter...Why? Only her color motivates your hate].

As for Mireille, with the introduction of Ouleymatou, the circle of abandonment, so deviously and deceptively introduced and enlarged, is completed. Unlike Ramatoulaye (*USLL*) and Ije (*Behind the Clouds*), Mireille, like Aissatou (*USLL*), never considers polygamy which she equates with adultery. To these two women, polygamy is infidelity, pure and simple. But Aissatou transcends her state of abandonment whereas Mireille lacks the necessary moral courage and family solidarity needed to survive. Like Ngoné War Thiandum (*White Genesis*), Nnu Ego (*The Joys*), Nwabunor (*The Victims*) and Perpétue, Mireille ends tragically. As Aminata Ka so rightly observes, Bâ writes with her heart rather than with her head. By a technique of rhetorical questions, Mireille's nostalgic ruminations, so reminiscent of Ramatoulaye's, underscore the poignancy of her loneliness. A brief note educates her ignorance that her husband has another love. Mireille takes immediate stock of the situation; a visit to the bank confirms a depleted joint account; she trails Ousmane in a taxi and beholds him with Ouleymatou and a young child that looks like Gorgui, her own child and the living evidence of her misalliance. She suffers horrible tortures: would her father accept her back? After her class, racial and cultural betrayal? What props does she have to fall back on? As Bâ puts it "derrière soi, on a tout brulé" (*Un Chant Écarlate* 242). Mireille truly has burnt all her bridges. Nerves become frayed and she tumbles into melancholia. Bâ's stylistic penchant for repetition can be related to Yu Sherkovin's theory that repetition is a technical ploy, adopted to emphasize a given situation (*Social Psychology and Propaganda* 10). She therefore effectively employs repetition to underline the pathos of Mireille's sad state as seen in "Mireille ne riait plus. Mireille ne parlait plus. Mireille ne dormait plus!" (243). [Mireille no longer laughed. Mireille no longer spoke. Mireille no longer slept]. She remembers her father's contemptuous "Tu connais 'ça'? [You know "that"?] Just as Ramatoulaye is forced by later events to agree with her mother's estimation of Modou Fall's personality: "too perfect...to be honest," Mireille agrees finally with de la Vallée's assessment of Ousmane as "ça". As Marie Gresillon has observed, good parents seem to possess the right instincts regarding their children's happiness wheras Bâ's young girls, because of extreme romanticism, lack foresight and good judgement (Marie Grésillon, *Une Si Longue Lettre de Mariama Bâ* 74).

Gorgui, Mireille's infant son, does not belong to this world of skunks and liars, she reasons; tumbling into dementia, Mireille kills her child - the reason she is tied down to an insupportable union. Mireille's act of infanticide has been read as a chimerical effort to extirpate even the next generation of patriarchy. To her maddened psyche, this act symbolizes the ultimate solution to her conjugal problems; like Medea's against her husband Jason, it is the ultimate act of revenge against a treacherous husband. Showalter believes that "madness is explicitly associated with female sexual passion, with the body and with fiery emotions" (*A Literature of Their*

Own 122). Madness is a commonly employed literary device. As used by Bâ in her works, it highlights cultural / gender polarities. Although it has been used extensively by other African writers, Chikwenye Okonjo-Ogunyemi explains its nuances of difference:

> *Unlike negatively presented white mad-women, the black mad-woman in most novels written by black women knows in her subconscious that she must survive because she has people without other resources depending on her: in a positive about-face, she usually recovers through a superhuman effort or somehow aids others.* ("Womanism: The Dynamics of the Contemporary Black Female Novel in English" in *Signs*, 11. 74)

Elizabeth in Head's *A Question of Power* recovers; Merle in Paula Marshall's *The Chosen Place, The Timeless People* pulls herself together; Ramatoulaye refuses to go mad and even Jacqueline decides to get well. In any case, the strong, nurturant instinct innate in the African would save her from such an act as Mireille's because as Ogunyemi goes on to explain, for the black woman, madness is "a temporary aberration preceding spriritual growth, healing and integration" (*ibid*).

Mireille now knows total liberation in madness, becoming "the avenging hand of God." She incarnates the furies pursuing Orestes / Ousmane. In wide-eyed shock, Ousmane is now confronted with the spectacle of the naked, maddened "fury" and wonders:

> *Par quell canal haineux avait-on prévenu sa femme?*
> *Par quelle voie calomnieuse avait-on drainé vers l'oreille de sa femme, sa trahison?* (246)

[By what odious channel had his wife been warned? By what calumnious path had his betrayal been whispered to his wife's ear?]

It is significant that he thinks in terms of "betrayal," corroborating Mireille's charges which she hurls at him: "Sale Nègre! Menteur! Infidèle! Adultère! C'est meilleur avec ta Nègresse, n'est-ce pas?" (*Un Chant Écarlate* 245) [Filthy Black! Liar! Infidel! Adulterer! It is better with your black woman, isn't it?"

Ramatoulaye, Lolli, Jacqueline, Ije - all these abandoned women consider infidelity an act of betrayal. Certainly, Mireille is still thinking of the primary circle of a couple and "adulterer" is the term of infidelity in the Western, monogamous, Christian concept of marriage to which she is accustomed. Thus, Edris Makward is proved right in his contention that Mariama Bâ is centrally preoccupied with "the pursuit of happiness" within the concept of the couple. ("Marriage, Tradition, and Women's Pursuit of Happiness in the Novels of Mariama Bâ" in *Ngambika* 273). Mireille transformed into the naked "furies" pursues and catches up with Ousmane on the staircase landing with a kitchen knife - an exclusive feminine weapon. In a telling description of haunting and lyrical splendor, Bâ weaves the title of her tragic tale into the flowing fabric of Ousmane's bleeding wounds:

Les blessures d'Ousmane, sourdait un chant profound, écarlate d'espérances disperses (*Un Chant Écarlate* 248).

[From Ousmane's wounds, welled up a deep song, scarlet with scattered hopes].

Mariama Bâ, the acclaimed highpriestess of family love, is concerned about marital peace and harmony. Possibly, she writes from a subjective standpoint. There is some validity to the criticism that her conception of feminism is personal and bourgeois like that of Betty Friedan, in contradistinction to that of Emecheta, Nwapa, or Alkali who portray both rural and less privileged women. An accommodationist, her docile, lovelorn, female heroes shy away from direct confrontation with their oppressors. They only wade into battle with men as soon as Bâ dons them with the mantle of madness, a device whih facilitates their emergence from their cloistered homes. They thus represent the author's crazed, but liberated doubles. In madness, Bâ's female heroes become assertive, action-oriented and tragically potent, a fact that bears out Phyllis Chesler's psychoanalytic observation that madness in women is as a result of "an intense experience of female biological, sexual and cultural castration and a doomed search for potency" (*Women and Madness* 6). Chesler analyzes how patriarchy shapes social definitions of madness, and of how psychiatry is used as a form of social control. Thus, women are defined as "mad" when they deviate from stereotypical sex role. Moreover, class, race, and especially sex wthin the maririage construct affect the likelihood of a woman being diagnosed as mad, and further determine her actual diagnosis, or her "type" of madness: <http://www.amazon.com/Women-Madness-Revised-Phyllis-Chesler.>

Finally, Mariama Bâ's style remains without parallel. Employing language that is aphorical, rhetorical, replete with repetition, she describes the joys of early love, the pains of betrayal, men caught in the quagmire of lust, vanity and duplicity, women abandoned even by their freely chosen partners. It is a credit to Bâ's optimism, positivism and romanticism that she still upholds the ideal of a mono-gamous family construct as the soulbeat and cornerstone of a healthy society. All these, she achieves in a language that is both "emotionally compelling and artistically excellent" (Charlotte Bruner, *Unwinding Threads*... xiv).

IV

I.N.C Aniebo's *The Journey Within* continues the literary exploration of the theme of infidelity as a destabilizing principle in marital unions and which keeps women in chains of abandonment, whether temporary or permanent. It is a rich narrative made striking by its superlative technical mastery. The story contains an indepth exploration of the relationship, attitudes and fate of husbands and wives in two marriages – that of Nelson and Ejiaka Achu, and Christian and Janet Okoro.

Christian and Janet's marriage, enveloped in an ambience of family bitterness and rancor, is irretrievably breaking down. Janet desperately wants a child since none of the five children she has had lived beyond five years. Besides desiring more children from him, Janet has the added misfortune of actualling desiring Christian physically for as she confesses, "she has been seduced by Christian's charms," causing readers to squirm as Janet, in self-abnegation, begs her husband for sexual favors. Her "almost superhuman...efforts to rouse Christian to make love to her" are thwarted and rebuffed by him with what the chauvinistic Chinweizu describes as "the guile and discipline of an Odysseus, the obduracy of a Gilgamesh turning down Ishtar's amorous advances" (Chinweizu 96-99). Janet thus suffers the agony of neglect and abandonment at the hands of her husband Christian, who, with the most unchristian spitefulness, taunts her with her barrenness, "his whole body gathering itself into a sharp instrument for hurting":

> There is something unhealthy in your womb that kills those babies even before they are born . . .
> Unfortunately your own children do not survive

because you boil the poor things too long in your hot womb (The Journey Within 79-128).

He refuses to cooperate with Janet for more children until she has her womb examined and treated. He philanders, preferring young adolescents and other men's wives, such as Angela, the pampered wife of a doting old man, Tom Big Harry, with whom he indulges his most orgiastic sexual fantasies. The irony is palpable as the syphilitic Christian is probably responsible for the early demise of Janet's children, rendered unhealthy by this disease. With an unnatural sentiment, he thanks his stars that none of his children survived:

> *He was glad his children had not lived long enough to become nuisances although he did not think Janet would have made him baby-sit with any of them. She would not trust him with them, knowing how much he disliked the squalling brats* (137).

Christian contrasts sharply with Nelson whom Janet sees "...vibrating with the happiness new fathers always had." This portrait of a child-hating, improvident and syphilitic husband, happy at having no encumbrances, is in Nnolim's opinion, anomalous, "heretical and scandalous... only an irresponsible, disoriented Igbo, nay African 'Christian' would rejoice at childlessness" in *Perspectives*. . . (233-237). The narcissistic Christian perennially preening before a mirror possesses a hard-core of selfishness. As Mrs Jeremiah would explain to Nelson and Ejiaka "when a person thinks only in terms of his life, he becomes envious and selfish" (115).

In this novel, sexual relationship is depicted as a means of exploitation and an assertion of dominace and gender superiority. For Christian (who persistently seeks sexual satisfaction outside marriage and corrupts others like the faithful Nelson to do the same), life has no morality and is, therefore, meaningless:

> [Life] did not always have a beginning and an end nor a progression. It picked you up and dropped you where it pleased. (The Journey Within 95).

Consequently, Christian lives in a meaningless fashion, sybaritically indulging his senses to satiety. The Journey Within, although one of the few African novels in which the sexual act is openly explored in explicit erotic terms, is yet a moral book. It is thus, appropriate that Christian suffers for irreverently flouting morality. For seducing Tom Big Harry's wife with impunity, he is severely beaten up by the man's thugs, his shop broken into and his goods stolen, leaving a significant message printed in bold letters for his illumination: "YOU TAKE, WE TAKE." For his promiscuity, he is afflicted with syphilis – *nshi nwanyi* - which makes him insane "so he did not know what he was doing when he ran out naked and was struck down by a car" – a violent death, but a fitting one; he hates children so, there are none to mourn him. It is a fitting act of poetic justice. Kenneth Little has described Janet as having firm views concerning the status of wives:

> She believes they ought to fight for their rights...she has all the instincts of a would-be 'liberated' woman (The Sociology of Urban Women's Image in African Literature 129).

Janet views marriage as an arena for the battle of the sexes. Hear her as she instructs Ejiaka, weeping for Nelson's infidelity and neglect of her:

Marriage is a place for doing battle, battle for supremacy. Unless you want to be defeated, you do battle every day, every hour. Sometimes, you lose, sometimes, you win. (The Journey Within 174)..

But Ejiaka, though illiterate, is intelligent and resourceful. She forgoes the combative stance and handles her problem with tact and forbearance, getting happy results for, "had she followed Janet's advice, she would have lost everything" (218).

And yet, Janet was not always aggressive. At the beginning, affairs between her and Christian had been different: "he had once been loving and always ready to please, to make one smile" (129). Now, paradoxically, there has been a role reversal for the two. She, who used to feign sleep in order to keep at bay the sexually indefatiguable Christian, is now the one who suffers nightly agonies of rejection, going to desperate length to arouse him to make love to her: "she would do all the work, cause him to have an erection, do all the movement" (74) if only Christian would make love to her. Wishing she were a hermaphrodite, she laments:

Was there no other way of getting pregnant? Really, why should she subject herself to this charade? (74)

She knows the cold waves of despair and loneliness of a woman whose marriage has broken down rretrievably, a union in which there is no longer any closeness or warmth and she wonders where love has flown: "where did I go wrong? What did I do to deserve this?" (129), she tortures herself. The way she sees it, it is now a case of unrequited love – "she loved him but he no longer loved her" (32). Early, in their warmly loving union, there had been mutual understanding for "in the beginning, we did not talk much yet understood each other perfectly. Now, we talk a great deal but somehow do not communicate" (183). Truly, her mother had been right when she insisted that Christian's type "was meant to be loved and not to love." Mireille's father and Ramatoulaye's mother have also been right in their assessment of the unsuitability of their respective daughter's choice of a husband. Janet yet vows not to indulge in adultery and Kenneth Little observes, "she retains, nevertheless, her self-respect" (*The Sociology of Urban Women's Image* 129).

The irony is sharply obtrusive as the author gives a backhanded reward to Janet. She, who is determined never to achieve motherhood through adultery, is now raped in a train coach by faceless soldiers. Out of this event, as traumatizing as that in Sembène's *White Genesis*, a fruitful legacy issues forth in the form of the much desired child. Without being a feminist, I.N.C.Aniebo has in this work, decried the socially-ascribed lopsided gender roles which in marriages produce so much emotional imbalance and despair. To be gleaned, equally, form this work, is his advocacy of female bonding. – a feminist prerequisite – as a source of solace. Ejiaka, although much younger, illiterate and quite without sophistication, warmly appreciates Janet's supportive care of her and comes to depend on it. She is sensitive to the contradiction in both their lives, as she feels Janet's agonizing desire for a child:

> ...how unfair and cruel the world was. Here was a woman who had helped many to deliver their babies safely now unable to have one of her own! How could God allow such a thing to happen? (*The Journey Within* 86).

And although, Christian devilishly attempts to seduce Ejiaka by continually visiting her in Nelson's absence, subtly flattering her while denigrating Janet, the warm feelings between the two women remain. It is on Ejiaka's recommendation that Janet undertakes the train journey to Zaria to consult the *dibia* who will treat her for *ume omumu* – the curse presumed to be responsible for her children dying one after the other. Ejiaka confesses her gratitude to Janet for treating her "like a sister." Truly, the secret of sorority is to be found in reciprocity as these women strive to soothe each other, faced with the dominant and destructive aspects of patriarchy and male infidelity. For the characters in *The Journey Within*, life is clothed in subtle ironies and does not yield easy answers. For Janet, in particular, marriage never becomes a haven of peace and self-fulfillment and like Bâ's heroines, she wonders what love truly means: "To be loved and not to love. What did it really mean? Did it paint the whole picture of relationships in this world?... Does this explain the numerous marriages that fail? Do they fall apart because the couples were mismatched?" (132). It is to her credit that she constantly strives to make sacrifices to bring companionate love back into her marriage, all to no avail. Janet therefore suffers total abandonment. Nelson and Ejiaka's pagan marriage proves to be a total contrast to Janet and Christian's union. Thus, Aniebo constructs literary structures through the use of such striking contrasts. As Nnolim summarily phrases it:

> *Hatred, the altercation, the rancour, the frustrations, the emptiness, the accusation and counter-accusations between Janet and Christian on their supposedly "Christian" family where there is neither charity nor peace, stand in trembling equipoise to the love and caring and the peace that exist in Nelson's and Ejiaka's pagan family (*"In search of Aniebo: The Craft of *The Journey Wthin*" 4-5).

Janet envies Ejiaka her luck and feels like shaking her

"out of that dream world of a doting husband and freedom from want" in order to prepare her for the time "when a doting husband would eventually cease to be so" (Nnolim 26). But meanwhile, for Nelson and Ejiaka in love, "the rest of the day flowed like a laughing mountain stream" (15). The two husbands are also total contrasts. Nelson loves his son, unlike Christian who hates children; and Ejiaka thanks her *Ngele-oji* for having given her such a good, understanding and caring husband.

Ejiaka is a traditional wife, unaware of her basic human rights; although submissive, she yet has a lot of innate self-confidence. Nelson, a fitter in the railway workshop, is competent, ambitious and anxious to secure promotions. He begins to change as soon as he starts to make more money: he would buy furniture and household things without consultation; whereas, previously, he had requested things, he now orders his wife to get them. Matters reach a crescendo on the night Nelson and the dog-butchers kill his pet dog who is hostile to Okechukwu and Ejiaka. The latter witnesses the scene and is shocked into immobility. To save her from the maddened dog, Nelson slaps her back to consciousness. She is upset. When he makes overtures to her at night, she, reacting against physical abuse, turns her back to him and resists with all her might. The battle for supremacy ensues. Nelson sums up his philosophy of marriage: "you must show your wife you are tough and you are her master;" he seeks therefore to physically overpower and rape her since failure would be tantamount to giving her control over the household and himself. *In Charlotte Brontë: The Self Conceived*, Helen Moglen's psycho-sexual analysis of the Byronic hero can in general be used to illuminate the male fear of inadequacy and of female moral, sexual and physical superiority over him:

> *Always instrinsically connected to man's insecurity concerning his own sexuality, the fear of women is particularly pronounced in the psychology of the Byronic hero whose need to prove his masculinity by sexual conquest drives him to extremes of behaviour (23-24).*

The above, aptly and succinctly explains Christian's orgiastic sexual dream fantasy in which he conquers his paramour, Angela, until she pleads for mercy, "Master! Master!" and his calculated denial of sex to his wife. The behaviourial psychology of the two men is what Millet describes as "sexual politics," a system of interpersonal power by means of which individual men seek to dominate individual women. But in that battle in bed, the quick-witted and strong-willed Ejiaka gets the better of Nelson, who, feeling sore, eyes her with distrust and skepticism. Obviously, his physical victory over his neighbor, Mr. Okonkwo, provides no soothing balm to his bruised machismo which he needed to prove his sexual potency and superiority over Ejiaka. And so, when Christian introduces him to the brothel of Madame Obo, an accomplished courtesan cast in the mould of Cyprian Ekwensi's eponymous Jagua Nana, Nelson immediately falls ready victim to the woman's practiced charms. The liaison calls forth in him "the rich taste and scent of the freedom of the senses, the liberating effect of experimentation and the joy of total abandon" (*The Journey Wthin* 20). Failing to get sensual satisfaction from his wife, he takes to coming home late, reduces her feeding allowance "less his stomach" in order to pay his bill where he eats. Like many abandoned wives before her, Ejiaka cries in words reminiscent of Ije (*Behind the Clouds*):

> *He has changed. Sometimes, I don't even recognize*

him and I start wondering if he is the same person I married. (The Journey Wthin 173).

Confronted with the specter of infidelity, Ejiaka uses her commonsense; and her forebearance assures her success. Disregarding Janet's advice to be aggressive, she encourages Nelson to bring the woman home. That way, she and the children will not starve to death. Intimate knowledge of your rival at close quarters will strip her of mystic qualities while endurance and resourcefulness could enable one to survive the ordeal. This proves to be the case, for shortly after, Madame Obo throws Nelson out and he is forced to reconcile with Ejiaka. Her mature competence and tolerance recall a similar response to infidelity in Ike's *Sunset at Dawn*. The heroine Fatima's discovery of Amilo's playing around shocks her. But, she gets over the shock and posts to her husband, a packet of condoms as a gift so as to safe-guard herself and him from venereal disease. Desperate situations require desperate measures. To both Ejiaka and Fatima, their marriages matter and their husbands are precious; no need losing them to transient female fancies. For Ejiaka, abandonment is temporary and her marriage re-establishes its once happy lines. Nelson pays for his infidelity and desecration of the marital home by having his next child still-born. It is punishment from the gods as the diviner, Okwomma informs him. Thus, it seems that immorality does have its drawbacks.

V

Continuing the theme of betrayed love, infidelity culminating in the abandonment of the woman, is further critically examined in Zaynab Alkali's *The Stillborn*. The guiding principle is one of accommodationism. The work fittingly brings to a close this chapter on infidelity. It is

(a) a critical assessment of the factors within society and patriarchy which seek to entrench the woman in the chains of immanent negation and a sub-category existence; (b) an assessment of the efforts of the female hero to transcend this immanence through a quest for self-definition and self-fulfillment under a harmonious conjugal construct.

The Stillborn is a significant first work of a lone female voice from Northern Nigeria, Zaynab Alkali, who seeks to expose from a female perspective, the norms and values that oppress women in a traditional, male supremacist society. Nevertheless, the novelist evinces some sympathy even for the men whose stereotyped existence does not offer adequate channel for talent or enough maneuvering space, and so, they too suffer. And because they suffer, as Emecheta insists, the women suffer as a result. Alkali is thus, concerned about the survival and the wholeness of the woman as well as the man. Her brand of feminism, therefore, accords with Alice Walker's definition of a "Womanist" as

> *a black feminist or feminist of colour... committed to the survival and wholeness of entire people, male and female...(and who) loves herself* (Preface to *In Search of our Mother's Gardens: Womanist Prose xi*)

In the *Stillborn,* the lives of Li's big sister Awa and, friend Faku represent polarities of experience – the one of domesticity and incessant motherhood, the latter of abject neglect in barrenness; between them, Li strives to steer her life into a median course. This story poignantly chronicles their stillborn dreams and shattered illusions in a society made by men and run for men.

At thirteen, Li is restlessly vivacious and eager for life, impetuous and self-confident – qualities that to the elders, especially her father, are translated to mean impudent, stubborn and rebellious. Baba, the father, is a patriarchal figure of repressive authority who is obsessed with discipline. Her mother, milked dry from incessant maternity is dominated by an overbearing, unsympathetic husband. Mama's reticence and partial deafness become a psychological defense mechanism against a claustrophobic marital incubus that tries to rob her of self-worth. Her husband constantly calls her a "heathen" woman. Awa is mortally afraid of Baba and wonders "where Li got the nerve to look their father in the face" (*The Stillborn* 13). Understandably, the irrepressible Li, accustomed to a life that is free and fun-loving at the boarding school, finds the atmosphere of her patriarchal homestead claustrophobic and feels trapped and unhappy. Falling in love at the village dance with Habu, "so confident and sure of himself...different, bold and aggressive" (17) provides Li with an avenue of escape from the restrictions of parental and traditional village life. She has glowing dreams:

> *She was going to be a successful Grade 1 Teacher and Habu a famous, medical doctor...*[with] *the big, European house full of servants, the smooth body, the long, silky hair... There was no end to the luxuries the city could offer...The world was full of wonderful and exciting things. And were they not young and eager and ready to enjoy life to the fullest.* (57)

She marries Habu at fifteen. Four years later, the dreams have evaporated for she is still in the village, waiting for a husband (now salesman instead of a doctor) to send for her. She is meanwhile the butt of derisive village gossip. Grown more beautiful and mature, fresh suitors flock around her. Smarting from the hurt of betrayal and abandonment, she curses Habu "who had come to her when she was ripe for love and deceived her". As Kaka, her grandmother, sympathizes with her, Li, indeed, does "carry a burden too heavy for (her) young shoulders" (63). When eventually, she gets taken to the city to her husband, the Habu she meets is now a sullen stranger whose treatment of her is totally devoid of the respect, love or companionship needed to strengthen a marriage. All her romantic dreams of a blissful marital union in which she would care for her man, cook for him, "cuddle him in her breasts," prove chimerical bcause that "former lion of the village" is now as "unapproachable as an angry god," sleeping away from home, her meals uneaten. Li indeed has lost her man to the ensnaring enticements of city life. Habu is entangled with a woman and false pride prevents him from confessing his confusion and guilt. Even Li's one child with him can only be conceived in a moment of drunken and violent intimacy:

> She bent her head and hot tears trickled down her cheeks. "Where is my man?" She wailed silently. "That boyish man with an incredible smile and a mischievous twinkle in the eye? Where is that proud, self-confident, half-naked lover that defied the laughter of the villagers and walked the length and breadth of the village just to see me? (70).

When Li dreams that her ancestral home is in a state of ruined desolation, she determines to leave the city for her home in the village. Patience and determination are qualities she inherits form her mother whose oppressed lot and dogged independence Li understands better as she herself is softened and matured by marital troubles. Back again in the village, she remains abandoned for another two years. Pride restrains her from going back to Habu. Another Efuru, Li's husband never comes to console her on her father's death, nor does he acknowledge the birth of their daughter Shuwa. Out of desperation born of Habu's scorn and repudiation of her, she throws caution to the winds, dressing "extravagantly" and enticing other women's husbands. Zaynab Alkali devices an artistic ploy to stem Li's slide towards moral degeneracy else she may, like Amaka, go in for "total annihilation of man" (*One is Enough* 73) and herself, while leaving a trail of destabilized homes in her wake. Li is therefore toppled from her false throne of glory and Alkali drives home her disgrace for "henceforth, she remained at home and could not venture out for shame" (*The Stillborn* 5). Germaine Greer emphatically maintains that

> *Women who fancy that they manipulate the world by pussy power and gentle cajolery are fools. It is slavery to have to adopt such tactics (The Female Eunuch 326).*

At this crucial point in her existence, those innate qualities of defiant courage, resourcefulness and independence of spirit re-emerge and Li decides to subvert those Muslim criteria of female beauty- inertia and suffering silence – which Fatna Ait Sabbah denounces as

> ...*l'ordre culturel musulman qui désigne le silence, l'immobilité spaciale (reclusion) et l'obéissance comme les canons de cette beauté* (*La Femme dans L'Inconscient Musulman:*. . . 16)

[Muslim cultural principle regards silence, spatial immobility and obedience as canons of female beauty].

Consequently, Li takes her life firmly in hand and redirects her future destiny. Habu's abandonment of Li has been on physical, emotional, financial, spatial and psycho-logical levels. Adversity now compels her to rise above these levels of dependency so as to survive; to depend on herself for the fulfillment of her dreams: "yes, he had fanned the flame of her love, but she was determined to quench its embers" (*The Stillborn* 63).

Zaynab Alkali demonstrates a literary advancement on the old theme of abandonment. The nascent feminism of the earlier generation of female writers – Nwapa, Emecheta – shows their early female heroes the Efurus, Idus, Nnu Egos, as women in chains, passively acquiescing to some aspects of patriarchal tradition unfavourable to women. For instance, all of the above women accept, with unquestioning obedience, that barrenness is a peculiarly female condition; the men were rarely asked to undergo treatment like the women. Now, Alkali infuses Li with **the will to change** her circumstances and this enables her to transcend being locked into an untenable position as a tragic victim of abandonment; she breaks the silence enshrined in Muslim ethics and defies patriarchy. Therefore, Li would not listen to Kaka's suggestion to wait. All these years, she had waited for a man who cared nothing about her. Should she die because her man no longer loves her?

> *Was she to spend the rest of her life waiting for a man like a dog waiting for the bone form its master's plate? Who says a husband makes for a guardian or a father? Certainly not the Hausas who would say "A woman who takes a husband for a father will die an orphan"* (*The Stillborn* 65).

Women sometimes develop these capacities of resistance to male abuse not out of choice but out of a necessity to survive. Li dusted her certificate and endured the rigours of college life. All feminists and gynandrists further attest to the liberalizing effects of education and the need for financial independence. In real life, Benazir Bhutto, the much maltreated, erstwhile woman Prime Minister of Muslim Pakistan insists:

> *I believe that women's financial independence is key to every other type of independence. If I hadn't been financially independent, I am sure I would never have been able to enter a political party ("Benazir Bhutto speaks at last!" Hello* Magazine*).*

Li does attain the apotheosis of her feminist aspirations – self-definition, self-realization, financial autonomy:

> *At thirty-three, she looked years younger than her age. The trim waist-line and the unlined complexion were signs of careful cultivation which belied years of fierce emotional struggle and hardwork. At last, she had accomplished her ambitions. She was a successful teacher and an owner of a huge, modern and enviable building (The Stillborn* 101).

When Li flees the village to embark on a quest for self-discovery and fulfillment, she joins the band of the fleeing female heroes of African literature. Ebla (*From a Crooked Rib*) feels freer the farther away she is from the village; Amaka (*One is Enough*) moves to Lagos for self-realisation; Aissatou leaves for overseas and achieves success there. As a necessary first step in the process of individualization, it may have been expedient for writers to remove their women from the system that has oppressed them. But, Helen Chukwuma opines that heroines should be situated

> *in their usual environment to fight out their battle for a voice... I t is now time to return the heroines back to base and test their acceptance by those they ran away*

from in the first place (Helen Chukwuma "Feminism and Femininity in African Literature," 11).

Amaka does come back to Onitsha to show off wealth, her twins and to build a house and Obiora does want her back. Likewise, Alkali does bring Li back to the village to be its toast and to be acclaimed "man of the house," superintending over her grandfather's funeral rites. She has wrestled recognition and acclaim out of the same milieu from where she escaped in shame and gossipy derision. It is, by no mean, an easy feat!

Of great significance is the role of the men in *The Stillborn*. They are shadowy figures and mostly failures. Baba incarnates patriarchal tyranny; Sule views life pessimistically: "it's a rotten life," and he appears dogged by misfortune even as he goes into self-exile; the would-be-hero Habu a "good for-nothing" husband, ensnared by the city, degenerates into a good-for-nothing husband whose infidelities do not allow his marriage to get off base; Dan Fiama, his hope of heading a modern secondary school disappointed, becomes a hopeless drunk as a way of blocking out a world with which he can not cope; Garba, lazy and rootless, proves to be an unreliable husband to Faku. In between such men, they render stillborn their dreams as well as those of their wives. The fault for their lack of success is laid squarely at their doors and the author's philosophy of life spells it out. As Alice Walker's Grange Copeland would put it, because a man owns his own soul; Or Henley, a man is master of his fate and captain of his soul. Alkali gets a villager, Audu, to define life and its chances:

Yes, my clans people... Seeds and roots are not important. What is important is what man makes of himself in this life. Can a man choose his parents? No. Can he help coming from a particular family, or clan?

No. But a man can help being who he is (52).

The women in the novel step into, and fill the lacuna left by the men. Faku overcomes her inertia and her disadvantaged background, abandons her polygamous marriage to train herself as a social welfare worker. Li, energetically makes herself a success and in the void created by masculine failure, assumes the headship of her family. She would not let the vagaries of life dampen her ardour or defeat her. The key to Li's success lies in the fact that she is a dreamer. Although her naïve, youthful dreams prove to be stillborn, her creative imagination is continually striving to bring to birth, living dreams which are symbolic, portending significant events. One can safely credit her with the strange gift of prescience through the medium of dreams.

To Li, life is a game in which one must struggle to overcome all obstacles through sheer endurance and determination. The mature Li has now become more tolerant and understanding because she has been tempered with harsh experiences. Her sister, Awa, realizes with surprise that in the process of maturing, Li has become a better person with a finer soul. To enjoy it, life must be worthwhile and for it to be so, one must have goals, "for that it is the only way life could be meaningful" (102). Now mature and self-realized, having achieved all set goals, Li becomes accommodationist and decides to salvage marriage for the sake of her child and society despite her emotional brutalization. Exponents of a radical feminist ending view with dismay the seemingly retrogressive ending of *The Stillborn*: that at the moment of her greatest triumph, psychologically strong, economically independent, Li yet goes to the city in search of habu and reconciliation. Omodale Ladele charges that

> *Li prevaricates out of mere sentimentality and all her achievements indeed become <u>stillborn</u>!...Li throws every-thing she had going for her away ... Li fails herself as well as the spirit of the future by not pressing her positive potentials to materialisation* (Omolola Ladele, "Zaynab Alkali;" in Perspectives on Nigerian Literature 330)

Also, Charles Nnolim, alleging "maudlin over-sentimentalism" likens the reconciliation between Li and Habu Adams to "the proverbial case of the winged termite that finally fell to the toad after first flying to the high heavens" (Charles Nnolim, "A House Divided: Feminism in African Literature" 9). But Zaynab Alkali has clarified her point. It is only the really strong who can, disregarding public opinion, show compassion to the weak. By means of the novelistic reductionist technique, the high-flying, libertine and feckless Habu is halted in his amorous wandering by having his legs badly crushed in a car accident. Thus, physically broken, psychologically handicapped and having "lost the will to live," Habu Adams is no longer a god but a frail mortal, now forced by circumstances to recognize qualities such as humility, respect and penitence. Habu's lameness, El Hadji's impotence, or Dozie's infertility like Rochester's (*Jane Eyre*) blindness, Tom Tulliver's wound (George Elliot, *The Mill on the Floss*) are

> *symbolic immersions of the hero in the feminine experience. A Man, these novels are saying, must learn how it feels to be helpless and to be forced into dependency...if he is to be redeemed and to discover his humanity, the woman's man must find out how it feels to be a woman* (Elaine Showalter, *A Literary of Their Own:* ... 159).

When Li and Habu finally come together, it will be a

more realistic love union, shorn of romantic fripperies, a union of equals mutually needing and accepting love and help because in accommodation, "there is no question of the male authority and hegemony over the family under a loving, mutually respectful relationship" (Charles Nnolim 4). In fact, Chikwenye Okonjo-Ogunyemi's definition of "womanism" aptly sums up Alkali's stance:

> *Womanism is black-centered: it is accommodationist. It believes in freedom and independence of woman like feminism (but) unlike radical feminism, it wants meaningful union between black women and black men and black children and will see to it that men will change from their sexist stand... This ideological position explains why women writers do not end their plots with feminist victories* (Ogunyemi, op. cit. 65).

Thus, far from "throwing sand into the feminist garri" (Nnolim *ibid*). Alkali's *The Stillborn*, like Ifeoma Okoye's *Behind the Clouds*, or even Emecheta's *Double Yoke*, is a womanist novel "committed to the survival and unity of males and females" (Marie Umeh, "Ifeoma Okoye" In *Perspectives* 265). It does not give victory to the woman. Habu and Li's reconciliation testifies therefore to Zaynab Alkali's restorative vision of the marriage institution, to her commitment to the wholeness of man and woman, to her determination that a woman should herself break the chains of oppression and transcend her state of abandonment as well as to her belief in the survival of the family for the good of society. African feminism, in the final analysis is shown not to be anti-male: rather it is geared towards the extirpation of ethos that brings about abandonment of women and destruction of homes. Li's gesture thus stands out as the hallmark of altruistic love and godly charity. St. Francis' prayer of love and forgiveness comes readily to mind:

> Lord, make me an instrument of your peace;
> where there is hatred, let there be love,
> where there is discord, union,
> where there is injury, pardon;
> where there is doubt, hope
> where there is sadness, joy,
> where there is darkness, light
> Divine Master,
> Grant that I may not so much seek
> to be consoled as to console,
> to be understood as to understand,
> to be loved as to love; for,
> it is giving that you receive,
> it is pardoning, that you are pardoned, *et cetera*, .
> (*The Sunday Missal* 793-4)..

Li admires Awa and Faku, who have "given for the happiness of others" (*The Stillborn* 102); so to make peace and love, Li stretches out a helping hand to the father of her child but from a position of strength. Employing a symbolism that is extraordinarily germane, eloquent, and evocatively resonant, Zaynab Alkali has her female hero declare her frim resolve to start life anew with the now handicapped Habu. Her surprised sister questions:

> "why Li? The man is lame."
> "we are lame, daughter of my mother. But this is
> no time to crawl. It is time to walk again."
> "so you want to hold the crutches and lead the way?"
> "No".
> "What then, you want to walk behind and arrest
> his fall?"
> "No, I will just hand him the crutches and
> side by side we will learn to walk."

And so it is that Li courageously walks into literary immortality. Her central message is one of Womanist accommodationism: endurance, courage, adaptability, kindness and forgiveness – all which translate to *agape*, or selfless love. We must strive to overcome handicaps, accept challenges. After all, what matters is "the ability to succeed in the game of life" (*The Stillborn* 93). In an interview, Emecheta talks about the writer's fidelity to truth and vision of the world:

> *If you are a writer, you have to be clear about your own truth. Just put it there as your own truth.... Your truth may be wrong, but you write that truth.*
> (Mike Awoyinfa, "Conversation with Buchi Emecheta" in *Weekend Concord*).

Akali's "truth" or "vision" encompasses the total well-being of society, the giving of "self" for the sake of the whole. She defends herself capably and with clarity:

> *The search for the independent "self" however, should not stop at finding the "self"... A total rejection of the marriage institution, an establishment of "alternative living arrangement," a world of "women without men" are no answers to our social problems. If anything, such as a stance is a compounding of our already deteriorating social conditions. We need each other – men, women and children* (*WAACLALS* 10).

Flexibility, accommodationism, complementarity of man and woman – in lauding these timeless virtues, Alkali echoes Mariama Bâ regarding the qualities a couples need to sustain a union. Finally, tolerance, self-knowledge, understanding, positivism – these are additional qualities of accommodationism which, in the artistic vision of the writers studied in this chapter, will cement happy marriages by breaking the chains forged by such negative vices as infidelity.

NOTES:

1. Sembène Ousmane, *Véhi-Ciosane ou La Blanche Genèse* (Paris: Présence Africaine, 1969). Subsequent references are to this edition.

2. Mariama Bâ, *Un Chant Écarlate* (Dakar: Les Nouvelles Editions Africaines, 1980). Subsequent references are to this edition. All translations are mine.

3. I.N.C.Aniebo, *The Journey Within* (London: Heinemann, 1978). Subsequent page references are to this edition.

4. Zaynab Alkali, *The Stillborn* (Essex, England: Longman Group Ltd., 1984). Subsequent page references are to this edition.

5. Norah Lofts, *Women in the Old Testament*. It is surely instructive that this statement credited to a Jewish society of yore, still finds a great deal of elevance in the twentieth century.
6. In her calculated chicanery, Ouleymatdu actually subsumes in one, at least, three archetypal anima images often ascribed to women - as (1) Eve, the temptress as she dresses to conquer; (2) Eurydice whose beheld image kills Orpheus as Ouleymatou seduces and destroys Ousmane and his family by her machinations; (3) Circe, who turns men into beasts as the Senegalese transforms and reduces Ousmane Guèye into an insensitive, chauvinist "pig", beast (or is it thing?) of a man.

7. Bâ, Mariama *Une Si Longue* Lettre (Dakar: Les Nouvelles Editions Africaines, 1980). Trans. by Modupe Bode-Thomas as *So Long A Letter* (Ibadan University Press, 1981). The novel will hereafter be referred to as *USLL* and page references inserted in the text.

Works Cited:

Alkali, Zaynab. "Keynote Address Delivered at the Second Annual Conference of the West African Association of Commonwealth Literature and Language Studies" (WACLALS), December 7th, 1989.

Awoyinfa, Mike. "Conversation with Buchi Emecheta in Weekend Concord, Saturday, August 18, 1990.

"Benazir Bhutto Speaks at Ldsti" *Sunday Champion,* Dec. 16, 1990. (Culled from *Hello Magazine*).

Berrian, Brenda F. "Through, the Prism of social and Political contents: Sembène's Female Characters in 'Tribal Scars'." In *Ngambika: Studies of women in African Literature.* Eds. Carole Boyce Davies and Anne Adam Graves. Trenton, New Jersey: Africa World Press, 1986.

Bruner, Charlotte. *Unwinding Threads: Writing by Women in Africa.* London: Heinamann, 1983.

Cham, Mbye B. "Contemporary Society and the Female Imagination: A Study of the Novels of Mariama Bâ. *African Literature Today,* 15, 1987.

Chesler, Phyllis. *"Women and Madness."* New York: Avon, 1972. In Barbara Hill Rigney's M*adness and* S*exual Politics in the Feminist Novel*: *Studies in Brontë, Woolf, Lessing and Atwood*. University of Wisconsin Press, 1978.

Chinweizu. *Aniatomy of Female* Power. Nigeria: Pero Press, 1990.

Chukwuma, Helen. "Feminism and Femininity in African Literature." *The Statesman,* Monday, March 18, 1991.

Greer, Germaine. *The Female Eunuch.* New York: Bantam Books, 1972.

Grésillon, Marie. *Une Si Longue Lettre de Mariama.* Paris: Les Classiques Africaines, 1986.

Kristeva, Julia. "A Question of Subjectivity – an Interview." In *Wonien's Review,* no. 12, 19-21. In *Modern Literary Theory,* eds. Philip Rice & Patricia Waugh. London: Hodder & Stoughton, 1989.

Ladelo, Omolola. "Zaynab Alkali." *Perspectives on Nigerian Literature,* vol. 11. Lagos: Guardian Books, 1987.

Little, Kenneth. *The Sociology of Urban Women's Image in African Literature.* London: Macmillan Press, 1980.

Lofts, Norah. *Women in the Old Testament.* London: The Religious Book Club, 1950.

Makward, Fdris. "Marriage, Tradition and Women's Pursuit of Happiness in: the Novels of Mariama Bâ." *Ngambika: Studies of Women in African Litekature.* Eds. Carole Boyce Davies and Anne Adams Graves. Trenton, Mew Jersey: African World Press, 1986..

Mill, John Stuart. The *Subjection of Women.* London: Everyman's Library, 1929.

Moglen, Helene. *Charlotte Brontë: The Self Conceived.* New York: W.W.Norton, 1976.

Nnolim, Charles. "A House Divided: Feminism in African Literature." *Perspectives on Nigerian Literature,* vol. 11. Lagos: Guardian Books, 1988.

_____ . "In Search of Aniebo: The Craft of *The Journey Within.*" In *Perspectives on Nigerian Literature*, vol. II. Guardian Books Nigeria Ltd., 1988.

O'Brien, Mary. *"Feminist Theory and Dialetical Logic"* in *Feminist Theory: A* Critique of Ideology. Eds. N.O. Keohane *et al.* Sussex: The Harvester Press, 1982.

Okonjo-Ogunyemi, Chikwenye. "Womanism: The Dynamics of the Contemporary Black Female Novel in English." *Signs, 11,* 1 (Autumn), 1985.

Peters, Jonathan. "Sembène Ousmane as Griot: *"The Money Order* with *White Genesis."* In, *African Literature Today,* 12, 1982.

Rowbotham, Sheila. *Women's Consciousness, Man's World.* London: Pelican Books, 1973.

Sabbah, Fatna Ait. *La Femme dans L'Inconscient Musulman: Désir et Pouvoir.* Paris: Le Sycomore, 1982.

Sherkovin, Yu, *et al; Social Psychology and Propaganda.* Moscow: Progress Publishers, 1985.

Showalter, Elaine. *A Literature of Their own: British Women Novelists from Brontë* to *Lessing.* Princeton, New Jersey: Princeton University Press, 1977.

The Sunday Missal. Great Britain: Collins, 1981. 793-794.

Umeh, Marie."Ifeoma Okoye. " *Perspectives on Nigerian*

Literature, vol. 11. Lagos: Guardian Books, 1988.

Walker, Alice. Preface to *In Search of Our Mothers' Gardens: Womanist Prose.* San Diego: Harcourt Brace Jovanovitch, 1983.

———. *The Third Life of Grange Copeland.* N.Y: Pocket Books / Washington Square Press, 1991.

CHAPTER FIVE

FEMINIST AWARENESS AND THE ABANDONED FEMALE

> *Honey, de white man is de ruler of everything . . . . So de white man throw down de load and tell de nigger man to pick it up. He pick it up because he have to, but he don't tote it. He hand it to his womenfolks. De nigger woman is de mule uh de world.* (Hurston, *Their Eyes Were Watching God* 14)

We have so far considered as principal factors that keep women in chains, cause marital instability and abandonment in love relationships, such issues as childlessness, polygamy, and infidelity. Within the theoretical framework in Chapter One, we had outlined three categories of the feminist ideology, *viz*: conservative, radical, and accommodationist. By evaluating the levels of awareness of the female protagonists of the works that follow, this chapter attempts to provide an answer to the crucial questions posed in Chapter One, viz: how aware is the abandoned woman of her condition *vis-a-vis* gender bifurcation in so far as it contributes to abandonment? To what degree is she conscious of her right to personhood? Does feminist awareness exacerbate the process of abandonment through creating rancor and dissatisfaction in the conjugal construct?

Furthermore, other societal mores such as bride price or the dowry system, forced marriage, issue of chastity, sex-role stereotyping/gender discrimination, sexual exploitation, whims and caprices of the cruel male suffering from superiority, or inferiority complex sometimes coalesce to create situations in which the female is easily exploited and abandoned. The fact of the women's awareness of their situation unifies these abandoned females. Abandonment, therefore, occurs in this chapter when:

(a) weak, irresponsible husbands, intimidated by an ambitious, strong-minded wife with a domineering personality (*Efuru*[1]) have recourse to traditional mores and decide to assert their manhood; the female's radical feminist proclivities prove fatal to the survival of such a marriage;

(b) traditional practices such as dowry system is abused and parents barter a young girl into a forced marriage, and when a husband's feeling of intellectual inferiority causes him to sexually exploit his wife (*Perpètue*[2]);

(c) over-sensuality and ego-centrism of the profligate male (*La Nouvelle Romance*[3]) destroy a union;

enforcement of societal mores such as sex-role stereotyping, gender prejudice and cultural myths propel wives into a state of abandonment as in Emecheta's *The Joys of Motherhood*[4] (1980), *Second Class Citizen*[5] (1989) *Double Yoke*[6] (1984).

In these novels, there is a conscious examination of how these social structures of male dominance oppress women, destabilize the nuclear family and lead to - abandonment. The books under discussion are considered in a temporal order which is determined by each protagonist's degree of dawning feminist awareness.

Surprisingly, despite Nwapa's over-preoccupation with "children" in marriage, neither the issues of infertility, polygamy nor even infidelity occasioned Efuru's abandonment at the hands of two husbands. Adizua for one does not worry unduly over the lack of children since he asks Efuru not to worry about her infecundity, reassuring her, "I cannot exchange you with a wife who would give me twenty sons (*Efuru* 26). And at the time Adizua abandons her for another woman, Efuru already has a child, Ogonim. Her second husband, Gilbert, equally does not abandon her because of her barrenness, but resolves the issue himself by having a son outside marriage. Besides, she accepts Gilbert's son by another woman. Infidelity, as well, does not trouble Efuru unduly for she bravely countenances the act from both husbands. If Adizua had come back, the marriage would have continued, for Efuru waits for him: "he is still pleasing to my eyes" (62). What rather devastates her morale is the total desertion by Adizua and the lack of trust by Gilbert for she is even ready to acclimatize to polygamy and *marry* another wife for Adizua; she, in fact, does marry another wife for Gilbert. So, Efuru unlike Aissatou (*Une Si Longue Lettre*) openly conforms to tradition in accepting polygamy as a way of life: "I don't object to his marrying a second wife, but I do object to being relegated to the background. I want to keep my position as the first wife, for it is my right" (*Efuru* 63). This bears directly on the rules of equity, which in Efuru's ethical viewpoint must be observed with honor between a couple for the man "must go about it in an open and noble way".

Why then do her two marriages fail? The reasons must be sought for: (a) in the very character and personality of each of Efuru's two husbands and (b), in Efuru's own character and personality traits which make her "a remarkable woman" (l). As Femi Ojo-Ade sums it up: "Those very qualities that dazzle both family and friends set Efuru up as a victim of tragedy" (Ojo-Ade 162). Efuru is the more dominant personality in each of her two marriages. Both her husbands are "too weak in character to withstand the force of Efuru's capabilities and personal worth." Besides, despite their earlier infatuation, the two men marry her for reasons other than just love. From Ajanupu's tirade against Ossai, the reader discerns Adizua's weak, irresponsible nature:

> *You are the cause of your chlld's bad ways... You failed to make him stand on his own so that boy he leans on those rich women, not because he loves them, but because they are rich* (*Efuru* 97).

Efuru's industry paid for her dowry. And when Adizua abandons her, it is not because she is barren but rather for another "woman .. well to do ... whose personality [wealth] is greater than" Efuru's (62-63).

Gilbert, her second husband and his relatives equally recognize that Efuru's hands make money. "Anything she touches is money .. Any trade she put her hand to was profitable" (156-170). Thus her beauty, industry and success in trading (very dazzling qualities which endow Efuru with a superiority and confidence usually found in a male), rather engender in her husbands an inferiority complex that robs them of a sense of self-worth. Harold Scheub recognizes this when he asserts that "the very goodness of the character is an ironic flaw" ("Two African Women" 50). Adizua resolves then to escape from the oppressively dependent position in which he finds himself and his desertion devastates Efuru's psyche as it reduces her to a state of submission, self-doubt and loneliness. When Gilbert's behavior, in turn, overshadowed by such a superior wife, becomes problematic, Efuru acknowledges an intractable trouble:

> *She was . . . angry because she had again loved in vain. She had deceived herself all these years, as she deceived herself when she was Adizua's wife* (*Efuru* 266).

In the eponymous Efuru, Nwapa has created a strong-minded, ambitious and decisive female hero who, though illiterate and rural, yet has an intuitive but definite feminist awareness of her right to personhood and to happiness for "Life for [Efuru] meant living it fully. She did not want merely to exist. She wanted to live and use the world to her advantage" (94). One observes, however, that in *Efuru,* Nwapa's feminism is as yet tentative, indeterminate and inconsistent. Squarely embedded within a traditional milieu, Efuru conforms to some aspects of tradition (she accepts clitoridectomy (10-11), she kneels before her husband during marriage rites, she accepts polygamy), yet she flouts tradition where it matters. It can be argued that Efuru is punished in part because she flouts tradition; as Taiwo states, "conformity is an important aspect of traditional life. Any girl who tries to upset societal values does so at her own risk;" in the traditional sense, marriage is a communal affair involving two families who conduct adequate investigation into each partner's background. This Efuru preempts by running away and she lives to rue the day; had the investigative check been done, she would have discovered that Adizua's father was an irresponsible vagabond who deserted his wife for a rich woman, only coming back to her to be nursed and to die. In short, "Adizua's waywardness is in his blood" (73). Like father like son! One is constrained therefore to agree with Taiwo when he observes that "Efuru fails partly because she tries to embody tradition and modernism in an extraordinary way" (Taiwo 51). Besides, her very character in its assertiveness and exercise of personal choice lacks tolerance, a spirit of compromise and subtlety - qualities which would have helped her to better handle her husbands, who by contrast were indecisive, unambitious and weak. This can be seen when she states categorically to Adizua: "If you like, go to the farm. I am not cut out for farmwork. I am going to trade" (*Efuru* 5). Adizua automatically becomes a trader. With Gilbert, Efuru is equally self-opinionated and unyielding as is evident when at Ndoni to buy groundnuts, she peremptorily refuses to "go farther. . . Gilbert looked at her, *shook his head and stepped out of the canoe* ... He did not come back until next morning" (176).

Clearly, marriage being a union that thrives on compromise and pragmatism, cannot survive when one partner is domineering and too inflexible to know when to concede a point. In a patriarchal society where rigid gender roles confer legitimate leadership on even a pauper or a foolish male "as lord of the manor" over his wife, Efuru's dazzling but intransigent superiority becomes too much to bear for these fickle-minded males. We disagree here with Taiwo who thinks Efuru is "perhaps too good ... almost perfect character" (55). In fact, Efuru appears to be lacking in the sorely needed sensibility and wisdom to know when to "stoop to conquer." The dire consequences are at once apparent. Adizua, to assert his manhood, disappears. Gilbert in turn, spends the night at Ndoni and from there, his trips alone to Ndoni become more frequent and "the result is a bouncing baby boy" (*Efuru* 241). And Efuru is thoroughly humiliated. As Eisenstein so well puts it:

> *Precisely because women derive so much of their legitimacy and value from their attachment to a man, in a male-dominated society, the loss of the partner's loyalty is much more grave for women than for men* (Eisenstein 183).

Thus it can safely be said that in a conformist milieu where a weak man is derided "for letting a woman rule him" (*Efuru* 221), Efuru's feminist tendencies prove fatal to conjugal harmony. The same qualities that make her a remarkable woman also strike a death knell to her marriages. However, Efuru's independent spirit, pride and resilience come to her rescue each time. Abandonment can only crush "women who can not stand by themselves" (76), women who are financially as well as emotionally dependent such as Efuru's mother-in-law to whom "perhaps self-imposed suffering appeals" but not Efuru. Her justification for leaving Adizua's house can apply equally to Gilbert:

> *I know I am capable of suffering for greater things. But to suffer for a truant husband, an irresponsible husband . . . is to debase suffering* (73).

So, without father, or husband, or child, Efuru returns to her father's house as a priestess of Uhamiri. Since much of her insecurity and misery stems from her state of barrenness, she now realizes that her life can not be entirely defined by motherhood. She achieves peace and contentment dreaming

> *Of the woman of the lake...she was happy, she was wealthy. She was beautiful. She gave women beauty and wealth but she had no child* (281).

Thus, Efuru's awareness of the cultural traps in society that deny women happiness in marriage and her need for autonomous self-definition constitute her feminism. This leads directly to the inability of Nwapa's weak, inferior men to accommodate such an overpowering personality. Efuru's feminist awareness, albeit ambivalent, does deny her happiness. As has been mentioned earlier, Nwapa's first articulation of feminism in the novel, *Efuru* is full of contradictions. As has already been noted, Nwapa's approach to feminism is later to flower in *One is Enough* and *Women are Different* into radical feminism. Efuru's indeterminate feminism is well-understood by Boyce-Davies who states that "this vacillation between independence and dependence, masculinity and femininity, characterizes Efuru's existence up until the end of the novel" (*Ngambika*: 250). The ambiguity is heightened when Efuru is contrasted with Idu, her fictive sister. Idu, closer to tradition, is equally devoted to her husband and when he dies, flouts tradition and joins him in death. Whereas, Efuru, who starts off by flouting tradition, ends up revering it in form of an escapist, superstitious myth. A re-reading of Efuru reveals Flora Nwapa's advocacy of a separate female existence as injurious to the durable structure of the marriage institution. It is clearly radical feminism, shorn of all compromise.

But it is our contention that Efuru's abysmal illiteracy plays a key role in denying her marital happiness. She has already had a child who died. Thus she is fecund and possibly suffers only from secondary infertility, which ought to have been medically corrected because she herself confesses:

> *I went to Onicha with Eneberi to see a doctor. He treated me and asked me to come again. I have not gone* (*Efuru* 182).

But bound by superstition, Efuru chooses to frequent *dibias* to no avail. Education is clearly a *sine qua non* in any process of cultural re-evaluation because it will help the woman not to accept easily the limitations imposed on her by traditional society. Therefore, Efuru's decision not to consider reconciliation, but to renounce marriage and motherhood *in toto* appears pusillanimous in its extremism. It negates her declared intention to live life fully "and use the world to her advantage." She accepts meekly the dictates of an unreasoning fate: "It is the will of our gods and *my chi* that such a misfortune should befall me" (280). Amaka (*One is Enough*) proves fate and her *chi* wrong when she acquires both wealth, beauty and children at last. She, at least, is not afraid of living. The really positive, feminist character in *Efuru* is a subsidiary but strong figure, Ajanupu, who embodies the feminist spirit of economic and social independence: Ajanupu appears to be the hidden voice of the author in this work in her assertion of the rights of women (Taiwo 53). The novelist denigrates Ossai for her inability to face life, while Ajanupu is adulated:

> *when misfortune came, instead of fighting against it as Ajanupu would have done, she [Ossai] succumbed to it. She surrendered everything to fate. Ajapupu would have interfered with fate. She would have played her own tune and invited fate to dance to it* (*Efuru* 96).

A similarly spirited woman ready to do battle even with psychic forces, defy destiny and bend life to her terms is Agom (Onuora Nzekwu's *Highlife for Lizards*), who declares that "when one sees what one never saw, one does what one never did" (Boyce-Davis 25). Davies terms Agom "a woman who controls her life" (69). Agom does dominate her own story as Efuru and Idu do theirs, faces the same problem of infecundity but optimistically and with disciplined vigor "interferes with fate" and overcomes her handicaps - societal, natural or mystic.

Ajanupu, bonding with Efuru, provides the needed support in times of trouble. She denounces men's ingratitude and irrational caprices: "Some men are not fit to be called men. They have no sense. They are like dogs that do not know who feeds them" (*Efuru* 69). In Efuru's greatest moment of need, maliciously persecuted far adultery, it is Ajanupu who comes to the rescue. She tells Gilbert off for his betrayal of Efuru. He deals her a slap that makes her fall down. Quicky, *Amazonia,* stands up to and defeats exploitative patriarchy, for

Ajanupu got up quickly for she was a strong woman, got hold of a mortar pestle and broke it on Gilbert's head. Blood filled Gilbert's eyes (*Efuru* 276).

The pestle, like Mireille's kitchen knife, a symbol of female yokedom and domestic immanence, becomes the instrument of revolt. Nwapa's radical intent is loud and clear. Like Agom, Ajanupu represents "the matching human force that, effectively shatters the fetters of traditional, supernatural machinery that overwhelms Ihuoma (Elechi Amadi's *The Concubine*), Idu and Efuru" (Acholonu, "Love in Nigerian Fiction"). Agom, Ajanapu, Ramatoulaye, and Li are the literary opposites of those Chukwuma terms "the fleeing female heroes" such as Ebla *(From a Crooked Rib),* Naim's wife *(Mission Terminée),* Amaka *(One is Enough),* and Aissatou (*Une Si Longue Lettre*). Idu and Efuru withdraw from the struggle to change the world for the better - Idu escaping into death, and Efuru into a watery female kingdom where the goddess of the Lake is worshiped by barren women, who have sacrificed motherhood for wealth. By this turning away from confrontation with patriarchy and with the possibility of effecting a lasting social change, Nwapa clearly advocates a female sub-cultural universe of "women without men" -

the women's literature ghetto - separate, autonomous and far from equal [which merely reduplicates the central assumption - of woman as the "other" - that we are trying to change (Greene & Kahn, "Making a Difference" 24).

As Efuru defiantly provides what seems to be a valid option for herself, the perceptive reader feels that Nwapa actually still believes motherhood to be the ultimate good and infertility the ultimate affliction because her ambivalence persists to the end. Uhamiri, the river goddess gives beauty and wealth. But we have already been told that money can not buy children and that Uhamiri "had never experienced the joy of motherhood. Why then did women worship her?" (*Efuru* 281)". Is Efuru's contentment as a votary of Uhamiri then hollow? Nevertheless, Nwapa receives kudos for being the first African writer to present, from a gynocentric perspective, woman's efforts (however chimeric} to achieve plenitude, fulfilment and domestic serenity. She shows how those efforts are frustrated by patriarchal mores and mystic forces pitched against a nascent feminist awareness of auto-determination. But, Efuru's lack of subtlety and accommodationism unwittingly join with these forces to lead her into abandonment. Although marital happiness and motherhood elude Efuru, she however, in her own way, bravely decides to survive and live a meaningful life in terms of traditional society. Efuru is resilient because she has financial independence.

But, in the work that follows, other cultural strictures as well as human factors coalesce to snuff out the life of a promising Perpétue, easily sexually exploited because she is emotionally immature as well as economically dependent.

II

In *Perpétue,* Mongo Beti, erstwhile mysogynist who

depicted women in sexually derogatory terms, undergoes a transformation. Gone is the irony, the Horatian satire that marked his earlier works - *Mission Terminée, Le Roi Miraculé, Le Pauvre Christ de Bomba*. Fernando Lambert has observed that *"L'intérêt de ses oeuvres réside dans l'image qu''il retire de son peuple et dans le parti qu'il prend de rire dans une tentative pour échapper au tragique* (Lambert 194) - [The interest of his works rests in the image he creates of his people and in his determination to laugh in an attempt to escape the tragic]. The interest in his character's fate remains but grimness now replaces laughing satire as, finding congenial company with Ousmane Sembène, Henri Lopes. Ngugi Wa Thiong'O, Ayi Kwei Armah, Okpewho, etc., Beti deftly links the oppression of women to the oppression of the masses by a neocolonialist decadent regime and a patriarchal system redolent of retrogressive social mores. In the story of Perpétue, the primary theme - the debasement of women that leads to abandonment, and the secondary one - the corruption perpetuated in the Cameroun by the regime of Baba Tura - are interwoven as features of a corrupt system in which marital happiness becomes impossible.

The eponymous Perpétue, the focal point of the story is dead. Her favourite brother, Essola Wendelin M'barga, a Reubenist political activist imprisoned for many years and recently released from the concentration camp, undertakes a quest to uncover the details of her unhappy married life. A reconstruction of her Calvary forms the kernel of the story. The first of the cultural mores responsible for Perpétue 's unhappiness to be indicted is the lack of free choice of a marriage partner, usually dictated by an abused dowry or bride price system. Essola, the author's persona indicts a situation in which greed and selfishness impel women to barter their own daughters into virtual conjugal slavery, thereby depriving them of full human status. Essola denounces his mother:

> J'avais juré que Perpétue n'épouserait jamais que l'homme qu'elle voudrait épouser... que Perpétue ne serait pas vendue - que personne ne toucherait un centime sur sa tête... Alors, je déclare ceci, Maman, parce que tu as vendu Perpétue, eh bien, l'assassin de Perpétue, c'est toi.

[I had sworn that Perpetua would never marry unless she wanted to . . . That Perpetua would not be sold, that no one would touch a penny on her head . . . well, I tell you this mother: because you sold Perpetua, the murderer of Perpetua is you.]

Joseph Owono *(Tante Bella)* was one of the earliest opponents of the dowry system which he likens to slavery:

> Dans ce forme dotale . . . l'enjeu de ce commerce honteux est la personne humaine vendue ou achetée à prix d'argent ... la personne humaine est une merchandise ... la conséquence est l'aliénation de la liberté d'une créature de bon Dieu (*Tante Bella* 279-80)

[In this dowry form, the stake of this shameful trade is the human being sold or bought for a price ... a human being becomes an item of merchandise ... the result is the loss of the freedom of a creature of God.]

An analogous denunciation of a forced marriage contracted because of a heavy dowry system occurs in Sedou Badian's *Sous l'Orage (Under the Storm)* where Birama objects to his sister Kany being bartered off to polygamous Famagan:

> *Vous agissez comme si Kany était non une personne, mais un vulgaire mouton. Ce qui vous intéresse, c'est combien vous en tire. Vous la livrez au plus offrant et vous ne vous souciez plus de savoir ce qu'elle devient* (Badian 54).
>
> [You behave as if Kany was not a person but a common sheep. What interests you is how much you get out of it. You offer her to the highest bidder and are not concerned about what becomes of her.]

Other authors have spoken out against the dowry system. René Philombe in *Sola ma Cherie* (1966) attempts to conscientize society by outlining the evils of the dowry system. In the Anglophone sector, T. M. Aluko, *One Man, one Wife,* (1976), Grace Osifo, *Dizzy Angel* (1985), ensure that their heroines escape such a fate when they run away from a tradition in which women are regarded as saleable property with a specific financial value. Adah / Emecheta, (*Second Class Citizen*) equally takes a vow against the dowry system:

> *my daughters ... God help me, nobody is going to pay any bleeding price for them. They will marry because they love and respect their men not because they are looking for the highest bidder or because they are looking for a home* (133).

Elaine Showalter caps it all when she observes in a feminist critique of Thomas Hardy's *The Mayor of Casterbridge* that "patriarchal societies do not readily sell their *sons,* but their *daughters are* all for sale sooner or later" ("Towards a Feminist Poetics" 34-36). Essola Wendellin therefore represents the new African man seeking to liberate women like Perpétue from such oppressive cultural mores that have for centuries silenced and marginalized them into an abandoned existence.

Essola's flashback quest places him squarely at the centre of the action as he goes from one person to another piecing together the strings of Perpétue's life - his cousin Amugu and the wife Katri, his mother and brother, Perpétue's schoolfriend Crescentia, Perpétue's neighbor's and friends, Anne-Marie and Jean Dupont, Zeyang Le Vampire, a football hero who later becomes Perpétue's lover and unsuccessfully tries to refund Edouard's dowry only to be arrested for conspiracy against the government and executed. From these multiple viewpoints, Essola at last, gets the full story of Perpétue's unhappy life.

Maria, Perpétue's mother, comes across as a gruesome, unnatural and despicable woman; she epitomizes the culturally, and mentally castrated women who superintend over the destruction of their own kind and in the process attenuate strength and bonding among womankind as she denies Perpétue the education that could have liberated her; thus, her mother vitiates Perpétue's efforts at chastity by pushing her into a man's bed before marriage. Beti views Perpétue's ordeal in biblical terms: it is a "calvaire - [calvary]": "Devina-elle alors qu'elle était vouée au sacrifice?" (*Perpétue* 8) [Did she already guess that she was destined to be sacrificed?] The girl's antipathy to pre-marital sex draws from her mother the exasperated complaint: "Ne dirait-on pas qu'on te conduit à l'abattoir pour t'égorger comme une bête de boucherie" (114) [Anyone would think you were being taken to the slaughterhouse to have the butcher cut your throat.]

Beti attempts to provide extenuating reasons for women like Maria even when they actively promote sado-rituals. He believes they are not responsible for their actions but are rather the victims of an alliance of patriarchal ideology and a capitalist system that exploits both sexes, particularly women, while reducing them to a state of "robotitude[7]" (Daly 59). He even paints a grim picture of what Perpétue would have become (had she lived) by graphically describing the type of environment that produces clones like Maria:

> *Zombotown, ce cimetière de morts vivants du sexe féminin grouillant de fantômes éloquents de Perpétue - malaxée, broyée par la vie, avilie, aveulie* (Perpétue 265)
>
> [Zombotown, the graveyard of the living dead women, swarming with ghosts that spoke eloquently of Perpétue - battered, broken by life, demeaned, deadened].

In Zombotown, deprived of medicare and other basic infrastructural facilities, brutalized and terrorized by a corrupt leadership that turns young girls into prostitutes as they are [passed from official to official - from Baba Tura to his henchmen] (*Perpétue* 153), sucked dry by the greed and egocentricism of grown-up children like Martin, this wonderful Perpétue could only have survived to become this vulgar re-incarnation of degraded womanhood (265). Beti would here obviously agree with Germaine Greer that "the wrinkles which disfigure women are lines of strain and repression" (*The Female Eunuch* 270). Idealists like Reuben and Perpétue can hardly survive in such an environment; they become the twin victims of an unjust patriarchy and a decadent regime. Perpétue's mother and others like her are victims of such a system. Functioning from a twisted mentality, they constitute one of the forces that deprive women like Perpétue of any happiness in marriage.

Bright, quick and even-tempered, Perpétue is determined to make a success of her new life. The arranged marriage goes on smoothly enough until an unexpected incident brings out from Edouard - a plodder - a latent inferiority complex that flames up to become a virulent hatred of his wife. Here, Beti true to his cultural, nationalist feelings indicts assimilationist French colonialism that sacrifices indigenous language to turn young Camerounians into Frenchmèn expected to master the complexities of grammar and sentence structure. Edouard fails his promotion examination and while reviewing the questions, Perpètue unwisely answers amd explains the questions thus showing up Edouard's ignorance in his friend's presence. As the author remarks, this incident

> *sonna sans aucun doute le debut de sa debacle en assommant publiquement Edouard de la révélation insupportable que sa femme lui ètait supérieure. N'allait-il pas tenter, à tout prix, de dementir cette è vidence? de voiler en quelque sorte l'éclat du soleil?* (*Perpètue* 138)

> [signals without doubt the beginning of the breakdown, confronting Edouard in public with the intolerable knowledge that his wife was his superior. Would he not try at all costs to disprove this plain fact and cover up what was clear as the day?]

It would appear that de Beauvoir's observation regarding the intelligent woman's dangerous position *vis-à-vis* the men very aptly describes Perpètue's situation for "en se faisant ... femme de tête, elle dèplaira aux hommes ... elle humiliera son mari par une rèussite trop èclatante" (*Le deuxième sèxe* 621) [in becoming a woman of brains, she will make herself unattractive to men ... or she will humiliate her husband by being too outstanding a success] (708). No doubt, Beti aims at debunking the myth of patriarchy that intelligence is gender-dependent. In *A*

Room of One's Own, Woolf hypothetically presents the story of a fictional sister of Shakespeare called Judith who is wonderfully gifted but is faced with unequal social and educational opportunities. She runs away to escape a forced marriage and failing to find suitable outlets for her talents and repressed by socio-cultural conditions this gifted sister gets pregnant and commits suicide (Woolf 70-73). The point is clear: inequitable circumstances inhibit the talents of many a budding female genius from seeing the light of day. In *Dizzy Angel,* Nneboy, one of Dolise's wives, wonders how Ogbanje excels academically over her son: "How can a girl do better than a boy in book work?" In Emecheta's *Second Class Citizen*, Adah proves intellectually superior both to her brother and to her husband Francis. Even a patriarchal western-European frame of reference shows an internalisation of the same assumption of male superior intelligence. In George Eliot's *Middle March,* Sir James Chettam, trying to denigrate Dorothea's superior intelligence, rationalises in an interior monologue:

> *A man's mind - what there is of it - has always the advantage of being masculine - as the smallest birch-tree is of a higher kind than the most soaring palm - and even his ignorance is of a sounder quality* (Eliot, 16-17).

One can almost hear female Eliot's scornful laughter. Obviously, patriarchal, cultural discrimination and not nature has interiorized intellectual inferiority for women. As Mary Astell rather laconically puts it centuries ago, "sense is a portion that God himself has been pleased to distribute to both sexes with an impartial hand, but learning is what men have engrossed to themselves." Perpétue is Edouard's intellectual superior. She, however, lacks sufficient maturity to mask that fact. Consequently,

Edouard's conduct rapidly degenerates and he begins to subject her to all the conditions that debase a woman - infidelity (he brings the women home and she is forced to fight for him), polygamy - Perpétue returns from having her first baby to see a second wife installed in their already exiguous dwelling and finally, he deprives her of housekeeping money, the ultimate punitive weapon for the non-working wife.

Mongo Beti, in keeping with feminist and gynandrist ideology, recommends financial autonomy as a means of transcending a position of dependency. And emphasizing the need for paid work as a liberating process, Simone de Beauvoir observes in *Le Deuxième Sèxe:*

> *C'est par le travail que la femme a en grande partie franchi la distance qui la separait du mâle. C'est le travail qui peut seul lui garantir une liberté concrète. Dès qu'elle cesse d'être une parasite, le système fondé sur sa dependence, s'écroule.* (Simone de Beauvoir 597).

[It is through gainful employment that woman has bridged most of the distance that separates her from the male and nothing else can garantee her liberty in practice. Once she ceases to be a parasite, the system that is based on her dependence crumbles].

The socialist economic-class ideology considers the whole system of unpaid female labor as underlying the oppression and servitude of women. Women's work in the home, motherhood, childcare and homecare - all considered as domestic work - are not compensated in quantifiable financial terms. Hence, Perpétue like many a wife before her, has to secure outside self-employment to ward off starvation. Anna-Maria eventually effects a reconciliation between Perpétue and Edward and when Sophie goes (Edward is unable to pay her bride price), he and Perpétue co-habit once again as a couple. The stage is now set for the final tragedy. Perpétue possesses a definite consciousness of the cultural dichotomization of society into masculine and feminine spheres with its concommitant inequities. In answer to his plea for forgiveness, she realistically tells Edouard:

> *Et quand je t'en voudrais? Tu es le maître, tu es l'homme, tu fais ce que tu veux. La vie donne tous les droits aux hommes* (*Perpétue* 195).
>
> [what if I was angry about it? You are the master. You are man. You do what you like. Life gives all the rights to the man].

Unable to pass his promotion exams, Edouard arranges for the commissioner of Police, M'Barg'Onana, to seduce his wife in order to assure for himself a rapid promotion. Perpétue resists, Edouard insists. The Commissioner offers Perpétue a chance to enter into correspondence with her imprisoned brother, Essola. Without knowing that her letters and parcels do not even get to her brother, Perpétue succumbs to this ruse and ends up as a mistress, bearing him a son. Consequently, Edouard enjoys a meteoric rise in his profession. He turns into a terror in Zombotown, as he becomes Baba Tura's organizing agent and wears a gun in his belt. As Anne-Marie sees Perpétue and the entire set-up:

> *une embûche abominable la livra à un homme non en femme et en amante, mais en victime innocente et désarmée... (Perpétue* 195).
>
> [a dreadful trap had delivered her up to a man no longer as wife and lover, but as an innocent and unarmed victim... (130).

As Gayle Greene and Coppelia Kahn see it, "women are the gifts which men exchange between each other .... Men not women have the power to determine the value of women in the exchange and the meaning associated with them" (*Feminist Scholarship* 7). In this manner, Perpétue is sexually exploited and bartered into adultery in exchange for masculine benefits. Also, viewing sexuality from this perspective, Catherine Mackinnon opines that "sexuality is to feminism what work is to Marxism, that which is most one's own yet most taken away" (in *Feminist Theory...* 1). Perpétue's gesture on behalf of her brother extends the biblical symbolism of the sacrificial lamb offered to redeem another. Adisa's sacrifice of her chastity in order to look after the sick Idemudia (*Violence*) comes readily to mind. Hitherto quite passive, when Perpétue at last falls in love with the football hero, Zeyang, she transcends that passivity and in an act of revolt, determines to seek happiness with him. It is her first conscious act of will. When Anne-Maria warns her about its possible dangers, Perpétue explains, with exasperation:

> *Oui, je sais ... je sais que je suis la propriété d'un homme qui m'a payée cher, il y a quatre ans. Mais pour la première fois, j'ai envie de n'en faire qu'à ma tête. Jusqu'ici, j'ai fait tout ce qu'on me demandait de faire. On m'a dit:Perpétue, viens là, et je suis accourue. Perpétue, lèves-toi, et je me suis levée. Perpétue, couches-toi, et comme une idiote, je me suis couchée. Eh bien, je saurai pour une fois à quoi ressemble la saveur des choses qu'on accomplit de sa propre volonté* (*Perpétue* 238).

["Yes, I know" said the young woman with decision and a hint of impatience. "I know that I am the property of a man who paid a lot of money for me, four years ago. But now for the first time, I want to do what I desire. Up to now, I've done everything I've been told. I was told, "Perpetua, go there" and I ran there. "Perpetua, get up," and I got up. "Perpetua, get into bed, and like a fool I got into bed." Well now, for once, I want to feel what it's like to do something of my own free will).

This powerful feminist speech and the determination to self-define the terms of her own existence do prove an awareness of her right to happiness and auto-determination. The course she follows leads to tragedy for her happiness is short-lived; her rebellion is shortly crushed by the full weight of enslaving patriarchy. When Edouard discovers Perpétue's affair with Zeyang, he is consumed with hatred and jealousy and literally imprisons Perpétue in the house. He denies her even ante-natal care in her third pregnancy (this time for Zeyang). Zeyang's efforts to raise money so as to pay back the dowry and redeem Perpétue fail. Severely constrained by her womanhood and burdened further by her pregnancy, Perpétue loses the will to live and one morning, she is discovered stone-cold dead.

Perpétue is unable to exercise the will to *change* her circumstance because of her extreme youth, lack of maturity and sufficient education. Definitely aware of gender imbalance, she nonetheless, lacks the inner resilience, education, family solidarity and material resources with which to fight both an unjust, exploitative husband and a system which confers right of ownership of a woman on him. Towards the end only does Perpétue determine to do things her own way; this is her only exercise of free will and which seals her doom.

Essola Wendelin has now fully reconstructed Perpétue's calvary. The novelist now uses him to mete out various acts of retributive justice. Essola gets Martin drunk and hangs him on the nearest tree in order to spite their mother to whom he gleefully informs, "je t'ai frappé dans ce que tu avais de plus cher, ton fils adoré. Nous nous sommes quittés" (*Perpétue* 294) - [I've hit you through what was nearest to you, your precious son. Now, we are quits] (212). Thus, Essola avenges Perpétue's death by indicting a patriarchal milieu with its enslaving cultural mores personified in people like Maria, Edouard, Commissioner M'Barga-Onana, who complacently accept the murder of Progressives like Reuben and Perpétue so that they can perpetuate age-old practices that should fall into desuetude. These practices reduce womanhood into a state of robotitude; therefore, marriage, which should be a co-operative union of mutually loving partners, becomes that of master / slave relationship in which the master "à se repaître en quelque sorte du sang de ces malheureuses, comme des cannibales" (295) - (in a way, feeds on the blood of these wretched women like cannibals] (212).

Essola reports himself to the Police Brigadier, who makes light of the murder, knowing Martin's worthlessness. The two philosophize on life which is "une sorte de mécanique" (302) [kind of a state of automaton] in which people passively allow themselves to be buffeted by an unjust and murderous fate without putting up a fight. Essola / Beti objects:

> *c'est stupide, c'est désespérant; et c'est que je n'arrive pas à accepter chez nous ... pourquoi ne pas essayer de briser cette malediction?* (302).

[it's meaningless, heart-breaking. And it's the thing I can't accept about our people ... why not try to break the curse?] (218).

Beti thus advocates breaking the curse of bad leadership, fighting unjust patriarchal mores in order to build up a new social order in which marriage can thrive as a compassionate union of a mutually contributing couple; in which children care grow up into men and women of dignity and worth without being traumatized and automatized. On that positive note of concern and advocacy of auto-determination, resistance to brutalization, Mongo Beti ends the sad story of Perpétue. With Perpétue, Beti redeems his erstwhile chauvinistic image and equally lives up to the artist's functions "as the record of the mores and experience of his society and as the voice of vision in his own time."

III

In *La Nouvelle Romance,* Henri Lopes continues the indictment of an exploitative patriarchy and corrupt political leadership which promote gender bifurcation - all of which make marriage a very unequal partnership. Wali, the female hero of Lopes' novel, possessed as a child only a dim consciousness that men are everything and women are their negation. This nascent awareness, later flowers into active feminism as positive as it is action-oriented towards eradicating the ignorance that gives rise to sexual imbalance and which in turn, creates familial disharmony. Etched in Wali's infant brain are memories of an unjust, laborious life that is the lot of women symbolized by her mother, who would get up early dawn (Wali, the child, trotting after her) to traverse miles to reach their farm where she would work all day under the scorching sun. In the evening, bent under the weight of farm produce, she would return to prepare meals and do other chores while the men would sit "sous un hangar à toit bas, les calebasses de vin de palme à leurs pieds .... Quelque-uns, las de la palabre, s'endormaient sur leur chaise longue." (*La Nouvelle Romance* 15) - [under a low-roofed shed, pots of palm wine at their feet .... Some, fed up with the palavar, would fall asleep in their long chairs]. Often, Wali's mother would stop and stare at them, sigh, shake her head and turn to continue with her work. Lopes' description calls to mind a similar scathing portraiture in Amah's novel, of indolent men who sit

> *in the shade of large bodwe trees or beneath the cool grass of huts built by women, drinking ahey, breathing the flattering air of the shade* (*Two Thousand Seasons* 10).

It is a universe with lop-sided values where women work and men rest; black patriarchy had allotted to itself the tasks of conducting only tribal warfare and hunting - two distinct spheres of existence which Wali could never really understand, for as the novelist quips satirically:

> *Mais puisqu'on ne se battait plus entre les tribus voisines, mais puisque les blancs avaient tué tout le gibier, que pouvaient donc faire les hommes?* (*La Nouvelle Romance* 15)

[But since there are no more inter-tribal wars, since white men have killed all the game...What work would the men do then?].

It would seem then that in African patriarchal ideology, the true meaning of gender is not simply "difference" but inequality, division, oppression and interiorized inferiority for the females. Women constitute the core of the rural labor force - farming, tending animals, nurturing children and looking after the home - work rendered invisible because it is relegated to the personal realm. In addition to sexual and political considerations, Okonjo-Ogunyemi's "womanism" takes cognizance of the peculiar issues of race and culture. In Wali's adolescent viewpoint, the African cultural cosmology considers woman not only as a second class citizen, to be seen not to be heard, but burdens her further with masculine tasks while the man has traditional society structured to pander to his leisure. Like all black women in the diaspora, the African woman is suitably covered by Hurston's Nanny Crawford's metaphor of the black woman being the "mule of the world" (quoted in the opening page of this chapter). In Wali's budding feminist consciousness, this abject "muledom"- domestic drudgery - makes marriage a very unequal affair, devoid of the principles of mutual tolerance, compromise and accommodation which should all add up to mean complementarity - a *sine qua non* for a thriving love relationship. Thus, divided into male and female spheres, it was a society with lopsided ethos in which "l'homme doit toujours domine.et la femme ... était l'esclave" (16-17) - [man must always dominate ... and woman was the slave]. It would require an exceptionally fair-minded man to cooperate with his wife to build a companionate union in a milieu so heavily redolent of sexism. And certainly, Bienvenu N'Kama, with his outsized, egocentric personality, is not such a man.

La Nouvelle Romance is a sort of bildungsroman. At the beginning of her marriage, Wali is enthusiastic and idealistic but encounters disillusioning experiences of societal prejudices (against the infecund woman), marital infidelity and the loneliness of the abandoned which prepare her for the illuminating and liberating experience of feminism. At Brussels, the lonely Wali has an encounter with the feminist ideology. She meets the Impanis, "si heureux, si forts et si bons ... ce couple si ouvert sur les autres" (130) - [so happy, so fine and so good ... this couple so open-minded towards others]. Their ideal marriage of complementarity and appreciation of the dignity of labor seems built on a bedrock of freedom from exploitation which Marxism, as a doctrine, preaches. Wali accompanies Jeanne to a conference organized by l'Union des Femmes Belges (Union of Belgian Women) and listens to a lecture titled "Woman Across History." She is thus introduced to *Le Deuxième Sexe* of Simone de Beauvoir. She learns of the universalism of womanhood - the thesis of de Beauvoir that one is not born but rather becomes a woman, that sex differences - the main source of female control and oppression - are socially constructed, that ultimately, that gender behavior, being a social artifact, is the psychology that keeps women subject to the rule of patriarchy. Having traced the history of woman across centuries through the various realms and modes within which patriarchy functions, de Beauvoir, in her lofty ideals, repugns the patriarchal familial structure that so marginalizes woman.

For Wali, it is an illuminating experience that impels her to undertake a review and revalorisation of "la vie des femmes de son pays, puis même à ses rapp6rts avec son mari" (132) - [the life of her country's women, and even of her relationship with her husband]. Her budding feminist consciousness now develops fully. She communicates her thoughts to her academic friend, Awa. As we have already read, Wali confesses to Elise, still at home, "mon séjour chez les Européens m'a ouvert les yeux . . . j'ai beaucoup appris" (192) - [my stay in Europe has opened my eyes...I have learnt a lot here]. Henri Lopes takes the reader through Wali's intellectual thought processes as she reads, questions status quo and the redefines concepts. One thing is clear to Wali: she must arrive at a decision and she must herself define the terms of her own emancipation. But how will she live? She overcomes this intimidating prospect, "une forme de là cheté," (132) - [a form of cowardice] and decides that she must learn a trade and become financially independent. Like all advocates of feminine emancipation, Lopes believes that "the economic dependence of woman upon man makes her a child, or ward only, not an equal partner" (Fuller, *The Great Lawsuit*: 11). Deprivation of economic support is also the most compelling factor of female subjugation. So when Bienvenu refuses to pay for Wali's medical treatment, her friend Jeanne persuades Wali to enroll at "L'Université Populaire."

While still in Africa, Wali had given tutorial to analphabetic fellow women; that she was able to inculcate knowledge to old mamas and to women of her generation had made her feel useful and had awakened in her a love of learning. Awa had encouraged her:

> *Je ne crois qu'il faille être specialement intelligent pour obtenir ces diplômes. C'est une question de volonté. Lorsqu'on est motivé, on arrive à bout de tout* (*La Nouvelle Romance* 47)
>
> [I do not think that one needs to be especially intelligent to obtain these diplomas. It is a question of will power. When a person is motivated, one always gets to the goal]

Consequently, Wali's adventures into the fascinating world of "belles lettres" transport her to horizons far removed from the mundane world of marital troubles and heartaches. Thus she learns that her disappointment in love is neither "faiblesse, ni vulgarité " (49); that even famous writers had traversed the same lonesome, loveless pathways and left in immortal print, the lessons of courage and resilience. Bâ's Aissatou travels the same route and emerges independent with head unbowed by betrayed love. Bâ has left a panegyric on books, an ode to knowledge flavoured with poetry, "...moyen inégalé de donner et de recevoir ... Les livres ... te permirent de te hisser. Ce que la société te refusa, ils te accordèrent' [*Une Si Longue Lettre* 51) – [... unequaled means of giving and receiving.... Books... enable you to better yourself. What society had denied you, they would give you]. Wali has occasion to lock intellectual horns with Zikisso, an investigating inspector, and personification of sexual exploitation and male chauvinism. She comes up the winner. Wali, thereafter, repulses the sexual advances of this lout who reminds her that in Africa a girl who refuses after she has accepted three beers, has earned a slap.

That Wali decides to leave Bienvenu and that the marriage ends in separation does not mean that Lopes espouses radical feminism. In fact, Wali's feminism looks rather more like womanism. Her womanist awareness does not lead to a break-up of her marriage for she, like Lopes, believes in the concept of the couple in a stable, loving union which yet allows for growth and maturity through education and worthwhile existence. Her awareness of the feminist ideology, rather than destabilize her home, contributes instead to a lucid apprehension of the female condition and the urgent need for men and women to build a more meaningful love union. The difficulty resides in finding the ideal partner. She, however, leaves the door open. Henry Lopes like Ousmane Sembène, Beti and others make the claim that mankind's social problems are traceable to the FVVA[8] principle - *femme, villa, voiture, argent* [woman, villa, car and money]. All of the above rest on the sex question - women's inferior position. Women must be educated and allowed to function freely as independent beings. Men must also evolve and learn alongside women in order to achieve the desired complementarity in conjugal relationship. Thus, Lopes releases Wali from the patriarchal prison of emotional and economic dependency. If only Bienvenu had enough literacy and the capacity for intelligent, self-evaluation like Dozie Apia, or Ete Kamba, he would have been an ideally re-socialized new African man, worthy of the new African woman into which Wali matures -- intelligent, giving, motivated, determined not to be circumscribed by limitations imposed by an unjust social order. Unlike Efuru, for instance, Wali does consult a specialist and finds out that her state of barrenness is reversible. Not for her, any fatalistic resignation to an unjust fate or *chi* or god:

> *Je devais me dresser contre cette condition, dût même le scandale en naître . . . je sais que ta (Elise) situation dans la société, celle de Bienvenu même, mon mariage, la condition de la femme ne pourront être changés sans transformer la société. Mais, nous les femmes avons un rôle particulier à jouer dans cette entreprise. Car les véritables esclaves qui ont intérêt à la grande lessive de l'Afrique, ce sont les femmes. Pour cela, je rentrerai un jour* (*La Nouvelle Romance* 193).

[I must make a stand against this condition from which this scandal emanates . . . I know that your situation in society, even that of Bienvenu, my marriage, the female condition will not be changed without transforming society. But, we the women have a particular role to play in this venture . . . the real slaves who have a stake in this grand purging of Africa are the women. For that I will return one day].

Wali restates the urgent need for social transformation. Ignorance which gives rise to basic injustice must be eradicated. Wali, Lopes' "femme des temps modernes" - this positive, reasoning, compassionate and liberated womanist who bends Europe's Marxist-feminist ideology to reflect and encompass Africa's peculiar cultural realities - would return undoubtedly like Ama Ata Aidoo's Sissie, full of love and reformative zeal for "Africa . . . crazy old continent" (*Our Sister Killjoy* 133). And like the befuddled Elise (to whom Wali confesses her grand plan for Africa), we have intimations of traditions to be transformed with the gynocentric values of nurturance, intimacy, fidelity and enlightenment which make a happy conjugal existence the necessary and legitimate goal of a revamped, human society. Thus, the woman's chains of immanence and abandonment will forever be broken and family unity restored.

IV

In *The Joys of Motherhood, Second Class Citizen* and *Double Yoke,* Emecheta continues the indictment of a tyrannical, patriarchal social order whose value system encourages female exploitation and tends to perpetuate the woman's state of enslavement, thus leading to abandonment in marriage. Such a system produces women in chains, abandoned to loneliness. The female heroes of Emecheta's stories, while playing their various roles as wife, mother or fiancée, assert their individuality to the degree that they are aware of their predicament and have therefore set goals.

Emecheta's characterization has plausibility because of the environments in which the female heroes find themselves: in *The Joys of Motherhood,* Nnu Ego plays out her role in the semi-rural slums of Lagos; in *Second Class Citizen,* Adah and Francis, both educated, live first in Lagos and later in the emancipated London metropolis where Adah finds it easier to strike out on her own; in

Double Yoke, the intellectualized university milieu provides the proper liberal backdrop enabling Emecheta to achieve a calculated, highly radical feminism as she shatters quite a *few* of the myths which traditional society has hitherto exploited to render more painful, the chains of woman's objectification. In *Double Yoke,* the author makes a *volte-face* as she pitches in for the concept of the couple in an attempt to achieve for Nko and Ete Kamba, a workable union built on mutual consideration and respect for human dignity.

In Emecheta's universe, marriage can paradoxically be both sublime and submerging. Nnu Ego, steeped in traditionalism, acquiesces in the cultural norms and traditional beliefs about marriage and makes motherhood the pivot of her existence. Consequently, imprisoned by her love for her children, imprisoned in her role as the senior wife (*The Joys of Motherhood* 137), she is submerged under the deluge of sexist societal mores. To Emecheta, the actual test of feminism is the marriage institution and as Chioma Opara observes of Emecheta's fictive world, "the family is the matrix of sexual discrimination, female oppression and the concurrent woman-as-slave mentality" ("Towards Utopia:" 144). Nko, for instance, brought up to recognize the primacy of wifehood and motherhood but who yet wants to be an intellectual with a good degree, is forced by harsh existential realities to choose between being "a good loving wife" and having "a good honors degree;" she determines to give a good fight and "manoeuvre these men to give her both" (*The Joys of Motherhood* 133).

At the root of the woman's problems is the premium which African societies place on the male sex. Adaku (*The Joys of Motherhood*), Nnaife's wife by levirate, goes into deep depression when she loses her baby son, "my only *man* child" and to Oshia's commiserating, "but you still have Dumbi," she snaps: "You are worth more than ten Dumbis" (128). Nnu Ego's inordinate pride in her boys make them realize that they are "rare commodities." Similarly, Adah in *Second Class Citizen* believes she was such a disappoint-ment to her parents because "she was a girl who arrived when everyone was expecting and predicting a boy" (7). To such people, though a girl may be counted as one child, "a boy was like four children put together" (8). The Ibuza men in Lagos thus settle the quarrel between Nnu Ego and Adaku by deciding in favor of Nnu Ego because she is a mother of sons. As Nwakusor lectures Adaku:

> *Our life starts from immortality and ends in immortality. If Nnaife had been married to only you, you would have ended his life on this round of his visiting earth. I know you have children, but they are only girls, who in a few years, time will go and build another man's immortality. The only woman who is immortalizing your husband, you go and make unhappy with your fine clothes and lucrative business* (166).

Such lopsided gender morality naturally culminates in the female no matter how enterprising or intelligent being relegated to a marginal existence and subjected to unequal educational opportunities. In *Second Class Citizen,* Adah's younger brother, Boy, is sent to school before her and only Adah's extreme, ruseful stubbornness earns her the privilege of also going to school. Ada's harassed mother's bitter comment, "to school, you must go until you go grey" (15) later proves prophetic. When Adah proudly shows Francis the manuscript of her first novel, his piqued indifference reminds her that

> *His ideas about women were the same. To him, a woman was a second-class human, to be slept with at*

> *any time, even during the day, and if she refused, to have sense beaten into her until she gave in; to be ordered out of bed after he had done with her; to make sure she washed his clothes and get his meals ready at the right time. There was no need to have an intelligent conversation with your wife, because you see, she might start getting ideas (81).*

Whereas in *Double Yoke,* both Ete Kamba's and Nko's parents are models of a new social order shorn of gender prejudices against educated girls; they pose no obstacles to their children's love union unlike Dozie's mother *(Behind the Clouds)* who believes that "educated girls were in most cases wayward and often childless, they were also headstrong and disrespectful (40). Judith Van Allen tries to explain this gender discrimination rampant in traditional Igbo society:

> *Education is also suspected as making a woman 'troublesome, without manners' which means that she will not show the proper deference of the 'ideal' village girl [who may not ever have existed.]* --- (African Woman's Modernization and National Liberation" in *Women in the World: A Comparative Study,* 43)

Emecheta therefore uses Adaku to make a propagandist statement in favor of equal education irrespective of gender. An ideal, futuristic society will value education for girls as highly as for boys. Adaku, not having "formed roots," understands her transient position of being only a lodger in Nnaife's household as a second wife and decides to make the best of what she has. So, she tells Nnu Ego

> *I will spend the money I have in giving my girls a good start in life. They shall stop going to the market with me. I shall see that they enrolled in a good school. I*

think that will benefit them in the future. Nnaife is not going to send them to any husband until they are ready. I will see to that (*The Joys of Motherhood* 68).

And Adaku does send them to a convent school. Nnu Ego, however, has a slowly developing consciousness of the dawn of this new era when she ruminates: "But who made the law that we should not hope in our daughters?" (187) and later openly acknowledges to her co-wife: "I am beginning to think that there may be a future for educated women. I saw many young women teaching in schools" (189). Obviously, women can equally make as meaningful a contribution to a people's progress as the men.

Thus, despite traditional society's predilection to downgrade a woman along sex lines, a character such as Adah in *Second Class Citizen* possesses a heightened sense of her self-worth. In England, Adah refuses the "second-class" status of working in a shirt factory which Francis and other Nigerians try to pressurize her into. She struggles and gets a job as a librarian; with her pay she refuses to foster out her children but puts them into nursery schools, with the *famous* vow that "nobody is going to pay any bleeding price for them" (133). As Taiwo puts it, Ada "readily throws overboard some traditional customs and beliefs when they clash with her new orientation in life" (*Female Novelists of Modern Africa* 104).

This socially constructed gender superiority builds up in man an inordinate self-conceit. It creates an imbalance in familial structure as man regards himself as a god to be worshipped and served. The slave motif thus runs through Emecheta's *oeuvres*. Where Adah dreams of an ideal home in marriage and "not just any home where there would be trouble today and fights tomorrow" (*Second Class Citizen* 25), Francis proves to be a thorough African male. Like Nnaife, he wants to assert his manliness and dominance without its concomitant financial responsibilities. As a result, Adah plays the role of the breadwinner and works to send Francis to London. A thinking being, she carefully lays her plans and decides early on to be "as clever as a serpent but as harmless as a dove" (22). Eventually, she on her own terms achieves total assimilation into British society on a first-class status. Like Nwapa's women, Emecheta's female heroes are full of initiative and are very determined.

The same delusions of male grandeur are discernible in Ete Kamba *(Double Yoke)* who, nourished on this masculinist ideal, has chimerical visions of his ideal wife who will be as adoring as his mother but educated to boot:

> *Yes, that was the type he would like. A very quiet and submissive woman, a good cook, a good listener, a good mother with a good education to match. But her education must be a little less than his own, otherwise they would start talking on the same level* (*Double Yoke* 32).

The irony is deep as Nko not only joins him at the university as a fellow student but proves far from his idealized image of a love partner. Gradually, she sloughs off the headscarf that gives her that unspoilt, madonna-like image, a symbol of repression since she has been dressing to fit the mold of Ete Kamba's ideal girl. She not only metamorphoses into a new woman with straightened hair and high-heeled shoes, determined to have her degree, be "a bad, loose, feminist, shameless career woman" (135), she conceives a child by the hypocritical Elder Professor Ikot and ends up reconciling with Ete Kamba after all.

Nko's new consciousness is a result of patriarchal double moral standard and the social tension produced from cultural myths that perpetuate man's exploitation of woman. For Nko does start off wanting a compassionate love union with Ete Kamba, "a marriage in which the two would complement each other" (95). When Ete Kamba gains admission into the university, she makes a love gift of herself. The ungrateful lover wallows in traditionalism as he unreasonably scorns Nko's generous sacrifice of herself by calling her a "whore;" he regrets that she is not a virgin and "was desperate for that blood she ought to have shed" (59). But the mystified and hurt Nko is far from being "quiet" and "submissive" and she answers back:

> *you did not sleep with me, you stood with me ... you called me a prostitute ... but you forgot that it takes two people at least to make any woman a prostitute, by your definition. You seem to be forgetting the men who slept with the woman. So, if I am one, then what are you?* (63).

She later unmasks Professor Ikot's hypocrisy - as she reminds him that if most girls who come to the university to read end up being "prostitutes Nigerian style, it is because people like you made them so" (140). Here, Emecheta shatters quite a few myths: (1) the myth of the virgin bride - the author never quite, discloses whether Nko is a virgin or not just as Sembène does in *Xala* with Ngone. As Nko sniffs laughingly to her roommates, "he wanted enough blood to float his whole village" (151); (2) the myth of female fidelity - men usually are the unfaithful partners; (3) the myth of the unmarried mother - Nko is pregnant and decides to keep the child. As Miss Bulewao reminds Ete Kamba who insists on upholding the male right to produce bastards:

> *Nko is going to be a graduate from this university. She*

too can afford to look after her own bastard.
Or you mean to tell me that having children out of wedlock is another masculine preserve? (*Double Yoke* 157).

It is indeed a changing world in which the traditional values come into conflict with new ones and none feels it more than the two lovers. Nko has earlier cried in anguish to her mother:

> Oh mother, I want to have both worlds. I want to be an academician and I want to be a quiet, nice and obedient wife, the type you all want me to be. I want the two, mother. 0 please, mother, help me (*Double Yoke* 55).

Nko's mother, an enlightened traditionalist, deeply feels for her daughter who suffering under a double yoke. Nko fails in all the traditional expectations but she emerges as an independent, young African woman, aware of all the pitfalls but determined to have both education and financial autonomy so as not to "reduce her family and herself to being beggars at Ete's table" (133). Defiant, she decides to take her chances at marital happiness with Ete Kamba but "she was not going to kill herself" for any man. Nko may not set about it the right way, she may have made mistakes but far from being a passive victim of patriarchal dominance like Nnu Ego, she self-determines her own destiny. She not only has the spunk but possesses "the will to change" and succeeds in actualizing her wishes in spite of obstacles.

This conflict between the old cultural mores that gave great advantage to men and the new Western ways that in some ways such as education favors women is also at the root of the couple's problems in *Second Class Citizen* for Francis is unwilling to let go the old and change with the times. Adah, toughened in the cruel school of adversity and privations, is aware of the harsh realities of life and is determined to survive. Dominant, decisive and cunning, she patiently rides the storm of patriarchal exploitation to gain greater ends. For most of her married life, she works to maintain Francis who "was only good at giving her children nothing else" (*Second Class Citizen* 61). Early in her marriage, she sheds her romantic illusions though "she still yearned to be loved, to feel really married, to be cared for;" but these are romanticised notions of love that Francis, nurtured with traditional practical values of a woman's place and role that are clearly at variance with those of the liberal English society, does not possess. Like Nnaife (*The Joys of Motherhood*) Francis "was not the type of a man who would go and look for a job unless pushed to it. He was the type of person who believed the world owed him so much that he need not put anything back" (*Second Class Citizen* 131).

In her long sojourn abroad, Emecheta has been deeply influenced by British and Irish feminism. She thus has a clear perception that much of the oppression women suffer from African men stems from the fact that the men themselves have been oppressed by colonialism and neo-colonialism - the fourth mountain on the African woman's back as delineated by Molara Ogundipe-Leslie: "her men, weaned on centuries of male [colonial) domination who will not willingly relinquish their power and privilege." Emecheta emphasizes the slave motif when, in *The Joys of Motherhood*, she makes Cordelia explain to Nnu Ego that the men "are all slaves, including us. If their masters treat them badly, they take it out on us. The only difference is that they are given some pay for their work, instead of having been bought" (51); and of course, Nnaife, the washer of white women's undies, in turn brazenly asks Nnu Ego, "did I not pay your bride price? Am I not your owner?" (48) Nnu Ego, fettered and frozen in her motherhood role gives in, saying, "He has made me into a real woman - all I want to be, a woman and a mother" (53).

But Emecheta /Adah, espousing Friedan's view that "marriage and motherhood are an essential part of life but not the whole of it" (Friedan, *The Feminine Mystique* 376), undoubtedly has other aspirations in life. Having sought in marriage mutual love and lost, Adah decides "to live, to survive, to exist through it all" (*Second Class Citizen* 164) and, the means she chooses is education. Education will enable her "stretch and stretch" like Friedan's "high-dominance" women until she can not only discover herself but force life to yield to her its sweet juices of success and abundance. Adah succeeds in achieving her dream of being able to write; she gets a good job as well, defying Francis' threat to stop her from working: "this is England, not Nigeria. I don't need your signature to secure a job for me" (177). Expectedly, Adah self-emancipates, becoming an independent woman, aware of her rights in a milieu in which Francis' African patriarchal claims lose their validity. She tries to explain the tragedy of Francis' life, "Francis was not a bad man, just a man who could no longer cope with the over-demanding society he found himself in." Soon, the marriage, based solely on economic and sexual exploitation of Adah, breaks down as she refuses to maintain him any further. When Francis burns the manuscript of her novel, she decides that the marriage is over because he has killed what she regrds as "her brain-child" - her manuscript.

Though brutally beaten up by Francis while pregnant with his fifth child, Adah yet accepts motherhood and financial responsibility for her children. Francis had long ago abandoned all care and support of the family, had destroyed all fidelity and trust that form the basis of any marriage. Divorce, though initiated by Adah, merely confers an official seal on the fact of abandonment. Adah's marriage is really over. In *Second Class Citizen*, Buchi Emecheta shows that it is possible to transcend near-insurmountable obstacles, physical and psychological battering, and still achieve intellectual and economic success by dint of *hard work and effort of will* without compromising one's dignity and pride of womanhood. In *La Nouvelle Romance*, Awa had encouraged Wali -"C'est une question de volonté. Lorsqu'on est motivé, on arrive à bout de tout" - ["It is a question of will power. When one is motivated, one ends up achieving everything]. Adah, being motivated, achieves success – self-actualisation.

Adah's feminist awareness is of the radical kind and it does contribute to her being abandoned by Francis in so far as it sharpens her clear perception that the type of marriage she has is inimical to her effort at self-definition, that though a woman, she has basic inalienable human rights to happiness, self-fulfilment, that some of Francis' African patriarchal expectations are repressive to her female self and are clearly at variance in the English society in which they both live. Similarly, Adaku *(The Joys of Motherhood)* possesses a radical feminist awareness; although illiterate, Adaku recognizes when it is time to call it quits with Nnaife; as a result of her drive and resourcefulness, she ends up a thriving business woman and *not a prostitute,* though she threatens to be one.

Thus, it seems that in Emecheta's feminist ideological universe, morality has very positive values. She balks when it is contravened. In *Double Yoke*, Nko, through prostitution tries to achieve academic success. Emecheta uses Mrs. Nwaiwu as her mouthpiece to pass strictures at this moral laxity while encouraging learning and self-actualization through hard work. Mrs. Nwaiwu counsels Nko to get a good degree by working hard for it. It is easier to get a good degree using one's brainpower than bottom power (152). Certainly, Emecheta believes this and creates the figure of Miss Bulewao *(Double Yoke)* to prove it. Miss Bulewao represents Emecheta's exercise in literary narcissism. In creating the character of the mature lecturer, Emecheta vaingloriously proclaims that she herself has attained the height, the ultimate in her ambition (a process started by her autobiographical persona, Adah) and that it is feasible, for

> ... *this plump woman, who with her books had almost transformed herself into a super human being ... the most talked about female writer in Nigeria, and maybe in the whole of Africa (13).*

From her autobiographical sketches in *In The Ditch* and *Second Class Citizen*, Emecheta's success is no mean feat: it must have been a hard struggle getting out of the ditch of patriarchal and racial ghettoes. Miss Bulewao is therefore, the mature fulfilment of Adah's youthful intellectual yearnings. From learning how to set about writing in *Second Class Citizen,* Adah/Emecheta ends up in *Double Yoke* as Miss Bulewao, giving a course in creative writing. Ete's story, *Double Yoke,* is the outcome.

Critics, like Charles Nnolim, have decried the curious rigor and ambivalence with which Emecheta treats her female heroes to whom she denies the same "success and freedom'" she gives to Adah/Emecheta. This, in part, can be attributed to the developmental nature of the author's feminist ideology. In *The Joys of Motherhood,* for instance, the radical feminist notions, clearly well--enunciated in her later works, are merely mooted at the beginning of the novel. Nnu Ego's feminist consciousness is at first, non-existent; then it slowly evolves as she encounters mind-boggling experiences; then it flowers into radical mythic feminism at her death as she denies her votaries all *joys* in wifehood and motherhood, not having known any herself. In Nnu Ego, Emecheta strongly indicts those features of patriarchy that deprive women of all joys in living, condemning them to the chains of abandonment and, at times, death. Her message is clear: times change and one must be prepared to make the necessary adjustments or face catastrophes; children may disappoint one. As Nnu Ego's children become a disppointment to her, her troubles with Nnaife increase correspondingly culminating in total alienation when Kehinde, the "deep one" of the twins, runs away to her Yoruba lover, who pays no bride price. Thus, the "dirty" children which the slave woman, or her "chi" had given Nnu Ego in profusion, have evidently been of no use to her. Has it all been worth it? In an interior monologue, the sad Nnu Ego philosophizes:

> *She had been brought up to believe that children made a woman. She had had children, nine in all . . . how was she to know that by the time her children grew up the values of her country, her people and her tribe would have changed so drastically to the extent where a woman with many children could face a lonely, old age, and maybe a miserable death, all alone, just like a - barren woman* (*The Joys of Motherhood* 219).

So, what really are the joys of motherhood? The sad paradox dawns on Nnu Ego that "it was true what they said; "if you don't have children the longing for them will kill you, and if you do, the worrying over them will kill you" (212). Already schizophrenic, she loses her mind entirely and dies quietly by the roadside. The irony is complete when her sons, who have never cared for her, all come home to give her the noisiest and most expensive burial in Ibuza.

Certainly, the author has treated Nnu Ego with undeserved rigor and injustice. An explanation comes readily to mind. Adah / Emecheta's early "low opinion of her sex" *(Second Class Citizen* 12) arises from her uneasy real-life relationship with her mother; she has never felt comfortable with members of her sex. She does acknowledge this in her novel. Any wonder that in the character of Nnu Ego, she piles up all the factors which make for the African woman's exploited existence and lack of marital serenity - infertility, polygamy, over-fecundity, the evils of the dowry system, marital and filial abandonment, just name it, Nnu Ego suffers it. Emecheta's tactics here is the same as in *The Bride Price* - expository rather than prescriptive - to demonstrate to the world that it is by means of superstitious myths, gender-based exploitative, cultural mores such as these that women are chained to an immanent existence, of which abandonment is an example. The need for a revision is all the more cogent. In the case of Nnu Ego, Nnu Ego, understandably, turning radical in death, abjures marriage and denies worshipers at her shrine the joys of motherhood, not having known the *joys* and not wishing to inflict her unenviable destiny on other women. The later Nnu Ego may well agree with Shulamith Firestone that only with the abolition of women's physical and psychological responsibility for the repro-duction of the species could women's liberation be accomplished. Hence Nnu Ego's lonesome feminist plaint, "God, when will you create a woman who will be fulfilled in herself, a full human being, not anybody's appendage?" (*The Joys of Motherhood* 186). Nnu Ego's feminist awareness of her right to individuation and self-reclamation comes too late to do her any good. Her life is already over. Consequently, a re-reading of the novel concludes that though Emecheta's feminist conception of Nnu Ego, indeterminate at the beginning and evolving slowly, becomes negatively radical at the heroine's death. More than any of her other novels, it can safely be said that *The Joys of Motherhood* marks the apogee of Emecheta's feminism by Nnu Ego's repudiation in death, of not just marriage, but motherhood as well.

By the time Emecheta comes to write her later novels, the sweet smell of success has undoubtedly softened her radical feminist stance sufficiently. Arguably, Nnaife is irredeemable because of his utter illiteracy and Francis, because of his indolent, intractable and cruel nature. It is in *Double Yoke* that Emecheta employs the reductive technique to positive use. Unlike Nnaife and rather more like Francis, Ete Kamba is young, literate and handsome. There, the analogy ends, for unlike Francis, Ete Kamba is redeemable and Nko loves him. Emecheta, now successful, generous and mature, having overcome her early bitterness about life (see the autobiographical *Head Above Water*), makes a plea for the concept of the couple. In *Double Yoke*, Emecheta's *persona* - Miss Bulewao goes to work resocialising Ete Kamba. The process is admirable:

> *"Suppose,"* she questions, *"you get a village girl and she is not a virgin, what will you do?"* He climbs down a little: *"I don't care if Nko were a virgin or not. But this child she is carrying...."* "There, you are growing up, Ete Kamba. When did you realize you were no longer looking for a virgin to pluck ...But, suppose by mistake one of the girls you sleep with on campus becomes pregnant and you don't want to marry the mother because you don't love her; how will you feel if Nko rejects you on that account?

Ete clutches at the last vestiges of the fast dissolving myth of masculine arrogance and dominance: "Madame, you seem to be forgetting that *I am a man"* (157). There it is out, at last! To be the new African male, the traditional cloak of male arrogance, cruelty and double moral standard, has to be shed. Ete Kamba, finally resocialized, demonstrates his new humanism when he stands by Nko in her bereavement, thus bringing to an end, their estrangement. Their reconciliation presages a new fruitful relationship. Like Idemudia, in Iyayi's *Violence* or Dozie in *Behind the Clouds* and unlike Ibekwe in *Estrangement,* Ete Kamba realizes, at last, the true reason for marriage - need for love and companionship, an egalitarian and complementary union in a new social order in which social prejudices will give way to ensure conjugal peace. Emecheta (a devoted mother herself) and now mature with experience, writing *Double Yoke,* appears to agree in *The Feminine Mystique* with Friedan that it is not difficult "to combine marriage and motherhood and . .. a "career"... it merely takes a new life plan." Nko is already equipped for that.

In closing this chapter, it is necessary to reiterate what has been repeatedly stressed in this work, *viz*: that the hallmark of radical feminism is divorce, or separatism - a feature that augurs ill for the familial structure of society. Most of the novels studied in this chapter end in separation through divorce (Adah/Francis, Wali/ Bienvenu) or, death (Perpétue, Nnu Ego) excepting the *Double Yoke* where a love relationship, beleaguered with so many obstacles, yet survives and promises to be a truly compassionate marriage. Henri Lopes and Mongo Beti, far from recommending a separatist existence, make a plea for the concept of the couple by advocating the eradication of those exploitative features of patriarchal

/modern society which make conjugal happiness a mirage. Consequently, we decry the kind of radical feminism which Nwapa's Amaka (*One is enough*) epitomizes and of which Uhamiri (Efuru) in her separatist, watery kingdom becomes the ultimate symbol. And while we may agree with Emecheta that marriage is an optional venture, we re-emphasize that it is also a healthy and necessary feature of society. All it requires to succeed is one golden rule as expressed by Miss Bulewao to Ete Kamba: the ability to "try and put yourself in place of the other" (*Double Yoke* 156). This golden rule, seemingly simple, yet difficult to put into practice, requires discipline, immense forbearance, humility and sincerity of purpose to make conjugal living truly successful.

NOTES

1. Flora Nwapa, *Efuru* (London: Heinemann, 1966). Subsequent page references will be to this edition.

2. Mongo Beti, *Perpétue* (Paris: Buchet/Castel, 1974). Translated as *Perpetua and the Habit of Unhappiness* by John Reed & Clive Wake (London: Heinemann, 1974). Subsequent page references will be to these editions.

3. Henri Lopes, *La Nouvelle Romance* (Yaounde: Editions CLE, 1976). Subsequent page references will be to this edition. Translations are mine.

4. Buchi Emecheta, *The Joys, of Motherhood* (London: Heinemann, 1980). Subsequent page references will be to this edition.

5. Buchi Emecheta, *Second Class Citizen* (London: Fontana Paperbacks, 1989). Subsequent page references are to this edition.

6. Buchi Emecheta, *Double Yoke* (Great Britain: Fontana Paperbacks, 1984). Hereafter, page references to this book will be inserted in the text.

7. Mary Daly in *Gyn / Ecology*: The Metaethics of Radical Feminism states that patriarchy feeds parasitically upon women, their lives and their energies. Thus women are "victimized into a state of living death."

8. FVVA – The Highligfe Principle – is a prize winning movie at the Third PanAfrican Film Festival at Ougadougou and directed by Niger filmmaker Mustapha Alassane.

Works Cited:

Acholonu, Rose. *Love in Nigerian Fiction: Feminist Perspectives.* Owerri: Achisons Publications, 1995.
Armah, Ayi Kwei. *Two Thousand Seasons.* Ibadan, Nigeria: Heinemann Educational Books, 1987.
Astell, Mary. *Some Reflections Upon Marriage.* (Cited by Catherine Belsey in *The Subject of Tragedy*). In *Modern Literary Theory*. Boston: Beacon Press, 1978.
Badian, Seydou. *Sous L'Orage.* Paris: Présence Africaine, 1964.
Davies, Carole Boyce. "Motherhood in the Works of Male and Female Igbo Writers." *Ngambika: Studies of* Women in African Literature. New Jersey: Africa World Press, 1986.
Beauvoir, Simone de. *Le Deuxième Sexe II* Gallimard: 1976.
Chukwuma, Helen. "Feminism and Femininity in African Literature." Owerri, Nigeria: *The Statesman,* March 18, 1991.
Eisenstein, Hester. *Contemporary Feminist Thought.* London: Unwin Paperbacks, 1984.
Eliot, Geogre (Mary Ann Evans). *Middlemarch: A Study of Provincial Life.* London: Oxford University Press, 1961.
Emenyonu, Ernest. "Who Does Flora Nwapa Write for?" *African Literature Today, No. 7.* London: Heinemann, 1975.
Firestone, Shulamith. *The Dialectics of Sex: The Case for*

Feminist Revolution. N.Y.: Bantam Books, 1970.
Fuller, Margaret. "The Great Lawsuit: Man versus Men, Woman versus Women." In *The Dial* (July) 1843.
Friedan, Betty. *The Feminine Mystique.* New York: W.W.W. Norton, 1974.
Greer, Germaine. *The Female Eunuch.* New York: McGraw-Hill Book Co, 1971.
Greene, Gayle & Coppelia Kahn, eds. *Making A Difference: Feminist Literary Criticism.* London: Methuen & Co. Ltd., 1985.
Hurston, Zora Neale. *Their Eyes Were Watching God.* New York: Harper & Row, 1990.
Kern, Anita. *Women in West African Fiction,* (unpublished Ph. D. Dissertation of the University of Toronto). 1978.
Lambert, Fernando. "Mongo Beti: La Dialectique du tragique et du comique." *Research in African Litterature* Vol. 2, no. 2, 1871.
Ojo-Ade, Femi. "Female Writers, Male Critics" in *ALT* 13. London: Heinemann, 1983.
Osifo, Grace. *Dizzy* Angel. Ibadan University Press, 1985.
Owono, Joseph. *Tante Bela.* Yaounde, Cameroun: Librairie "Au Messager" 1959.
Philambe, Rene. *Sola ma Cherie.* Yaounde, Cameroun: Edition CLE, 1966.
Scheub, Harold. "Two African Women." *Revue des Langues Vivantes,* Vol. 37. 1971.
Showalter, Elaine. "Towards a Feminist Poetics," in *Woman Writing about Woman,* ed. Mary Jacobus. London: Croom Helm, 1989.
Taiwo, Oladele. *Female Novelists of Modern Africa* (London: Macmillan Publishers, 1984.
Van Allen, Judith. "African Woman's Modernization and National Liberation." In *Women in the World: A Comparative Study* Ed. Iglitzin Lynne and Ruth Ross. Oxford: Clio Books, 1976.
Woolf, Virginia. *A Room of One's Own.* London: Hogarth's Press, 1929.

CHAPTER SIX

CONCLUSION: THE WILL TO CHANGE

> *But women's literature must go beyond these scenarios of ...madness and death. Although the reclamation of suffering is the beginning, its purpose is to discover the world...[go] beyond reclaiming suffering to its reinvestment ... a new women's writing, which explores the will to change.*
> --- (Showalter, "Towards a Feminist Poetics" 98-9).

In the preceding chapters, we have endeavored to synthesize thematically into a coherent critical corpus, many of the factors that keep women in chains by making them victims of abandonment in love relationships. These factors, singly and/or severally, destabilize and destroy familial peace and unity. The resultant portraiture of the woman suffering in abandonment is as depicted in the works of Nwapa, Mariama Bâ, Emecheta, Okpewho, Aniebo, Beti, Lopes, Sembène, Ifeoma Okoye and Zaynab Alkali – vibrant writers with an active social conscience who have uniformlly anchored their writings on the woman question. Thus, sharing similar thematic concerns, they have questioned age-old patriarchal and cultural assumptions of gender dominance and sex-role stereo-typing, have demythified superstitions, cleared the mists of ignorance that have beclouded many issues which only need enlightenment, tolerance and humane consideration for effective resolution. At issue is a crucial point: how can the tide of abandonment within the familial construct be stemmed? How realizable is the quest for individuation and autonomy within the familial construct, especially when faced with problems arising from barrenness / motherhood practices, polygamy / marriage practices, *et cetera*?

The answers the authors proffer differ as they treat one aspect or the other of the factors that threaten the familial harmony of the couple. But on one vital point, they are in accord: that abandonment is an aberration from a love relationship and needs to be corrected because it creates disequilibrium in a family. It does unquantifiable psycho-logical, physical, economic and emotional damage to adults and children alike, robbing all concerned of happiness. So, these writers of different sexes who come from different geographical, linguistic, cultural and religious groupings, nevertheless, agree on one general premise – that the quest for female self-realization and familial happiness pre-supposes a negation of sexist cultural restrictions. This quest must consider all matters that affect the "estate" or well-being of the woman; hence this work has feminism or the woman question as its backdrop.

Evaluating the authors' reactions to the issue of marriage, the question is posed as to whether a woman in a bad marriage should leave her husband? In other words, should marriage be considered sufficiently binding to couples who should work to repair damage to the structure, or, should couples separate if and when love dies? What about the sorrow and grief which separation or divorce causes? Far from being old-fashioned, the writers give serious consideration to these enduring, moral questions about the nature and responsibilities of human relationships. Divorce is always an extreme step in any society. Although Nwapa, Emecheta, Sembène seem to favor this step, most Africans are conservative and would rather opt for compromise. Mongo Beti in *Perpétue*, Aminata Sow Fall in *La Grève des bàttu* and Ousmane Sembène (surprisingly) in *Xala*, argue for the women to remain in a failed marriage, but simply because the women have little or no education, in addition to being both financially and emotionally dependent on their husbands. As both Sow Fall's *Lolli* and Sembène's Adja Awa Astou helplessly ask their daughters, "Où irai-je à mon âge?" These conservative women, handicapped by lack of financial autonomy (we shall treat this as a separate issue), are literally cudgeled into the immanence of submission by traditional societal and peer pressures. Truly, they become what we have seen Jarmila Ortova call them, *les femmes résignées*. As Taiwo aptly sums it up: Tradition has become too much a part of [their] life for [them] to change now" (Taiwo, *Female Novelists of Modern Africa* 217). The women mentioned in this section constitute the first group.

Nwapa, Emecheta (though literary success and maturity conduce to the latter attempting to reconcile a young couple in *Double Yoke*), Mariama Bâ (with Aissatou), Lopes (reluctantly so) and Sembène (categorically so in other works), endorse the exercise of women's rights to auto-determination which includes the right to end impossible marriages. The female heroes of these writers become assertive and pack up their marriages. They therefore fall into the category of radical feminists who are both emotionally and financially independent. A third group are the accommodationists who prefer to patch up matters so that they can keep the family hearth warm and stable. Thus, if the ultimate aim of radical feminism is a separatist, idyllic existence away from men – women *without men* like the Efurus, Adakus, Amakas, Adahs, *et cetera* – the ultimate aim of female accommodationism becomes the unity of enlightened men and women, working together for the good of the family and society. Consequently, this study endorses this group's ideal and advocates this principle of human responsibility by which a couple learns from their mistakes and as a result, enjoy a richly invigorated marital life.

This position naturally begs the question: does

accommodationism encapsulate a belief in conservative traditionalism, a retreat from that egalitarian concept (advocated by radical feminism) which aims at freeing women from politico-cultural, socio-economic and gender-constructed oppression, all of which lead to the abandonment of the woman? On the contrary, accommodationism as delineated and espoused by writers such as Okoye, Alkali, Aniebo and Bâ accords to women equal human value; it rather demythifies superstitious, cultural taboos which have hitherto fettered women as the veiled, the voiceless, the "*ou*;" it posits as well that men just like women are products of social conditioning and therefore are susceptible to transformations, hence the accent of accommodationism on compromise and reconciliation, on complementarity of the sexes rather than on divorce and separatism. For instance, a marriage such as Efuru's might have been saved if Nwapa had invested her female hero with a little more sensibility and spirit of compromise rather than a dogmatic adherence to her own wishes which consequently makes her undesirably intimidating to her husbands; though weak-willed, these me are yet reared in a patriarchal milieu where masculine dominance is an article of faith. Anyway if put into practice, these qualities demanded by accommodationism would obviate the necessity of divorce.

An interesting area of correspondence is these writers' technique of narration. All, whether avowed radical feminists, gynandrists or implied, adopt the gynocentric viewpoint. Traditionally, as this work has reiterated, both Western and African male-authored works are replete with negative, sexist portraitures. Now, there is evidence of a deliberate reversal as these revisionist writers, male and female alike, seem to put into practice Dale Spender's view that a one worldview, the androcentric view of literature *was simply not enough to provide full understanding about the way the world worked. It was too limited. It was the very perspective of those who did not exercise power, over whom power was exercised and who were defined as alien, other . . . that was needed for a full world view.* (*Mothers of the Novel* 143).

As Tillie Olsen says about American culture, "there is a wide discrepancy... between the life of women as conceived by men and the life of women as lived by women" (*Silences* 179). Male dominance and oppression mean women's silence and suppression and society can no longer afford to neither hear nor heed the voice of half of humanity. This is the rationale for the woman's point of view, with women as principal actors seen grappling with the harsh exigencies and vagaries of life rather than as marginalized, shadowy creatures hovering on the fringes of an androcentric cultural world. Thus will a full worldview emerge.

Arising from this androcentric viewpoint is an analogous technique of characterization. Admittedly, male writers like Sembène and Okpewho employ more telling dramatic symbols, but all the authors featured in this work resort to the use of reductive imagery to get back at chauvinistic man. Male characters as in Zora Neale Hurston's *Their Eyes Were Watching God* are forced to make do with subordinate roles. Insufferably chauvinistic males such as Jody Starks of that novel are psychologically dethroned from their "lord of the manor" pedestal. For instance, Janie at last finds her voice and uses it to deride her husband's impotence, and "Joe Starks realized all the meanings and his vanity bled like a flood. Janie had robbed him of his illusion of irresistible maleness that all men cherish, which was terrible" (*Their*

Eyes Were Watching God 75). Artistically, this verbal castration is a ploy to cut down to size man's traditionally oversized ego and render him more sage and more amenable.

Reductive imagery is designed in some cases to usher in a process of psychic renaissance considered necessary for the resocialization of oppressive male. For instance, El Hadji (*Xala*) is physically and psychologically castrated; Habu (*The Stillborn*) is made a cripple; Dozie (*Behind the Clouds*) is presented with the bitter pill that his lack of virility is really responsible for the couple's state of childlessness; Ete Kamba (*Double Yoke*) is humiliated by Nko's infidelities; Christian (*The Journey Within*) is stricken mad with syphilis; Modou Fall (*Une Si Longue Lettre*) in quest of the elixir of youth and struggling to keep up with the fun-loving zest of his young bride suffers a stroke induced by over-exertion; Ousmane Gueye (*Un Chant Écarlate*) as does Jason from Medea suffers torture with the death of his son at the hands of his wife Mireille, while narrowly escaping death himself; Mour Ndiaye (*La Grève des Battus*) is publicly humiliated by both the government and the wretched of the earth, while Obanua (*The Victims*) effectively comes across as a drink-sodden, improvident wastrel. In consonance with their actions, these male characters veritably can be said to belong to Northrop Frye's ironic mode since they prove themselves

> *Inferior in power and intelligence, so that we have a sense of looking down on a sense of bondage, frustration or absurdity* ("Fictional Modes and Forms")

In the light of the above-outlined treatment of male characters, it can be deduced that practically all the feminist and gynandrist authors studied make their female protagonists near perfect creations. This is compensatory mechanism at work, a way of taking revenge on chauvinistic male authors for the neglect, denigration and abuse of women hitherto seen in their writings. The eponymous Efuru for instance is introduced as a remarkable woman from a distinguished family who is distinguished herself. In the author's opinion, she has no fault, and is in fact a perfect character. Similarly, Amaka (*One is Enough*) is idealized while her subsequent immorality in Lagos, being glossed over, yields rich dividend – wealth and children. These attract to her not only the admiration of, and overtures from her erstwhile fickle husband Obiora, but desperate marriage proposals as well from Rev. Fr. McLeod who readily abandons priesthood for her. Equally, Emecheta's Adah and Nnu Ego are perfect mothers who in the pelican image sacrifice happiness for their young while they work to maintain their respective lazy and loutish husbands. If Li (*The Stillborn*), Wali, (*La Nouvelle Romance*), Ramatoulaye (*Une Si Longue Lettre*), Mireille (*Un Chant Écarlate*), Adja Awa Astou (*Xala*), Lolli (*La Grève des Bàttu*) and the eponymous Perpétue have any faults at all, it is that of gullibility and loving unwisely (in some instances flouting parental wishes and traditional codes). Obviously, if male characters are reduced in size, the female characters are overinflated, larger-than-life beings. Thus, these writers' empathy with their female characters is unashamedly palpable. For the gynandrists, this portraiture of ideal womanhood illustrates their ideological stance of social realism which critic Irele describes as a ploy

> *whose conscious direction is toward the attainment of a social ideal established through the presentation of exemplary characters and situations* (*The African Experience in Literature and Ideology* 160).

Agreeing with this line of reasoning, Ojo Ade opines that it is only natural that the African female writer should depict the travails of her female character with empathy since the latter becomes a *doppelganger* used to work out the writer's own *angst* since "... the original coalesces with the double. Woman weeps with woman; for the life of woman is filled with worries" ("Female Writers, Male Critics;" in *ALT* 161). This lack of aesthetic distance naturally results in what we have seen William Morgan label existential female characters (who are capable of, and do respond to change and growth and are full-rounded), and essential male characters who are flat and consequently remain static. Thus, these empathizing authors work jointly towards achieving, fictionally at least, a sexually more balanced society.

A further concord in approach is to be found in the authors' active encouragement of sisterly solidarity or bonding as well as a meaningful male/female relationship. For this reason too, they generally decry both infidelity and/or polygamy which attenuate female bonding and love among children of the same parents.

A lot of emphasis has been placed on the relationship between the artist and the artist's environment. Achebe insists that "art is, and always was, in the service of man" (*Morning Yet on Creation Day* 19). The artists who live and move and have their being in society must produce works that will serve the interests of their society. This empowers the artist to function as a teacher. Therefore, from the creative works of these revisionist artists are distilled general guidelines to enable women transcend their state of abandonment caused by such factors as those studied in this work.

On barrenness, motherhood and marriage practices, pioneer woman novelist Flora Nwapa whose feminist consciousness is tentative at the beginning of *Efuru*, by the story's end and in *One is Enough*, turns radical and does away altogether with the institution of marriage. Her message: if a woman is unable to have children, her life is not ended for she can still be useful to herself and to society by doing her best in her chosen job. Veritably, Nwapa's panacea for woman's survival in a world of shifting loyalties and problematic realities is financial autonomy, especially, since some men (like Edourad in *Perpétue*) deprive their non-working wives of even house-keeping money in order to cudgel them into submission and subservience. And so, writers such as Nwapa argue, if the woman faced with an intolerable marriage had viable options she would opt out like Efuru, Amaka (*One is Enough*), Adaku (*The Joys of Motherhood*), or where the woman decides to accept matters as does Dora (*Women are Different*), or Li (*The Stillborn*), she would do so from a position of strength. This conviction possibly prompted Nwapa's dedication of *One is Enough* to "Ine, my husband's mother who believes that all women, married or single, must be economically independent." Objections to an extreme clause in Nwapa's philosophy have already been made in this work: not motherhood at all costs, nor financial autonomy by all means, either.

On the other hand, writers like Buchi Emecheta view the institution of marriage with a more open mind. Emecheta's attitude seems to be: if a woman is lucky to be fertile and has children, she should enjoy it, but if the reverse is the case, there are other avenues of being productively useful to oneself and to society. One's hopes and happiness should not be built entirely around one's children because times and values change and children may not live up to their parents' expectations; therefore, one should be sufficiently pragmatic to adjust to changing circumstances, have other absorbing and satisfying interests lest parents end their days miserable like Nnu Ego and Nnaife (*The Joys of Motherhood*).

However, Ifeoma Okoye's thesis like Nwapa's in *Idu* shows an advance on an old theme, which is: that a man too can be responsible for a couple's barren state. So, certain traditionally discriminatory, sexual practices which lead to a woman's marital misery need to be overhauled. Thus, the new consciousness engendered will prevent the excruciating agony of abandoned women like Nnu Ego, Ije, Janet, or, Amaka who have been socialized into believing that they are solely responsible for the couple's infertility. An awareness of male culpability will foster in men like El Hadji qualities such as humility and compassion needed to promote a companionate marriage. These new African men will then be better prepared to handle the primed new African women.

On polygamy, the findings from the books treated in this critical study serve as a strong indictment against this practice so out of tune with the realities of marital intimacy. The general consensus among the authors is that polygamy may have worked in the past when handled by masterfully strong and wealthy patriarchs like Okonkwo, Nwakibie, Ezeulu of Achebe's rural world even though in that world, there were obvious stresses and strains. But when ineffectual and impecunious wastrels like Okpewho's Obanua, Ake Loba's Païs (*Les Dépossédés – The Dispossessed*) or the hedonistic, morally unprincipled El Hadji, Mour Ndiaye, or, Modou Fall indulge in polygamy, a calamitous state of affairs is the result.

On this issue of marriage practices, there is evidence of intra-cultural influences amongst the Senegalese trio – Sembène, Aminata Sow Fall and Bâ. Unlike their Anglophone counterparts, they uniformly evince no obsession with the number of children nor with their gender. This, possibly, we attribute to the nature of their Muslim society in which the practice of multiple wives assures families of quite a litter of children. However, these novelists' extreme antipathy to polygamy in a milieu where this practice has religious sanction is demonstrably subversive. In their opinion, polygamy is part of an Islamic tenet that panders to the profligacy and hedonism of *nouveaux riches* husbands who consequently discard their older, doting wives in favor of younger girls whom they set up in separate villas. Thus, a new cultural archetype is created. But more than that, polygamy is a feature of cultural nationalism that needs immediate eradication because it objectifies women as much as it enslaves them.

But unlike Western feminism, African feminism contends with issues more complex than mere egalitarianism between man and woman. The most striking contribution of these pioneer African female writers and gynandrists is that they recommend for retention in African culture only those traditional practices that are of real value to African societies. The greatest of these is their commitment to the maintenance of a happy home and hearth, a healthy environment in which to raise children. This is shown by their effort to lay down the principles of a stable, companionate marriage. A lot of adaptability, flexibility and understanding, they conclude, are required from both partners in any marriage. These qualities will make of marriage "a commitment shared by two people that becomes part of their commitment to themselves and society" (*The Feminine Mystique* 367). Ifeoma Okoye, Zainab Alkali, Mariama Bâ, Henri Lopes, Sembène and Mongo Beti stand out as advocates of marital love, mutual growth rather than mutual destruction. Their women characters operate from a position of superior, or at least, equal status.

One question that impinges on the consciousness of the reader is whether the female authors are closer to their female characters than are the male authors. One accepts that these male authors have, with their own *ouvert esprit*, manifested extreme empathy towards their female creations. It should be noted that one of the major contributions of Marxist thinking to this debate is the connection it made between economics and politics which allows us to interpret a correlation between economic/political power with woman's exploitation and oppression. Stylistically, using a lot more complex symbols than do their female counterparts, the male writers have dexterously linked the travails of abandonment suffered by their women characters to class exploitation and oppression. Thus, it is with surprise that this female writer acknowledges that Okpewho and Beti have evinced as much conscience and commitment to the socialist cause as Ousmane Sembène and Henri Lopes – avowed Marxist-socialists that they are. Their female characters are readily credible, be it Beti's Perpétue crushed by the weight of unjust patriarchal and neo-colonialist system represented by Edouard, or Okpewho's Nwabunor laboring vainly in a rural milieu steeped in poverty, ignorance and fetishism, or Sembène's Adja Awa Astou, innately compassionate and resiliently accommodating but forced into passive acquiescence because she lacks sufficient education and a solid material base to be independent of her husband, or even Lopes's Wali, coerced into self-emancipation by Bienvenu's unremitting profligacy.

Yet, it can be validly stated that female writers are generally closer to their female characters. Acknowledging the principle that the personal is political, women authors' predilection for fictionalized autobiography – semi-confessional in nature – becomes an attempt to work out the relationship between self and society, between sense and sensibility. Writers write best about what they know best. Mariama Bâ's outpourings of sensibilities come across convincingly and movingly because they contain elements of real-life experiences. Also, in her gifted prose and across a wide thematic, literary canvas modulated by well-crafted artistry, Emecheta's characters almost leap out of the pages of her fiction and come alive because the empathy with her fictionalized *doppelganger* (a double self) is in some aspects based on personal experiences. In other words, women get into fellow women's skins. Consequently, we readily accept Ojo-Ade's statement that

> *[i]t is only natural that the female African writer should depict the travails of female characters. The creator exhibits deep empathy for her heroine, who, to a large extent, is a mouthpiece for her personal notions on life, a sister in suffering....* (161).

Ultimately, the literature of abandonment is a literature of suffering and oppression. The title of a work by feminist writer Dame Rebecca West, "Unhappily Ever After" (*TLS* 779) denotes that unhappiness is still the keynote of contemporary fiction by and about women. But this literature of abandonment is also protest literature which fits neatly into the Feminist phase or second stage of Showalter's category of Western Women's writings. It is literature used to dramatize the ordeals of wronged womanhood. This protest literature is generally used to fight against sexism and the abuses emanating from patriarchal power structures. It is literature used to redefine and revise a male-dominated literary canon. It asks that readers – male oppressors as well as the female oppressed – be aware of the causes of abandonment and of oppression, and the implications to the family. Widespread awareness, it is hoped, will stimulate a change, enliven social consciences, illumine the sources of human weaknesses and strengths, and by so doing, ginger up efforts to construct a better world. Yet, the import of the literature of abandonment still remains at the level of a consciousness-raising ploy.

A recurrent feature of this literature of abandonment is the madness motif. In African literature, it is amazing the number of female characters who lose their sanity: from Emecheta's unfortunate Nnu Ego, Okpewho's Nwabunor, Bâ's *maddened* angels to include (outside of the purlieu of this work) Njau's Selina (*Ripples in the Pool*), Bessie Head's Elizabeth (*A Question of Power*), and others. The number includes suicide victims: Nwapa's Idu, Sembène's Ngoné War Thiandum, Yvonne Vera's Phephelaphi (*Butterfly Burning*). Consequently, I argue here that suicide actually raises the notion of a pusillanimous escapism from harsh, intolerable realities. And whereas nineteenth-century Western novelists used madness to symbolize repression and loss of identity, and whereas diasporan black female writers employ a similar motif to express female oppression and sexual exploitation (Pecola in Morrison's *The Bluest Eye*, or even Fern in Jean Toomer's *Cane*), male and female African writers used madness as a symbol of self-expression and reconquest of the lost self. It would appear though that female characters (especially Bâ's maddened angels) can summon up courage to rebel against social injustice and patriarchal repression only when in the unfettered, safe and unheeding world of unreality. This is pure escapism. Just as fleeing heroines should be brought back to base to work out their problems within the context of their human society (which Bâ's Ramatoulaye and Alkali's Li did), authors should endeavor to create strong-minded female heroes, endowed with the perquisites of fortitude, resilience and resourcefulness needed to grapple with life's sometimes-heartbreaking problems, but *without going mad*. In this regard, it denotes a healthy progress in fictional development that Bâ makes Jacqueline recover, and that Ramatoulaye resolutely refuses to go mad with grief and loneliness, wisely recognizing that "pour vaincre la détresse quand elle vous assiège, il faut de la volonté" – "to overcome distress when it sits on you, demands strong will" (*Une Si Longue Lettre* 63). Jacqueline's doctor urges her to react, be resilient, have courage and find a reason for living. I argue that female writers and gynandrists ought to endow their characters with sufficient *will to change* the negative factors in their existence, and rather than remain passive receptacles of inequities, victims of loneliness, abandonment and death, to become assertive, dominant, strong-minded survivors and pace-setters and thus, a source of inspiration to others.

Therefore, Showalter insists that writers must go beyond the reclamation of suffering to its re-investment. Nwapa's eponymous Efuru believes that people whether fictive or real should not suffer uselessly. Suffering must be re-invested to serve an experiential, indeed, redemptive purpose both for the sufferers and for other people's education. To escape the immanence of a tangential, oppressed existence, to be able to exercise that will to change, the keys to this gate of freedom as this work continues to emphasize can indeed be found in education, the courage that emanates from self-knowledge, and financial autonomy.

The writers studied in this work largely agree (with the exception of Nwapa who promotes liberation *via* economic power, no matter the means) that rather than mere financial autonomy realizable sometimes through prostitution, or other forms of immorality, there is a more worthwhile alternative – enlightenment which only *education* can confer. Lopes (Wali), Alkali (Li), Okoye (Ije), Sembène (Ramat and Tioumbe), Bâ (Aissatou, Daba and Ramatoulaye), Aminata Sow Fall (Raabi), and Emecheta (in her remarkable portraits of Adah Obi and Miss Bulewao), testify to the fact that education is the *desideratum* for an enlightened, independent and self-fulfilled living.

Education heightens self-awareness, defines goals, fosters self-discipline and forges a will of steel. It equips women for a good job and a future that can enable them take care of themselves and their children, and do so independently if the need arises. Education also empowers them to transcend imaginatively if not physically the constraints of their patriarchal world. Furthermore, as Katherine Frank puts it:

> *Education gives women a vision of human existence beyond the confines of their own lives; it bestows a kind of imaginative power, a breadth of perspectives, an awareness of beauty, dreams, possibilities* ("Women Without Men..." 23).

Li, the inveterate dreamer, achieves her heart's set goals and a chance to reconstruct life on her own terms. Aissatou is saved by her books; Wali staves off despair and loneliness through lessons learnt through reading, and is inspired to go up to university level in order to prepare herself for a future job of emancipating her fellow countrywomen from sex-biased prejudices which have kept them in chains. For this reason too, all the Senegalese authors featured in this study have created models of *évoluées* – the Ramas, Dabas and Tioumbes – all endowed with the *will to change* and transcend their mothers' state of thraldom and abandonment, because equipped by education, they now symbolize the future hopes of their respective society. These young models of new African womanhood vindicate Betty Friedan's theory that girls should

> *Stretch and stretch until their own efforts will tell them who they are ...by participating in the mainstream of society, by exercising their own voice in all the*

decisions shaping that society (*The Feminist Mystique* 377-85)

The keys to freedom's gate therefore are education and the ability to earn a meaningful living. *Education* and *money*! Literary histories of Western women reveal that these two imperatives re what saved many literary women from obscurity and frustrated destinies. Virginia Woolf stresses these when she recommends for every woman – a room of one's own and five hundred pounds:

> *A woman must have money and a room of one's own . . . women have had less intellectual freedom than the sons of Athenian slaves. That is why I have laid so much stress on money and a room of one's own* (163).

As early as 1787, Mary Wollstonecraft Godwin, mother of feminism had in her novel, *Mary*, revealed her unconcealed contempt for the languorous, indolent, society woman who skims across the surface of life, and who *will not think*; she wondered how else people can think, exist, fulfill themselves if not from education and its benefits. When wives are uneducated, they have no rights. Men and women who lack education are "condemned to ignorance, unawareness: this makes for brutality in men and pretty lisping in women"(Dale Spender, 251-3). As if to reinforce this thesis, Betty Friedan insists:

> *I think that education, and only education has saved and can continue to save...* (*The Feminist Mystique* 357).

Thus, we see the importance of Bâ's often quoted panegyric on the power of books as an instrument of knowledge, as a means of transmitting culture and as a social lever. Emecheta's Adaku (by sending her daughters to school) acknowledges it; even the blighted Nnu Ego, at the end, begins to see the use and power of education for women. Birth, ancestry/caste pride are of no consequence. What matters is what one makes of one's life. And it all resides in the **will to change** – *la volonté*, achieved through *education*. Even for people of middle years, the writers seem to imply, education is illimitable. It has no barriers. As Friedan puts it, it is actually only

> *When women as well as men emerge from biological living to realize their human selves, those leftover halves of life may become their years of greatest fulfilment* (Friedan 357).

Therefore, every woman who successfully fights these barriers to a life of transcendence opens the door wider and makes it easier for the next female victim of abandonment to throw off her chains. I echo Bâ's Ramatoulaye's magnificat:

> *Mon Coeur est en fête chaque foir qu'une femme emerge de l'ombre* (*Une Si Longue Lettre* 129).

[my heart rejoices each time a woman emerges from the shadows].

Finally, *Women in Chains: Abandonment in Love Relationships* ...must be seen as a pioneer work in a new field. It is the first, comprehensive, booklength attempt to thematically group together many of the traditional, socio-cultural factors as well as the defects from the human personality which cause so much distress to families and give rise to the abandonment of the woman in a love relationship. These factors are delineated and critically assessed in the light of evolving feminist awareness, though it should be stressed that the kind of feminism which this work has sought to highlight is the accommodationist kind which aims at the wholeness and happiness of both man and woman. Writings of authors from disparate cultural, religious, linguistic backgrounds have been studied. The common bond uniting these writers is their love of humanity, concern for the democratic ideals and rights of man and woman to individuation and self-realization, a burning desire to see the woman – the suppressed half of the human species – achieve happiness within the conjugal construct. When more families are united in love and harmony, our world will be saner and happier.

And so, this work can not pretend to be the last word; the field is new and leaves much room for exploration. More and newer factors that militate against the flourishing of women's capacities and against the attainment of peace in the home – factors which can lead to abandonment such as the stigma attached to illegitimacy, female genital mutilation, *et cetera* - need to be highlighted in more critical studies. We therefore anticipate further critical researches that would widen the perspective of African literature to include writings from other parts of Africa – East, Southern and Northern Africa. Literary appreciation of works from these areas as well as from the diaspora, with comparisons, analogies and contrasts of women seeking to find their *voice* and to occupy their proper place in the canon will deepen the richness and unique beauty of African literary heritage as well as contribute to the establishment of a concrete and well-articulated female literary culture.

Furthermore, a documented literary history of African feminist writings will undoubtedly plug holes and hiatuses in the continuum of such women's writings, obviating any future efforts to rescue and re-establish these writings – an exercise currently going on in Western feminist literature, despite its long literary history. Certainly, a woman's history of African literature will have to be written.

Finally, creative writers should produce more challenging works depicting vigorous and purposeful female characters who are ethically well-integrated, enlightened and financially autonomous, seen operating from a stable, familial base and launching forth even into the public realm to contribute meaningfully to society. Quoting Friedan again, in order to safeguard the family,

> *It is better for a woman to compete impersonally in society, as man do, than to compete for dominance in her own home with her husband . . . and so smother her own son that he cannot compete at all* (257).

In conclusion, we anticipate the next phase of African feminist literature – the literature of reconstruction and reinvestment of fulfilled womanhood. In this wise, of all the authors studied, Zaynab Alkali, Buchi Emecheta (with *The Rape of Shavi, Destination Biafra*), Sembène (as always) have launched themselves on this prescriptive track. They project the future as it could be. This is the artist's peculiar and unique gift – to be visionary, to protect new realities. Carole Boyce Davies words it succinctly:

> *But we already recognize that the artist has the power to create new realities; to represent male-female relationships and the role of women as . . . they have been in the past and might be in the future* (In Ngambika 86).

Creations of new realities may smack of chimera, but out of utopian dreams new societies can emerge for

Worlds would varnish but for thinking
Glory is not but in dreams. . .
Dwell in thought upon the Grandest
And the Grandest you shall see;
Fix your mind upon the Highest
And the Highest you shall be
(James Allen, *The Secret of Happiness* 46-7).

In other words, if the mind can envision it, it can also be achieved: a safer, more harmonious society in which the concept of the couple can thrive - men and women loving and being loved, a society which is free from domination, exploitation and oppression, a love union in which a fulfilled, actively contributing woman will be free from the chains of abandonment.

Works Cited:

Achebe, Chinua. *Morning Yet On Creation Day*. London: Heinemann, 1987.
Allen, James. *The Secret of Happiness*. Lexington, Kentucky: Successful Achievement, Inc. 1971.
Bâ, Mariama. *Une Si Longue Lettre*. Dakar: Les Nouvelles Éditions Africaines. 1980.
Davies, Carole Boyce. "Maidens, Mistresses and Matrons: Feminine Images in Selected Soyinka's Works." In *Ngambika: Studies of Women in African Literature*. Eds. Carole Boyce Davies and Anne Graves. New Jersey: Africa World Press, 1986.
Irele. Abiola. *The African Experience in Literature and Ideology*. London: Heinemann, 1981.
Frank, Katherine. "Women Without Men." In *African Literature Today*. Trenton, NJ: Africa World Press, 1987.
Friedan, Betty. *The Feminine Mystique*. London: W.W. Norton & Co., 1974.
Frye, Northrop. "Fictional Modes and Forms." In *Approaches to the Novel: Materials for a Poetics*. ed. Robert Scholes.

CA: Chandler Publishing Co., 1966.
Hurston, Zora Neale. *Their Eyes Were Watching God.* New York: Harper & Row, 1990.
Olsen, Tillie. *Silences.* New York: Delacorte Press / Semour Lawrence, 1978.
Rice, Philip and Patricia Waugh, eds. *Modern Literary Theory: a Reader.* Great Britain: Hodder and Stoughton, 1989.
Ojo-Ade, Femi. "Female Writers, Male Critics." In *African Literature Today*, 13. London: Heinemann, 1983.
Showalter, Elaine. "Towards a Feminist Poetics." In *Women Writing and Writing About Women.* Ed. Mary Jacobus. London: Croom Helm, 1980.
Spender, Dale, ed. *Living by the Pen: Early British Women Writers.* New York: Teachers College, 1982.
_____. *Mothers of the Novel.* London and New York: Pandora, 1968.
Taiwo, Oladele. *Female Novelists of Modern Africa.* London: Macmillan Publishers, 1984.
Vera, Yvonne. *Butterfly Burning.* Harare: Baobab Books, 1998.
West, Dame Rebecca. "And They All Lived Unhappily Ever After." In *TLS.* London (26 July),1987.
Woolf, Virginia. *A Room of One's Own.* Great Britain: Hogarth Press, 1929.

BIBLIOGRAPHY
PRIMARY SOURCES.

Alkali, Zaynab. *The stillborn.* Essex, England: Longman Group Ltd., 1984.
Aniebo, I.N.C. *The Journey Within.* London: Heinemann, 1978.
Bâ, Mariama. *Une Si Longue* Lettre. Dakar: Les Nouvelles Editions Africaines, 1980.
_____. *Un Chant Ecarlate.* Dakar: Les Nouvelles Editions Africaines, 1981.
Beti, Mongo. *Perpetue.* Paris: Editions Buchet/Chastel, 1974. Trans. as *Perpetua and* the *Habit* of *Unhappiness.* London: Heinemann, 1978.
Emecheta, Buchi. *Joys of Motherhood.* London: Heinemann, 1980.
Second Class Citizen. London: Allison and Busby, 1975.
_____. *Double Yoke.* London: Ogwugwu Afar Ltd., 1982.
Fall, Aminata SOW. *'La Greve des* Bàttu. Nouvelles Editions Africaines, 1979. Transl. as *The Beggars Strike* or *The Dregs of Society* by Dorothy S. Blair, Longman, 1985.
Lopes, Henri. *La Nouvelle Romance.* Yaounde: Editions CLE, 1976.
Nwapa, Flora. *Efuru.* London, Heinemann, 1966.
_____. *Idu.* London: Heinemann, 1981.
_____. *One is Enough.* Enugu, Nigeria: Tana Press, 1981.
Okoye, Ifeoma. *Behind the Clouds.* London: Heinemann, 1982.
Okpewho, Isidore. *The Victims.* Nigeria: Longman Drumbeat, 1979.
Ousmane, Sembène. *Véhi-Ciosane ou Blanche Genèse.* Paris: Presence Africaine, 1969 Trans. by Clive Wake as (*White Genesis).* Heinemann: London, 1977.
_____. *Xala.* Paris: Presence Africaine, 1973. (English Trans. by Clive Wake, *Xala.* Heinemann, 1976).

SECONDARY SOURCES

Achebe, Chinua. *Things Fall Apart*. London: Heinemann, 1958.
_____. *Arrow of God*. London: Heinemann, 1964.
_____. *Morning Yet on creation Day*. Essays. London: Heinemann, 1975.
_____. *Anthills of the Savannah*. U.X.: Heinemann Ltd., 1987.
Aidoo, Ama Ata. *Our Sister Killjoy*, London:. Longman Drumbeat, 1981.
Amadi, Elechi. *The Concubine*. London: *Heinemann*, 1966.
_____. *Estrangement*. London: Heinemann, 1986.
Anozie, Sunday. *Sociologie du roman africain: realisme, structure et determination dans le roman moderne ouest-africaine*. Paris: Aubier Montaigne, 1970.
Armah, Ayi Kwei. *The Healers*. London: Heinemann, 1978.
_____. *Two Thousand Seasons*. Nairobi: East African Publishing House, 1973.
Badian, Seydou. *Sous L'Orage (Kany)*. Paris: *Presence Africaine*, 1963. (Written in 1954).
Bebey, Francis. *La Poupée Ashanti*. Yaounde: Editions Cie, 1973. Trans. as *The Ashanti Doll* by Joyce A. Hutchinson. London: Heinemann, 1978.
Bestman, Martin. *Sembène Ousmane et L'Esthetique du Roman Negro-Africain*. Quebec: Editions Naaman de Sherbroke, 1991.
Brown, Lloyd. *Women Writers in Black Africa*. Connecticut: Greenwood Press, 1981.
Bruner, Charlotte. *Unwinding Threads: Writing by Women in Africa*. London: Heinemann, 1983.
Chevrier, Jacques. *Littérature Nègre*. Paris: Armand Collin Collection, 1974 (pp. 97-153).
Chinweizu, *Anatomy of Female Power: A Masculinist Discussion of Matriarchy*. Lagos, Nigeria: Pero Press, 1990.
Coghill, Nevil. *Introduction to the Cantebury Tales*. London: Penguin Books, 1958.
Cornevin, Robert. *Littérature d'Afrique Noire de Langue Française*. Paris: Presses Universitaires de France

(Collection SUP), 1976.
Daly, Mary. *Gyn/Ecology: The Metaethics of Radical Feminism.* Boston: Beacon Press, 1978.
de Beauvoir, Simone. *Le deuxième Sexe 1 & 11.* Paris: Editions Gallimard. 1976. Trans. *The Second Sex.* H.M.Parshley, New York: Alfred A. Knopf. 1951.
_____. *Tout compte fait.* Coll. Folio. Paris: Gallimard, 1972. Trans. as *All said and Done.* Patrick O'Brian. Harmondsworth, Middlesex: Penguin, 1987.
_____. *La femme rompue.* Paris: Editions Gallimard, 1967. Trans. Patrick O'Brian. *The Woman Destroyed.* London: Fontana, 1987.
Desalmond, Paul. *L'Emancipation de la Femme* en *Afrique et dans le Monde.* Dakar: Les Nouvelles Editions Africaines, 1977.
Diallo, Nafissatou. *Le Fort Maudit.* 1980.
Egejuru, Phanuel Akubueze. *BlackWriters: White Audience; A critical Approach to African Literature.* Exposition Press, Hicksville, New York, 1978.
Eisenstein, Hester. *Contemporary Feminist Thought,* London: Unwin Paperbacks, 1984.
Eliot, George. *Middlemarch: A Study of Provincial Life.* London: Oxford University Press, 1961.
Emecheta, Buchi. *The Slave Girl.* Glasgow: Fontana/Collins, 1977.
_____. *The Bride Price.* Fontana/Collins, 1978.
_____. *Destination Biafra.* Glasgow: Fontana, 1982.
Farah, Nuruddin. *From a Crooked Rib.* London: Heinemann, 1970.
Firestone, Shulamith. *The Dialectics of Sex: The Case for Feminist Revolution.* New York: Bantam Books, 1970.
Forster, E.M. *Aspects of the Novel.* Harmondsworth: Penguin Books Ltd., 1974.
Friedan, Betty. *The Feminine Mystique.* New York: W.W. Norton & Co. 1974.
Fromm, Erich. *The Art of Loving.* New York: Harper & Row. 1974.
Frye, Northrop. "Fictional Modes and Forms." In *Approaches to the Novel; Materials for a Poetics.* Edited by Robert

Scholes. California: Chandler Publishing Co., 1966.
Fryer, Judith. *The Faces of Eve: Women in the Nineteenth Century American Novel.* New York: Oxford University Press, 1976.
Gilbert, Sandra and Susan Gubar, eds. *The Mad Woman in the Attic: The Woman Writer and the Nineteenth Century Imagination.* Haven and London: Yale University Press, 1979.
Goldman, Lucien. *Pour une Sociologie du Roman.* Paris: Gallimard, 1964.
Greer, Germaine. *The Female Eunuch.* 1971., reprinted, New York: Bentam Books, 1972.
Greene, Julien. *God's Fools: The Life and Times of St. Francis of Assisi.* Trans. Peter Heinegg San Francisco: Harper & Row, 1983.
Grèsillon, Marie. *Une Si Longue Lettre de Mariama Bâ.* Paris: Les Classiques Africaines. 1986.
Hooks, Bell. *Feminist Theory: From Margin to Centre.* Boston: South End Press, 1984.
Howe, Irving. *Thomas Hardy.* London, 1968.
Hunter, JiM. *The Metaphysical Poets.* London: Evans Brothers, Ltd., 1965.
Huraton, Zora Neale. *Their Eyes Were Watching God.* New York: Harper & Row, 1990.
Ijere, Martin. *Women in Nigerian Economy.* Ed. Martin Ijere. Enugu: ACENA Publishers, 1991.
Irele, Abiola, *The African Experience in Literature and Ideology.* London: Heinemann, 1981.
Janeway, Elizabeth. *Man's World, Woman's Place: A Study in Social Mythology.* New York: Ben Publishing, 1971.
Keohane, Nannerl O., Michelle Rosaldo Z. and Barbara Guelpi C. *Feminist Theory: A Critique of Ideology.* Great Britain: The Harvester Press Ltd., 1982.
Kesteloot, LiLyan. *Anthologie ̄Négro-Africaine.* Paris: Editions Gerard and Co. Verviers (Belgique), 1967.
_____ . *Les écrivains noire de langue française: naissance d'une littérature.* Brussels, Université Libre de Bruxelles, Institut de Sociologie, 1963. *(Black Writers in French: a literary history of negritude).* Philadelphia: Temple

University Press, 1974.
Kettle, Arnold. *An Introduction to the English Novel,* Vol 1. London: Hutchinson & Co., Ltd, 1951.
Konadu, *A Woman in her Prime.* London: Heinemann, 1967.
Kourouma, Ahmadou. *Les Soleils des indépendances.* Montreal: Presses de l'Université, 1968.

POSTFACE

Women in Chains: Abandonment in Love Relationships in the Fiction of Selected West African Writers
- A Review
by PROF. PETER I. OKEH
*Dean, Faculty of Arts,
University of Benin, Nigeria*

Women in Chains is the major title of this scholarly work written by Dr. Rose Ure Mezu of Nigeria. The title smacks of a deliberate exaggeration in terms which is hyperbole and an implicit comparison in ideas which is metaphor. When the eighteenth century French writer and philosopher, Jean Jacques Rousseau, came up with his *Discourse on Inequality (Discours our l'inegalite)*, (1749) and cried out that men (including women) were born free but that they were everywhere in chains, the powers that be at that time laughed because they believed he was crying wolf. Yet that unwelcome and unexpected idea gained ground with the participation of other great minds like Voltaire, Montesquieu and Diderot, and changed the French society by what is historically known as the French Revolution of 1789. We can see Dr. Rose Mezu as another Rousseau in West Africa crying out to many unbelieving ears, along with other enlightened women, joined by male defenders of women's cause, that a good many of African married women are in chains.

History is bound to repeat itself by bringing about the expected changes in our modern societies determined and governed by the males to their own advantage. Naturally we do not see women carrying chains around. Dr. Mezu is simply comparing implicitly the situation of chained prisoners to that of women suffering under male hegemony. The title with its double tone of hyperbole and metaphor therefore serves as an attractive beacon inviting the reader to penetrate the work and extract its useful substance in addition to enjoying himself according to literary mode. The minor title *Abandonment..*, is like a regulator channeling the imagery in the major title into its decoded and simple significance.

The depth, the finishing and the punching nature of Dr. Rose Mezu's book easily convinces one that it is best for women to speak for themselves, to set the time and the pace of their own emancipation. There is always something lacking when a man, with all the good will in the world, embraces women's problem and makes himself their advocate. Before a white American, John Howard Griffin, wrote his book, *Black Like Me* (1961) on the lot of Blacks in the United States, he temporarily changed his skin into that of a negro. It worked. He was able to have shocking experiences he never would have had as a white man or discover as a white investigator of black problems in the American society. Maybe, our men may have to change their sex and live for sometime like women in the society in order to appreciate what our women go through. This, of course, is not possible. Should we not then listen more to those who wear the shoes and who know exactly where they are being pinched?

The critical work has a wonderful display of significant men and women in literature and other disciplines, in Europe, America and Africa, in the ancient past, all through the ages and in the contemporary era who had spoken out or written in favor of womanhood in the man's world that has persisted throughout history. One has to give Dr. Rose Mezu a pat on the back for the time and devotion she put in the work so as to bring into fruition her wide research on the half of humanity. Her comparative stance enables her to do this with such .an ease and Swiftness that can hardly be paralleled. Acquaintance with her approach convinces one more than ever of the immense advantages of the knowledge of languages in literary appreciation. Although English is the linguistic medium of her writing, French chips in now and then to fortify her thinking and vary its expression while Latin, German and Igbo are captured and injected into the work as it pleases the critic.

Dr. Rose Mezu's book has a special advantage over the novels and the papers yet written on African feminism. It is critical in focus and so gathers and examines with care thematic and aesthetic contents of the existing creative works. It embraces details which one can only get through the reading of a wide range of publications. It goes into depths which only the extensive nature of a full book can tolerate. *It is the first of its kind by which she sets the pace for other researchers who are likely to follow her footsteps.*

In some unbalanced critical works, one often loses the impression that one *is* reading criticism of creative writings. This is not so with *Women in Chains*.... Dr. .Rose Mezu carefully remembers to put with her analysis of ideas in each book comments on the literary aesthetics exhibited by the writers. The result is that a constant equilibrium is maintained between instruction and entertainment as she discovered them in her readings. It is true that no amount of reading of comments on creative writings can replace the reading of the works themselves. However, Dr. Rose Mezu's analysis in *Women in Chains*.... are so forceful that one gets a reasonable degree of satisfaction obtained through the knowledge of original works. Thus while the book does not dispense one from reading the novels, it gives a functional competence which only needs to be completed 'later.

Dr. Rose Mezu handles her object of study with a clear and constant methodology. We are going, to follow her from the first chapter which forms her introduction to the sixth chapter which serves as her conclusion. She titles the first chapter, "The Universal Canvas". It starts off with abandonment in Western literature beginning with classical mythology captured by Homer and Virgil, through ancient Greece and Rome up to the middle Ages, the 19th century romantic and social novels and anchoring in the 20th century with the works of Simone de Beauvoir. She concludes:

> Thus, from the western literary history, it can be seen that abandonment and love have always gone hand in hand, and women have not always received a fair deal from patrimony.

Next, Dr. Rose Mezu makes a critical review of abandonment in African fiction where she demonstrates that this universal phenomenon "exists in African literature and in fact has developed into a significant corpus which may safely be termed a literature of abandonment". She goes on to expose the objective of her work which is the restoration of a healthy balance in the relationship between men and women among African couples. The fourth section of the chapter introduces the writings of both Anglophone and Francophone African authors treating feminism in their works. This gives a global idea of the contents of the novels that will be talked about later. This is an effective way of showing the reader exactly where he is going as he reads the work. The final section announces the remaining chapters in the book: Chapters two, three and four are devoted to the three major themes of infertility, polygamy and infidelity; chapter five looks at other causes of abandonment in marriage while concentrating on major abandoned women in West African fiction; chapter six serves as the conclusion of the whole essay. This long and detailed introduction aims at preparing the reader for a fruitful and guided study of the critical work.

The second chapter presents barrenness as a catalyst for self-discovery for African women who do not have children in their marriages. Although procreation is primordial in African societies, it often assumes the dimension of an obsession in wives, husbands and relations, and any lack of it spells disaster for women without fruitful wombs. This is worsened by the fact that our male-supremacist societies always hold, the woman responsible for childlessness no matter what science has to say to the contrary. Dr. Rose Mezu takes her time to expose this sad phenomenon with illustrations from various novels by African authors, male and female, particularly female - to show this destruction of marital happiness and resultant abandonment. Nnu Ego in Buchi Emecheta's *The Joys of Motherhood*, Amaka in Flora Nwapa's *One is Enough*, Bali in Henri Lopes' *La Nouvelle Romance*, Salimata in Ahmadou Kourouma's *Les Soleils des Indépendance*, and Ije in Ifeoma Okoye's *Behind the Clouds*, come into focus. Dr. Mezu, concludes this way:

> The awareness 'mriters are out to create is that the tragedy compounding the issue of infertility has more to do with ignorance, arising from superstition, cultural chauvinism, and

general societal intransigence. k consciousness of thesis factors, less interference from ill-motivated, overbearing relatives and inquisitive neighbours, and readiness by the couple to give and take-do - as you will like done to - otherwise called "accommodationism", will *go* a long way to ensure, peace and serenity in a conjugal construct ....

Chapter three takes up the issue of polygamy and traces the relationship between it and the perennial subjugation of women. Many African men still do not see anything wrong with this outmoded system. They are ready to say at any point in time: "It is part of our culture; it is allowed by Islam; man is a polygamous animal; it can be justified from the Bible". These statements are nothing but clever ways of avoiding the issue: Polygamy is outdated in the present age everywhere including West Africa.

One needs to read the other side of the story from Dr. Rose Mezu and the authors she introduces to us. We must listen especially to these women who speak the bitter truth with commitment although with a feminine bias which is understandable. The works considered in the chapter are: Aminata Sow Fall's *La Greve des Battu*, Mariama Bâ's *Une Si Longue Lettre*, Ousmane Sembine's *Xala*, Isidore Okpewho's *The Victims* and Ifeoma Okoye's *Behind the Clouds*. The highlights of this section are: African women do not find relief in polygamy and need to be emancipated from its restrictive forces. It dehumanizes them even though they traditionally do not place much premium on romantic expressions of love. They can transcend any state of abandonment by virtue of education, financial autonomy and female bonding. Partners in marriage can combat it and promote conjugal love and family unity by sincerity, fellow feeling, mutual acceptance, tolerance, patience, compromise, forgiveness and maturity "that come with the successful facing together of the harsh realities of life". Children born in polygamous families suffer definite disadvantages not found in monogamous ones. It is like a nail on the head of this age-long practice in our societies.

In chapter four Dr. Rose Mezu discusses the famous question of infidelity with its aberration, incest, in relation to the abandonment of African women in marriage. Strange enough, in the social diary of many African males, this vocabulary exists only for women: A man would be looking for a virgin to marry without worrying that he has slept with some other women in his life. Some husbands would punish their wives if suspected of infidelity but would not entertain any objection to their adventures with other women. In some villages married women must not make love to other men if they do not want to have problems at child bearing. In case such problems arise, they are made to make open confessions of other men who made love to them in order to facilitate delivery. Meanwhile, the men would go round with other women and this would not make any story for anybody.

It requires a woman to cry out against this double standard and apparent hypocrisy nonchalantly and arrogantly, maintained by our societies governed by men. And the malaise becomes more disgusting when some men in their sexual activities now turn to their own daughters. We easily agree with Dr. Rose Mezu that infidelity causes familial disunity, keeps the woman in chains of neglect and "brings about the abandonment of the woman who regards marital infidelity as an act of treachery - an infringement of mutual trust". Just as in chapter three, she picks up and analyses in detail some characteristic novels: Ousmane Sembène's *Vehl-Closane*, Mariama Bâ's *Un Chant Écarlate*, I. N. C. Aniebo's *The Journey Within*, and Zaynab Alkali's *The Stillborn*. We are instructed on how, in these novels, the writers, like Elaine Showalter, achieve:

> Symbolic immersions of the hero in the feminine experience. Men, these novels are saying, must learn how it feels to be helpless and to be forced into dependency.... If he is to be redeemed and to discover his humanity, the woman's man must find out how it feels to be a woman

In this chapter, Dr. Rose Mezu fine-tunes her thinking on African Feminism whose aim, according to her, is accommodationism and which, in the final analysis, is not anti-male but "is geared towards the extirpation of ethos such as can bring about abandonment of women and destruction of homes".

The fifth chapter of *Women in Chains...* is captioned "Feminist Awareness and the Abandoned Female". On following Dr. Mezu up to this point, one has the feeling that all is still not said about the factors responsible for the abandonment of women in wedlock. This last chapter comes to the readers' aid by its exploration of some other factors which contribute to this constant problem. The author calls them "social structures of male dominance (which) oppress women, destabilize the nuclear family and lead to abandonment". The chapter evaluates the levels of awareness of the female protagonists of feminist novels, makes a large scale study of both male and female characters, condemns the abuse of the dowry system and the enforcement of other societal mores that contribute to abandonment. Many of the novels studied in the preceding chapters are scrutinized once more but with new perspectives. Flora Nwapa's *Efuru*, Mungo Beti's *Perpetue*, Henry Lopes' *La Nouvelle Romance*, Buchi Emecheta's *The Joys of Motherhood*, *Second Class Citizen*, and *Double Yoke*, however remain the main focus. Here as earlier, Dr. Rose Mezu continues to expound her thesis on her preference for the survival of the family construct through accommodationism against radical feminism which tends to divorce or separatism.

Chapter six of her book serves as her conclusion to the work and she titles it, "The Will to Change". It is a retrospective look at what she tried to accomplish coupled with some suggestions for the way forward in the relations between men and woman in marriage. She recalls the authors visited in the course of her study: Nwapa, Emecheta, Okpewho, Aniebo, Beti, Lopes, Sembene, Mariama Bâ, Aminata Sow Fall, Ifeome Okoye and Zaynab Alkali. Then she recapitulates her treatise on the issue of abandonment in marriage. It is a befitting conclusion to an essay consecrated on writers whose common bond, to use the words of Rose Mezu herself is

> their love for humanity, concern for the democratic ideals and right of man and woman to individuation and self realization; a burning desire to see the woman - the suppressed half of the human species - achieve happiness

within the conjugal construct

With that, *we* come to our own conclusion of our study of *Women in Chains: Abandonment in Love Relationships in the fiction of selected West African Writers.* A French translator modulated the title of Peter Abraham's *Mine Boy* as *Rouge est aussi le sang des Noirs* which, given literally in English says, 'Black people's blood is also red'. The translator wanted to underscore the abnormality of racial discrimination whereby Whites treat Blacks as if their blood were different in color. It might be a good thing for those men who dump women into a common grave of despite and submission to remember that their blood, like ours, is also red. Then both Blacks and Whites, husbands and wives, all over the world will be creating a new and improved order in which men and women born free and equal will be living in free and equal associations. That is in essence the logical assessment of the giant effort made by Dr. Rose Ure Mezu and reflected in the work we have analyzed.

There is however a lacuna in Dr. Rose Mezu's book which every man reading it will not fail to notice. It is that the culpability of women at times in their own abandonment is not highlighted. This in a way makes married men scapegoats in the compound problem of incompatibility in marital relationship. She talks elaborately on the lack of female bonding and cites Dr. V. U. Ola's conclusion that "Achebe sees polygamy as a system of relationships which works or fails according to the character of each person involved" But there is need to show that polygamy has not always been bad in Africa for it functioned well before the advent of the white man and has still some pockets of success in the modern era.

There are empirical cases of unjustifiably abandoned men who are in chains of solitude and family burdens through the fault of the wives they married. The very concept of marriage, where two persons are supposed to be one, gives the husband the role of the captain and his wife that of an assistant. Failure to recognize this by some women in marriage has made many marriages hit the rocks. Although male chauvinism and African societal structures can be blamed for the break-down of some mixed marriages (between Whites and Blacks) as is the case in Mariama Bâ's *Un Chant Écarlate*, the main causes are generally racism and poor African economy. Inability to put marriage above pressures from these factors are more often traced to white wives than to black husbands. We stress however that we appreciate Dr. (Mrs) Mezu and that we can understand her position. It requires an extraordinary and unusual effort for one to be a self condemned culprit. That is why she stood firm for the cause of women in marriage outside the cause of men. The important thing is that what she did, she did very well. There is room for others - male and female to add more.

Printed in the United States of America

0-87831-179-3